The Lean Design Guidebook

Everything Your Product Development Team Needs To Slash Manufacturing Costs

Ronald Mascitelli

TECHNOLOGY PERSPECTIVES
Northridge, CA

© Copyright 2004 by Technology Perspectives

All rights reserved

Editorial and Sales Offices: Technology Perspectives
    18755 Accra Street, Northridge, CA 91326
    (818) 366-7488

Publisher's Cataloging-in-Publication
   (Provided by Quality Books, Inc.)

Mascitelli, Ronald.
   The lean design guidebook : everything your product development team needs to slash manufacturing cost / by Ronald Mascitelli. -- 1st ed.
   p. cm.
   Includes bibliographical references and index.
   LCCN 2004101401
   ISBN 0-9662697-2-1

   1. Design, Industrial. 2. Manufacturing processes -- Cost control. 3. Production planning. I. Title

TS171.4.M373 2004   658.5'752
                        QB104-200121

10 9 8 7 6 5 4 3 2 1
First Edition

This book is printed on acid-free recycled paper meeting the requirements of the American National Standard for Permanence in Paper for Printed Library Materials.

Manufactured in the United States of America

Dedication

*To my mother and father,
Rita and Louis Mascitelli,
for their love, guidance,
and unwavering support
of my goals.*

Table of Contents

Acknowledgments	ii
Introduction - About This Guidebook	1

Part I - The Business of Lean Design

Section 1.1 - Ground Rules and Basic Tools	7
Section 1.2 - What's "Lean" Mean?	15
Section 1.3 - When Is a Product Profitable?	21
Section 1.4 - Screening for Profitable Projects	33
Section 1.5 - Defining a Target Cost	43
Section 1.6 - Twenty Levers for Product Cost	51

Part II - Consider Cost From the Very Beginning

Section 2.1 - Capturing the Voice of the Customer	67
Section 2.2 - Prioritizing Customer Requirements	79

Part III - Reduce Cost Through Cross-Product Synergy

Section 3.1 - The Product Line as a "System"	95
Section 3.2 - Platforms Come in All Sizes	107
Section 3.3 - Modular, Scalable, and Mass Customizable	117

Part IV - Cost Leverage Is Greatest During Conceptual Design

Section 4.1 - Value Engineering and Analysis — 137

Section 4.2 - The Quick-Look Value Engineering Event — 145

Section 4.3 - Sponsoring a Design Challenge — 175

Part V - Preparing for Production: The "3P" Process

Section 5.1 - What's a Lean Factory Look Like? — 191

Section 5.2 - Overview of Toyota's 3P Process — 195

Section 5.3 - The "How's it Built?" Review — 201

Section 5.4 - The "Seven-Alternatives" Process — 211

Part VI - Attack Direct Costs During Detailed Design

Section 6.1 - What's a Process Capability? — 227

Section 6.2 - Six-Sigma / Robust Design — 235

Section 6.3 - Design for Manufacture and Assembly (DFMA) — 267

Section 6.4 - Achieving Continuous Cost Improvement — 281

Conclusion - A Word About Lean and Green — 291

Glossary — 293

Bibliography — 303

Index — 307

Books by Ronald Mascitelli -

Building a Project-Driven Enterprise:
    How to Slash Waste and Boost Profits Through Lean Project Management

The Lean Design Guidebook:
    Everything Your Product Development Team Needs to Slash Manufacturing Cost

The Lean Product Development Guidebook:
    Everything Your Design Team Needs to Slash Time-to-Market (Forthcoming 2005)

The Lean Innovation Guidebook:
    Everything Your Design Team Needs to Create Breakthrough New Products (Forthcoming 2006)

Acknowledgments

So many people and so little space! A book of this breadth benefits from a vast number of contributors, each of whom has provided a key element in the integrated approach presented herein. To avoid having this section sound like an Academy Awards "thank-you" speech, I'll demure on naming each individual who has inspired, supported, criticized, or otherwise contributed to this guidebook. Instead, I'll extend a hearty salute and my sincere thanks to all who have played a part in this work. That being said, there are a few truly unsung heroes who deserve a moment in the limelight. I would like to commend the originators of the concepts of Value Engineering and Value Analysis for envisioning the design of products in a fundamentally different way. Contributors such as Arthur E. Mudge and Lawrence D. Miles presaged the value-focused principles of "Lean Thinking" decades before Toyota and others turned "waste" into a four-letter word (actually *muda* is the Japanese word for waste). It gives me great pleasure to restore this powerful work to center stage, as one of the pillars upon which this guidebook is based. Similar accolades and appreciation are due the pioneers of Total Quality Management, Six-Sigma methods, Design for Manufacture and Assembly, Mass Customization, and of course, Lean Thinking.

On a personal level, I would like to thank my wife and business partner, Renee, for her hours of editing, proofing, critiquing, and generally supporting this effort. Her contributions can be seen on every page of this work. Finally, a tip of my hat to each and every student who has attended my seminars and workshops over the years for challenging my ideas, demanding ever more practical tools, and establishing a real-world context for all that follows.

Ron Mascitelli
April 10, 2004

"When one becomes adept at using a hammer, everything begins to look like a nail."

Abraham Maslow

About This Guidebook

There's waste in your product designs, and it's costing you a fortune! Oh, it may not look like waste to you...at least not yet. But soon you will begin to see the profits that are being squandered and the opportunities being missed. More important, you will learn how to *solve* cost problems at every stage of product development. You are about to begin a guided tour of product cost-reduction methods, beginning at the earliest stages of project selection, and ending with the launch of a successful and highly profitable new product. Along the way, I will introduce you to eighteen *lean design tools* that are practical, efficient, and immediately deployable. Each tool addresses a specific opportunity for cost reduction during product design: As a group they represent an integrated approach to achieving the highest possible product value at the lowest achievable manufacturing cost.

Before we go further, let's establish the intended audience for this book. This is a guidebook *for* practitioners, *by* a practitioner. All of the methods you will learn can be implemented at the level of an individual designer, a product development team, or even throughout an entire organization. In other words, these tools are meant to be *used*. If you are a member or leader of a product design team, welcome to the tour. If you manage an engineering, marketing, or manufacturing organization, please join the group. Improvement champions, manufacturing engineers, Six-Sigma blackbelts, quality specialists, procurement folks; you're definitely in the right place. If your firm is committed to lean manufacturing and looking to expand its success, you deserve a front-row seat; the tools in this guidebook are specifically designed to dramatically enhance your efforts toward a lean enterprise. Other interested readers are welcome as well...provided that you are comfortable with the pragmatic (and decidedly informal) tone of this material.

Just a few administrative details and we'll be on our way to the first stop on our journey. I've described this work as a guidebook, and that is the analogy you should keep in mind as you proceed. It is my intention that this book become dog-eared and worn through constant use. Graphics are used extensively to illustrate key concepts. Templates, forms, and worksheets are provided wherever possible to help you hit the ground running with your new knowledge. To assist you in expanding your knowledge, I've taken the liberty of providing lists of references (along with my personal ratings) at the end of

Introduction

each major section of the book. Even the chronological order of presentation is intended to convey the sense of a journey; from the soft and fuzzy world of conceptual design to the final traumatic birthing process that characterizes the transition of new products into production.

Well, the tour is about to leave the station (or terminal, or dock...choose whatever fantasy you wish). As you board, take a quick look at the summary of lean design tools provided in the two figures that accompany this introduction. The Lean Design Tool Quick-Reference Guide lists all eighteen tools, with a brief synopsis of each tool's applicability and an indication of where in the book it is described. The Timeline for Application of Lean Design Tools suggests the periods within a typical product development process during which each tool would be most beneficial. Naturally, your situation may be different from the "typical." Hence, these tools are designed to be flexible, scalable, and easily adaptable. I'll be providing hints on how to tailor them to your specific needs at every stop along the way.

Welcome to the world of lean design. I hope you enjoy your intellectual journey, but make no mistake: Your travels will be wasted if you don't commit yourself to *putting the tools you've learned to work!*

Lean Design Tool Quick-Reference Guide

Lean Design Tool	Overview	Section
Product Opportunity Ranking Tool	Enables rapid prioritization of new product opportunities.	1.4
Target Costing	Establishes a clear cost target for design teams early in development.	1.5
Twenty-Cost-Lever Tradeoff Tool	Tradeoff tool for comparing potential cost-reduction design alternatives.	1.6
Lean QFD	Method for capturing the "voice of the customer" with minimal time and effort.	2.1
Must / Should / Could Prioritization	Technique for the priority ranking of product specifications and features.	2.2
Product-Line Optimization Team	An ad hoc team dedicated to identifying cross-product-line cost-savings.	3.1
Product-Line Roadmap	A visualization tool that displays future line extensions, opportunities, etc.	3.1
Platform Plan	A project plan for implementing platform-based cost-saving initiatives.	3.2
Module-Optimization Checklist	Provides development teams with a way to optimize their platform designs.	3.3
Quick-Look Value Engineering Event	Powerful tool for identifying and screening possible low-cost design options.	4.2
Pugh Method for Concept Selection	A quick and easy method for evaluating several product design concepts.	4.3
Lean Design Challenge	Harnesses the "smarts" of an entire organization to solve cost problems.	4.3
"How's it Built?" Review	A producibility review that brings together product and process designers.	5.3
"Seven-Alternatives" Process	Optimizes capital investment by considering multiple process alternatives.	5.4
Cost-of-Poor-Quality Calculator	A template for calculating the benefits of increasing process "capability."	6.2
Six-Sigma Cost-Reduction Guide	Overview of Six-Sigma Design tools with a focus on their cost-saving impact.	6.2
Design "Best-Practice" Guideline	Template for capturing successful design techniques and cost-saving rules.	6.3
Lean Design "Maturity Model"	A guide to the staged implementation of lean design tools within a firm.	6.4

Introduction

Timeline for Application of Lean Design Tools

Lean Design Tool	Project Selection	Conceptual Design	Concept Validation	Detailed Design	Qualification & Pilot Mfg.	Production Launch
Product Opportunity Ranking Tool	■					
Target Costing		■			■	
Twenty-Cost-Lever Tradeoff Tool						■
Lean QFD		■	■	■		
Must / Should / Could Prioritization		■	■	■		
Product-Line Optimization Team	■		■			
Product-Line Roadmap			■			
Platform Plan			■			
Module-Optimization Checklist				■		
Quick-Look Value Engineering Event		■		■		
Pugh Method for Concept Selection			■			
Lean Design Challenge						■
"How's it Built?" Review		■			■	
"Seven-Alternatives" Process		■			■	
Cost-of-Poor-Quality Calculator						■
Six-Sigma Cost-Reduction Guide						■
Design "Best-Practice" Guideline	■					■
Lean Design "Maturity Model"	■					■

The Business of Lean Design

1.1 - Ground Rules and Basic Tools

1.2 - What's "Lean" Mean?

1.3 - When Is a Product Profitable?

1.4 - Screening for Profitable Projects

1.5 - Defining a Target Cost

1.6 - Twenty Levers for Product Cost

Part I

> *"Rule Number 1 -*
> *Never lose money.*
>
> *Rule Number 2 -*
> *Never forget Rule Number 1."*
>
> Warren Buffett

> *"Where profit is,*
> *loss is hidden near by."*
>
> Japanese Proverb

> *"Most of us don't recognize*
> *opportunity until we see it working*
> *for a competitor."*
>
> Jay Huenfeld

Section 1.1

Ground Rules and Basic Tools

This introductory section sets the stage for all that follows. The scope of this guidebook will be defined and several important ground rules will be discussed. But first, a note to the reader. As I mentioned in the "About This Guidebook" section, I've used a rather terse, "cut-to-the-chase" style throughout this book. This is intended to remove unnecessary "noise" so that the reader can focus on the critical information needed for successful cost improvement. That being said, a bit of humor might sneak in now and then. One cannot live by dry facts alone.

The Three Dimensions of Cost, Price, and Time

The product development process represents the most complex, challenging, and, sad to say, poorly understood activity in business. Unlike other business processes, new product designs cannot be developed without the involvement of virtually every function within a firm. Moreover, since each new development project is unique, it is impossible to define a fixed and standardized process flow (a high-level process can be defined, but at the detail level, each project *must* be treated as unique). To make matters worse, external customers are involved, making the development of product specifications something bordering on the mystical. Technology is continuously evolving, rendering great products obsolete at a frighteningly rapid pace. Finally, competition relentlessly drives firms to be better, faster, and cheaper.

A good first step toward getting a handle on this frustratingly slippery process is to recognize that there are actually three distinct dimensions to new product development, as shown in Figure 1.1. Achieving optimal profitability demands that all three aspects be addressed. *Price* must be maximized, requiring creativity, innovation, and an empathic understanding of market needs. *Time* must be minimized, both to stay ahead of the competition and to extend the profitable life of the product. And, of course, *cost* must be driven ever downward. The dimensions of price and time will be addressed in forthcoming guidebooks: the focus of this book will be on achieving the lowest possible manufacturing cost for any product, without sacrificing the high quality and breakneck speed essential to business success.

Why focus on cost reduction? Aren't the other dimensions equally critical? The answer is "yes...but." Depending on your business environment, it might well be true that slashing time-to-market or driving higher levels of innovation will give you greater overall benefit. However, *reducing manufacturing cost is the fastest and surest way to achieve a measurable increase in profits.* Speeding up the development process often requires disruptive changes in how a firm operates, and those changes can impact virtually everyone in the company. Moreover, the benefits won't be felt for months or years, depending on your typical development cycle-time. On the price side, finding new market niches and innovating high-value product solutions is tough and unpredictable work. Cost reduction, on the other hand, can apply to both new product ideas and existing successful products, requires minimal organizational change, and can yield immediate bottom-line results. Therefore, slashing costs is a great place to begin your journey toward lean product development excellence.

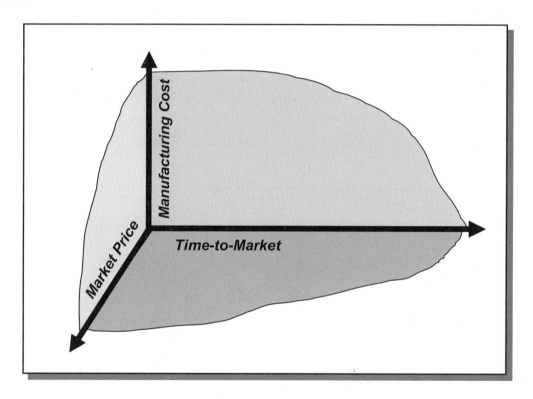

Figure 1.1 – The three distinct dimensions of new product development. The focus of this guidebook will be on manufacturing cost reduction.

Some Ground Rules for Design Excellence

Before we dig in, there are some fundamental ground rules that must be followed to play in the design-excellence game. The first rule is that *the value of a product, from the customer's perspective, can never be compromised as a result of cost-reduction efforts.* There is a big difference between optimizing production cost and cheapening your product. In the first case, the customer's true needs have been carefully interpreted and a product "solution" has been designed to fully address those needs in the most cost-efficient manner possible. In the second case, costs have been cut in a haphazard way in the hope that the customer "just won't notice" the compromises. This rule was violated by U.S. car manufacturers in the 1970's, for example, enabling Japanese firms to capture huge chunks of the

Western market. While U.S. manufacturers were cutting costs by sacrificing reliability and filling auto interiors with flimsy plastic, the Japanese were innovating the now legendary Just-in-Time (i.e., lean) production process that enabled high quality, and at the same time, dramatically lower costs.

The second ground rule is that *product development must be executed by a cross-functional team.* Most of us are familiar with the concept of concurrent engineering, wherein a team consisting of, at a minimum, marketing, engineering, and manufacturing, develop a product through parallel and collaborative efforts. It is important, however, to not treat this concept in a superficial way. Putting names on a roster and calling that a team is wholly inadequate. Having the team leader serve as nothing more than a liaison between high-walled functional "silos" is equally ineffective. A team must work like a team, with frequent interaction, shared responsibilities, open dialog, and sufficient autonomy to execute product development as a highly focused *project,* not a background process.

Our final rule is that *all product development work must be prioritized,* both within a given project, and across all design activities within an organization. Assuming that your firm does not have a surplus of designers sitting on the bench waiting to be called into play, your organization has *a finite capacity to perform new product development.* As is the case in your factory, the only way to maximize the profits resulting from finite capacity is to ensure that the highest value opportunities are always given priority. Moreover, priorities should not change from day to day, and they must be communicated to all involved parties within the firm. How best to accomplish this is beyond the scope of this book, but if you currently have no better way, just stick your finger in your mouth, hold it up to the wind and pick some potential winners. Any sane prioritization approach is better than no prioritization at all.

Some Tools to Go with the Rules

This is a book chock full of tools, but some are so fundamental as to be worthy of a front-row seat. Each of the following basic concepts should be kept in mind during every stage of product development, from the first dim glimmering of the light bulb to the pizza party after the first shipment.

The first tool is quite simple: *question your assumptions.* In my experience, a large percentage of the cost of most products is not intrinsically necessary. As you will soon learn, cost-reduction methods such as Value Engineering work to strip away all preconceptions so that designers can focus on the essential functions that a product must perform. In so doing, assumptions are scattered like so many cockroaches as new possibilities for simplicity and efficiency are brought to light. To me, it is like fingernails on a chalkboard when I hear designers say, "We have to do it that way!" The greatest enemy of innovation is a closed mind. Some examples of how the abandonment of assumptions has led to breakthroughs in product cost are provided in Figure 1.2.

Product – Classical Guitar
Cost Driver – The glue-up of a classical guitar typically requires up to 8 hours of a highly skilled craftsman's time.
Assumption – It would be impossible to create a time-saving jig for assembly, because the jig would need to remain inside the finished guitar.
Cost Breakthrough – By designing an injection-molded plastic jig that is acoustically tuned, the jig can be left inside the guitar…and the sound quality is actually *improved*. Garrison Guitar saved several hours of labor per unit and was able to use lower-skilled assemblers.

Product – Ink Jet Printer
Cost Driver – The carriage upon which the cartridges ride was originally machined out of solid stock to very high tolerances.
Assumption – The carriage tolerance must be as tight as the tolerance on the cartridges themselves.
Cost Breakthrough – By designing an "accommodating bearing" upon which the cartridges ride, the tolerances of the carriage could be dramatically reduced, allowing a cheap piece of extruded aluminum to do the job. HP saved enough cost to enable its entry into the home-office market for printers.

Product – Portable CD Player
Cost Driver – To achieve accurate sound reproduction, a precise drive motor was needed. Furthermore, any bumps to the unit would be heard by the user.
Assumption – The drive motor determines the quality of music reproduction.
Cost Breakthrough – Rather than depending on the precision of the motor, Sony incorporated a time delay into their electronics, so that music is initially read into a buffer memory. The memory is read out at precisely the right speed, and any noise from bumps can be filtered out before the user hears the music. This breakthrough enabled the Discman product to become a great success.

Figure 1.2 – Some examples of how the questioning of fundamental assumptions has led to breakthrough product cost reduction.

The next basic tool provides a way to crowbar open those closed minds that surround you. If you have lived in the "lean" world for any length of time, you have likely heard of "The Method of Five Whys." When you come across a stubborn assumption (or the person attached to it), try asking "why" several times, as illustrated in the following example:

Designer: "We have to make this product using high-cost materials."
Team Leader: "*Why* do you think that's true?"

Designer: "Because the customer requires that the product withstand a harsh use-environment."
Team Leader: "*Why* do you think that high-cost materials are essential to the product surviving in the specified environment?"

Designer: "Because when we tried using a cheaper grade of XYZ alloy, the test results were terrible."
Team Leader: "*Why* did we try a cheaper grade of the *same* material instead of performing a survey of possible *alternative* materials?"

Designer: "Because we have always made this type of product from XYZ alloy."
Team Leader: "*Why* are you convinced that the choices of our ancestors are still the best choices today? Hasn't material technology advanced dramatically in the past few years?"

Well, we've only used four "whys" in the above example, and have already uncovered the obstructive assumption (and probably driven our designer to profanity). Do keep in mind that asking "why" continuously can be extremely irritating, so be circumspect in your use of this technique. You might also look in a thesaurus for some synonyms for "why."

Our next basic tool is stated thus: *Avoid both overshoot and undershoot.* The concept of customer value is not monotonic; the more performance we provide the more our customers will pay. Actually, customer value is more like the pyramid shown in Figure 1.3. Virtually every product requirement can suffer from either overshoot or undershoot of some optimal level. Too little performance and the market will either reject the product or condemn it to the discount bin. Too much performance and the price will exceed the customer's budget for that particular product solution. In either case, your profits will suffer. Although it may be possible to coax more money from your customers with a breakthrough in performance, there is always a point of diminishing return for "gold-plated" products. A personal computer with a fast microprocessor is worth more than one with an inadequately slow one, but how fast is fast? Today, adequate speed is table stakes for PCs, and systems with more than sufficient speed have become low-priced commodities. Ask yourself this question: Is there *any* processor speed that would warrant your paying twice the current price for a PC? Likely not. Remember that trite-but-true old adage; when it comes to optimizing profits, *better is indeed the enemy of good enough.*

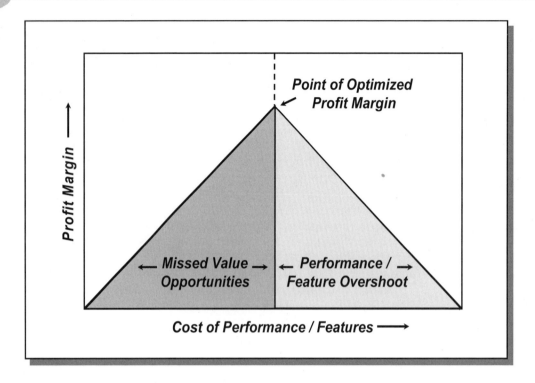

Figure 1.3 - It is possible to either *overshoot* or *undershoot* the optimal point for virtually any product specification, resulting in a loss of profits.

One last basic tool, followed by a warning. The tool is illustrated in Figure 1.4, by what appears to be a rather dazed airplane. The point is this; it is critical that several times throughout the development process, your designers pull their collective noses out of the trees and gain a "40,000 foot" perspective on the product being designed. Questions like, "Have we missed any opportunities to reuse previous design work?" or "Can we standardize a component across the entire product line?" won't typically be asked unless mandated by the team leader and upper management. As a good rule-of-thumb, either once per month or prior to every major decision point in your development process, a rapid climb to high altitude should be performed. As you continue your journey through this guidebook, you will discover that there is much profit hidden in the synergies of a multi-product system. You can't capture these profits, however, without the perspective of an eagle.

Now for the warning. This book has the word "lean" in the title, and the next section will explain why that word is warranted. Improvement programs, as you are no doubt painfully aware, come and go. "Lean Thinking" is yet another of those programs; perhaps one of the most powerful and broadly applicable in recent memory. With each such initiative there are benefits to be sure. However, it is all too common for improvement programs to become bandwagons, with an unnecessarily dogmatic life of their own. Proponents insist on using jargon and slogans. Methods which don't really apply are used indiscriminately (see quote by Maslow in the "About This Guidebook" section). Internal champions begin to take on the mantle of high priests, with all the anality of that exalted office.

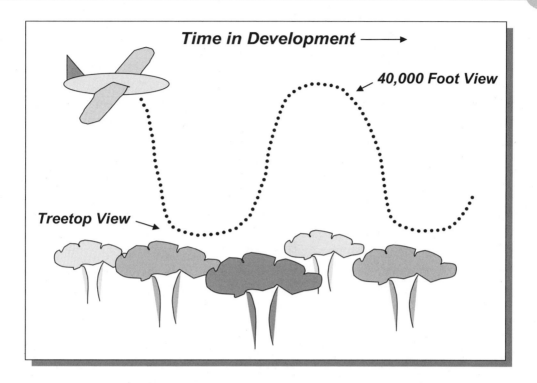

Figure 1.4 - It is critical that design teams consider synergies across all products within a firm to achieve breakthrough cost reduction. On a regular basis throughout a development project, the team should take a "high-altitude" look at their design to identify opportunities for optimizing the profits of an entire product line.

These occurrences undermine the true value of the improvement initiative, and generally make everyone sick to death of hearing about it. A good example of this trend is the deployment of Six-Sigma methods throughout the manufacturing world. An excellent methodology to be sure (see Section 6.2), but after some godlike executives gave it a rousing cheer in the press some years back, many companies embraced the methodology, only to find the tools either not applicable to their critical problems or too complex and time-consuming for their type of products. As with all improvement trends, the Six-Sigma bandwagon has been slowing a bit in recent years, much like those old familiar ones of the past (e.g., Total Quality Management). Hence, many Six-Sigma consultancies are now referring to the same basic toolbox as "Lean Six-Sigma," which only goes to show that even a bandwagon can hop on a bandwagon.

Notes

Section 1.2

What's "Lean" Mean?

The term "lean" has developed several meanings within the industrial world. For example, a number of firms have downsized in recent years, citing the need to "lean out" their organizations. This is certainly *not* the context in which lean is used in this guidebook. The "lean" I mean has a very specific and positive connotation; the act of eliminating non-value-added waste throughout an organization to enable higher productivity, increased profits, and improved overall competitiveness. This is accomplished through *improved processes and methods*, rather than a wholesale elimination of jobs. In principle at least, firms utilizing the lean design tools described in this guidebook will actually *create* jobs, increase shareholder value, and put a smile of satisfaction on the faces of their product designers.

The Basics of Lean Thinking

Long ago, at a university far, far away, a couple of bright guys asked a simple but loaded question: "Why are U.S. automobile manufacturers getting their butts kicked by the Japanese?" (Note that I am paraphrasing here, if that isn't obvious.) The answers that had been proposed up to that point included: A) unfair business practices, B) cheap labor and materials, C) some strange manufacturing methods that made no sense at all, or D) an unholy alliance with the devil. Our friends at the university quite rationally agreed that there must be something more to it than that. Were there underlying principles and techniques that the Japanese were using to dramatically improve their cost effectiveness in manufacturing? With this fundamental question in mind, they set off to understand how Japanese breakthroughs such as Just-in-Time (JIT) inventory management came to be.

The result was a landmark book entitled, *The Machine that Changed the World*, by James Womack, Daniel Jones, and Daniel Roos. Published in 1990, this book presents a very accessible account of both *how* the Japanese implemented what the authors call "lean manufacturing," and *where* these ideas came from. A subsequent book published by Womack and Jones in 1997, entitled simply *Lean Thinking,* goes somewhat further. The authors came to recognize that the value-focused principles upon which lean manufacturing was based could be extended to the entire enterprise, from the front office, to engineering, to the factory floor.

Today, the lean enterprise philosophy has become one of the most successful and broadly accepted improvement initiatives in history. Words like *kaizen*, the Japanese word for continuous improvement, and *muda*, the Japanese word for waste, have become embedded in the manufacturing lexicon throughout the world. More important, the concepts of value, waste, and the difference between them, have taken center stage in the building of manufacturing excellence. Despite well-documented successes in the manufacturing arena, however, Lean Thinking has been slow to migrate into the "office," and has made nary a dent in the world of product design.

End of history lesson. For our purposes, this is about as far as we need to go with the formal philosophy of Lean Thinking (not to mention our lesson in Japanese). In the remainder of this section, I will provide you with a quick and practical overview of the "best of lean." As you will discover, the commonsense methods and tools presented throughout this guidebook are intended to seek out and destroy waste in the design arena, thereby yielding products that maximize the cost efficiency of a lean factory. Beyond that, I will try to demystify both this and other major improvement initiatives by avoiding jargon and dogma in favor of directness and simplicity.

Getting a Grip on Value

We will spend a great deal of time in this book wrestling with the concept of value. Hence, this section is really just an *hors d'oeuvre*. In a nutshell, *value is what customers willingly pay for*. Since the whole point of new product design is to make money, the fact that customers pay for value should make us pretty excited about creating it. The first step in defining the value of a product is to identify the problem that it is intended to solve. Make no mistake about it; *every product is the solution to a problem*. The more *important* the problem, as perceived by customers, the more they are willing to pay. Likewise, the more *effective* the product solution, as perceived by customers, the more they are willing to pay. This behavior is illustrated graphically in Figure 1.5 and some examples are provided in Figure 1.6.

The most important aspect of value, from the standpoint of the product designer, is that there are no preconceptions built into the word. Value does not demand complexity, for example, nor does it imply technological sophistication. Even more important, *value is not directly correlated to cost*. All that matters in the creation of value is that customers perceive that their problem has been successfully solved. In a famous (but probably apocryphal) story, two astronauts, one from the Soviet Union and the other from the U.S., were discussing how their scientists had solved the problem of taking written notes in space. The U.S. astronaut was brimming with pride about the "space pen" developed by NASA that utilized a pressurized ink cartridge to enable writing at zero gravity. "A million dollars in R&D to be sure, but what a great solution, right?" said the American. The Soviet cosmonaut scratched his head and responded, "Very impressive, but our scientists came up with a different solution...we just brought along pencils."

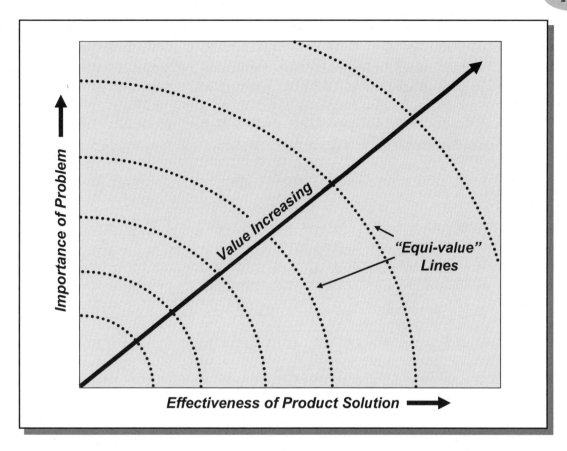

Figure 1.5 – The value (and typically the price) of a product is driven by two primary factors: the importance of the problem that the product addresses and its effectiveness at solving that problem, as percieved by the customer. Value can be enhanced by an increase in either factor.

Five Principles to Profit by

In the book *Lean Thinking*, the authors identify five fundamental principles that they believe were the fountainhead of all that Japanese enterprise had become by the early 1990's. The principles can be summarized as follows:

> *Principle #1* – Specify Value
> *Principle #2* – Identify the Value Stream
> *Principle #3* – Enable Value to Flow
> *Principle #4* – Establish the "Pull" of Value
> *Principle #5* – Pursue Perfection

These principles have served extraordinarily well as the foundation for waste-reduction initiatives and represent excellent rules to live by for any firm. In my opinion, however, they require a bit of elaboration and interpretation to make them applicable to the non-recurring world of product design and development. I have therefore taken the liberty of suggesting a new set of five principles, shown in Figure 1.7, that more closely reflects the tools and methods that will be presented in this guidebook.

Customer Problem	High-Value Solution	Lower-Value Solution
Need Flexible Personal Transportation	Performance Sports Car	Mass Transit
Need to Lose Weight	Doctor-Supervised Program	Diet Pills
Need Something to Drink	Chilled Champagne	Tap Water
Need Entertainment	Front-Row Seats at Theater	Television
Need a Place to Live	Beverly Hills Mansion	YMCA
Need a Better Job	Ivy League Degree	On-line Learning
Need Psychological Help	Respected Therapist	Radio Call-in

Figure 1.6 – Some examples of product "solutions" to customer problems. Evidently there can be a dramatic difference between the lowest and highest value solutions. It is also important to recognize that not all customers will perceive value equally (i.e., they have differing situations) – hence the need for differentiated products in several price and performance ranges.

The first principle that I propose recognizes the high leverage that exists at the earliest stages of product development. Tools such as Value Analysis and Value Engineering provide a powerful methodology to satisfy this initial mandate. Moving on to the second principle, once customer needs have been mapped into product functions, a process must be identified to deliver that set of functions to the market in product form. Speed is of the essence in product development, and a lean and efficient process is critical to sustaining competitiveness.

The third principle recommends that unnecessary or redundant cost items be stripped away. As the development process moves forward, there are many ways to eliminate wasteful design features, excess material, unnecessary direct labor, redundant testing, etc. Often, the best way to accomplish the waste reduction mandated in Principle #3 is through frequent consultations with real-world customers. This leads us to the iterative design approach recommended in Principle #4. Customer feedback can dramatically improve a design, both by fine-tuning the performance of the product and by uncovering ways to unobtrusively reduce cost. Finally, Principle #5 states that although embedding applicable

> **The Five Principles of Lean Design**
>
> ***Principle #1*** – Precisely define the customer's **problem** and identify the specific **functions** that must be performed to solve that problem.
>
> ***Principle #2*** – Identify the **fastest process** by which the identified functions can be integrated into a high-quality, low-cost product.
>
> ***Principle #3*** – Strip away any **unnecessary** or **redundant** cost items to reveal the optimal product solution.
>
> ***Principle #4*** – Listen to the voice of the customer **frequently** and **iteratively** throughout the development process.
>
> ***Principle #5*** – Embed cost-reduction tools and methods into both your **business practices** and your **culture** to enable continuous cost reduction.

Figure 1.7 – Following the above principles will empower a firm to eliminate waste and achieve excellence in new product design and development.

tools into your formal development process is important, it pales in comparison to the *necessity* of building a cost-conscious culture (sorry for the alliteration) throughout your organization. Policies and processes are no substitute for personal involvement and initiative, and there is no way to "proceduralize" the occurrence of breakthroughs in cost reduction. Creativity is born on the human side of business. Therefore, tips on how to foster innovations in low-cost design have been sprinkled into every section of this book.

Now that we have a basic understanding of how lean thinking can be adapted to the product-design function, let's dig deeper into the concept of value and see what it takes to launch a financially successful product solution.

Notes

Section 1.3

When Is a Product Profitable?

It has become fashionable these days for management teams to focus on revenue (i.e., sales) growth rather than profitability, particularly among high-tech start-up firms. Amazon.com is famous for its lack of profits, yet has managed to excite the stock market merely by reducing how much money they *lose* from year to year. It seems that some managers and investors believe that if a firm is well-positioned within a high-growth sector, profit growth will naturally and automatically follow revenue growth. This logic may make sense for a few hyped-up darlings, but for firms that are in business for the long haul, profit growth is *at least* as important as boosting sales. Hence, it is critical that designers understand where costs come from, how they build up to determine profit margin, and what a design team can do to influence them.

One of the key challenges facing designers is that by far the greatest leverage for cost reduction occurs early in the product development process, as shown in Figure 1.8. Decisions made during concept development can inexorably freeze many of the critical cost factors in a product, making it impossible to significantly reduce these costs later on. Materials and processes are selected, suppliers are identified, complexity is established, and synergy with other products is considered (or totally ignored, as is the case in many firms). In particular, it is a dangerous fallacy to believe that cost- reduction activities should be reserved for products already in production. Like it or not, cost must be a primary consideration even before a team understands a product's detailed design; most profit opportunities have already left the barn before the first drawing is created.

Building up Costs to Determine Profit Margin

The following discussion is somewhat simplified, but the important factors are all present. Since every firm has its own cost-accounting structure, it is important that design teams take the time to understand their specific situation. The easiest way to accomplish this is to invite your firm's cost accountant (if you have one), or some other finance representative, to meet with your team immediately after project kickoff. These folks can help you understand how things work in your neck of the woods (and your engineers will appreciate meeting someone with even worse interpersonal skills than they have).

The first step in understanding product cost buildup is to recognize that costs fall into a two-by-two matrix, as shown in Figure 1.9. The first bimodal dimension is *fixed costs versus variable costs*. A fixed cost is volume independent, meaning that the cost to

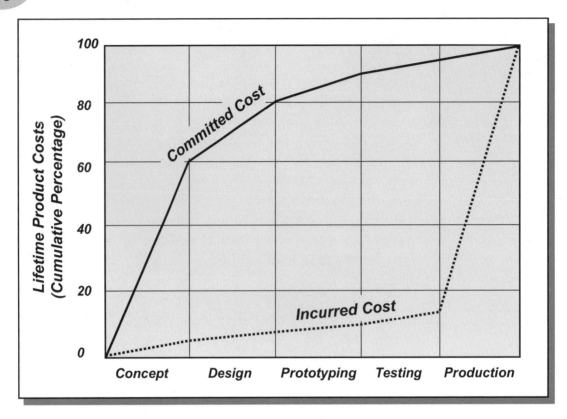

Figure 1.8 – The majority of product costs are committed early in the design process, even though the expended costs are quite low. Once a product reaches production, there is frustratingly little that can be done to affect its fundamental cost structure.

the firm is the same whether a million units of the product are produced or only one. A variable cost, as the name implies, scales with product volume, although the scaling factor may not be linear (economies of scale often apply to variable-cost items). The other dimension of product cost is *assignable versus overhead*, also referred to as *direct versus indirect*. An assignable cost can be directly associated with a specific product (or at least to the product line as a whole), whereas an overhead cost is spread like peanut butter across all products within a given business unit.

Now we can begin to build up our product's cost structure, starting with the most obvious costs: production materials and labor (often referred to as "direct materials" and either "direct labor" or "touch labor"). Both direct materials and direct labor are *variable assignable costs*. Hence, anything you do to reduce these costs will be multiplied by the volume of the product produced. Because these costs are the most familiar, it is common for cost-reduction initiatives to stop right here. Bad idea. Although materials and labor are critical considerations, they often represent only a fraction of the total cost buildup, as shown in Figure 1.10.

Under the category of *fixed assignable costs* are items such as dedicated capital equipment and the non-recurring design cost of a product. Unfortunately, many companies lump both equipment and design costs into indirect overhead, thereby hiding them from view (and often from consideration). If a piece of equipment is needed only for a specific product, that product should absorb all of its depreciation. Unfortunately, equipment that will be shared across multiple product lines is not so easily allocated, as will be seen in the next section. Likewise, non-recurring design costs can and should be directly assigned to a specific product, and should be amortized over the volume of the product produced.

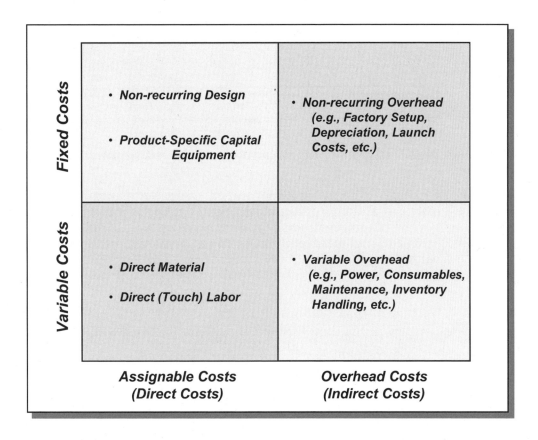

Figure 1.9 – The two dimensions of product cost are: i) fixed versus variable, and ii) assignable versus overhead. It is important that designers understand how their actions influence the cost factors shown above.

Things get trickier when we try to deal with the overhead (indirect fixed and variable) costs of a product. A firm's operational overhead is really just a big trash bin into which all costs other than assignable costs are tossed. Items such as maintenance, inventory carrying and handling costs, factory utilities, sustaining engineering, and so on, are all components of operational overhead. Since (presumably) these costs are applicable to all products within a factory, they are typically allocated by some "logical" accounting scheme, most often as a multiplier on top of direct labor (and sometimes direct materials).

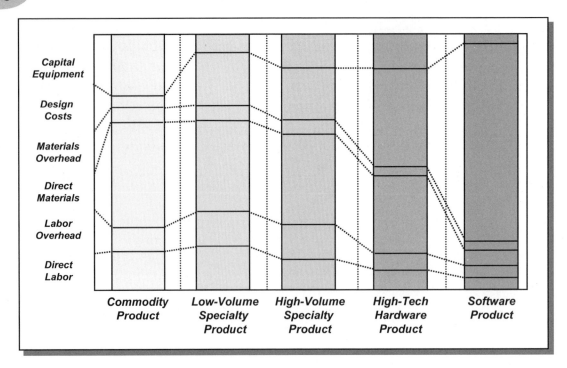

Figure 1.10 – Typical cost buildups for several categories of manufactured products. Note that although direct materials and labor represent a significant portion of total cost, some types of products are dominated by capital costs and non-recurring design costs. In all cases, the applied overhead cannot be ignored.

Thus, to summarize, there are five primary categories of cost that can be affected by a design team: 1) direct materials, 2) direct labor, 3) assignable capital equipment, 4) assignable non-recurring design, and 5) operational overhead.

This jumble can best be untangled through a simple example. Your firm produces thingamajigs (sorry, but the market for widgets has been in the dumpster in recent years) at a sale price of $200 per unit. The cost of materials to make a thingamajig is $10.00 per unit at a given production volume. Note that the cost of scrap and wasted materials must be included in this direct material cost. The direct labor cost to produce one thingamajig is $8.00 per unit at the same production volume. It took 5000 hours of design engineering time to get this particular model into production, at a cost of $250,000 (this is the "fully burdened cost" for the nitpickers among you). Finally, the cost of fixtures, tooling, and dedicated capital equipment was $1,000,000. Note that the latter two costs are volume independent.

Well, that's four out of five. Operational overhead at your firm is treated as a multiplier on top of direct labor at a 100% rate and as a multiplier on direct materials at a 50% rate. We now have everything we need to calculate gross profit margin. Or do we? It's easy to see how the direct labor and material costs build up, and even how overhead would be calculated. But how do we allocate the fixed costs of capital equipment and non-recurring design? We need one more number: *the breakeven number of units produced.* Once we've chosen this number, we can simply divide the assignable fixed costs by the breakeven number to determine a per-unit allocation, as shown in Figure 1.11. (Note that it is actually the *depreciation* of capital equipment that is allocated over the breakeven units, but I'll leave it to your charismatic finance person to explain the distinction.) Obviously, a higher breakeven number gives you a better gross margin. So how should that number be selected? Ideally, it is a very conservative estimate of the total sales volume for the product. Please, please, please be *conservative* here. If you guess low (and make no mistake, it is a *guess*), your firm will still make all of its profits. If you guess high, however, your firm could end up developing a low-profit, or even a no-profit, product.

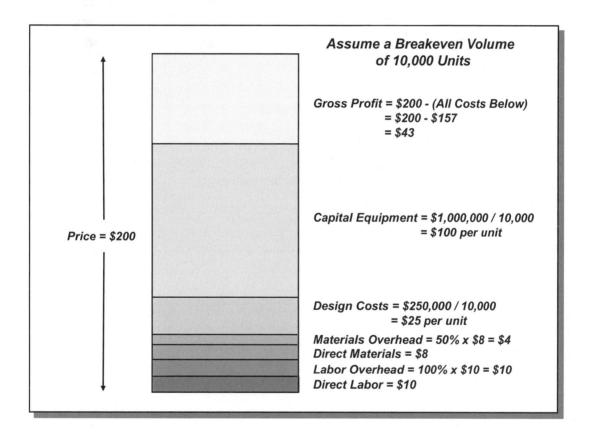

Figure 1.11 – An example of how a cost buildup is calculated for the case of a thingamajig. Your firm's buildup structure may be slightly different.

The moral of this section is that designers basically have five "knobs" that they can turn to reduce product cost. They can decrease direct labor or direct material costs. They can cut back the non-recurring hours required to design the product. They can shrink the capital investment required to produce the product. Finally, they can drive down the factory's operational overhead rate. Some examples are provided in Figure 1.12. Any of these actions will reduce the cost of a product and increase its gross margin, *provided that*

Cost "Knob"	Possible Opportunities for Design Team
Direct Labor	• *Simplify product assembly* • *Automate manual operations* • *Reduce test and inspection requirements*
Direct Material	• *Use lower-cost materials* • *Use higher-volume materials* • *Reduce scrap and wastage*
Indirect Overhead	• *Simplify initial factory setup* • *Reduce number and variety of parts used* • *Reduce material handling and storage*
Design Costs	• *Reuse existing design elements* • *Purchase commercial-off-the-shelf components* • *Accelerate design process*
Capital Equipment	• *Design product for existing processes / equip.* • *Select processes with low tooling costs.* • *Reduce product tolerances*

Figure 1.12 – Some examples of how a product design team can favorably impact the five cost "knobs" of a product.

the other cost factors are not negatively impacted. These five cost knobs are often connected to each other in subtle ways. For example, in the case of a high-volume product, it may actually make sense to *increase* assignable capital investment (e.g., by purchasing automation equipment), because the resulting drop in direct labor would more than make up for the increase. Nothing is ever easy, is it?

Better Costing Is as Simple as ABC

The control of product cost is absolutely critical to business success, yet it is essentially impossible for firms to know *exactly* what a given product costs to produce. To be sure, you can determine direct costs such as labor and materials to a fairly high degree of accuracy. Likewise, if your accounting system is sufficiently sophisticated, non-recurring design cost can be assigned its own general ledger account and captured on a product-by-product basis. Even the cost of assignable tooling and machines can be well-established, although capital equipment is frequently shared among several products. So where is the ambiguity?

Well, it lives in a dark and fearsome place known as the overhead hole. As I indicated earlier, many of the operating costs of a factory are lumped together into the indirect overhead rate. The reason is simple; it is assumed that allocation of these costs to specific products is just too difficult and time-consuming to be worth the effort. Moreover, Generally Accepted Accounting Principles (GAAP) embraces the scheme of indirect overhead allocation by labor hour (along with several other equally inadequate methods), leaving little room for a more accurate approach. Yet it is entirely possible, due to the inherent ambiguity associated with indirect overhead allocation, for companies to develop, manufacture, and sell products that are losing substantial sums of money, *and not even know it!*

This can be seen by considering the example shown in Figure 1.13. Although products are assigned indirect overhead as a multiplier on direct labor, it is entirely possible for two products that consume the same direct labor hours, and even the same direct material costs, to utilize overhead resources in dramatically different ways. In this example, Product A is just a little sweetheart, demanding relatively little power or consumables, taking up minimal floor space, employing standard parts and processes, and requir-

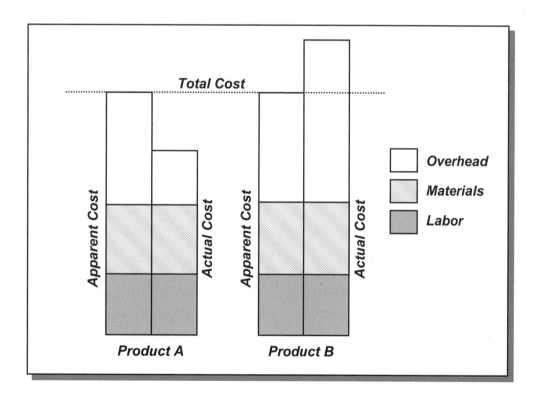

Figure 1.13 – An example that illustrates how the traditional methods of overhead allocation can lead to poor decisions regarding which products should be developed and sold. Product A and Product B have identical labor and material costs, and their sale price is the same. The difference between their allocated and actual overhead costs, however, makes Product A appear to be less profitable than it really is while Product B is actually losing money.

ing no new equipment. Even the supply chain and customers for Product A are tame and well-behaved...nothing like its evil cousin, Product B.

The case of Product B is a sad one. It looked so good on paper, and even the market demand has been impressive. It is, however, a big fat money-loser. The machining operations demand high levels of power and consumables, it is a large product that demands almost half of the factory's floor space, no parts or processes are shared with other products, and a large percentage of the general capital equipment within the factory has been co-opted by this beast. Furthermore, the suppliers for Product B are irresponsible, and the largest customers are demanding, annoying, needy, and generally pathological. The actual cost of producing Product B *should* be dramatically higher than Product A, but since indirect overhead is spread like peanut butter across all products, their cost buildups look exactly the same. Tragically, due to the high demand for Product B, the Sales Department is pushing to increase production at the expense of the far more profitable Product A; a recipe for cash-flow disaster.

So is there a better way? Several years ago, a new accounting method was proposed that recognizes the inequity in conventional overhead allocation and attempts to rectify it. The system is referred to as Activity-Based Costing (ABC) and it has shaken up the stogy cost accounting world like a 9.0 earthquake. ABC uses a two-stage approach to allocate overhead costs to individual products, as shown in Figure 1.14. The first stage carves up traditional overhead items such as maintenance and depreciation into *activity centers*. These activity centers are not real physical entities; they are a construct that allows the overhead peanut butter to be heaped in a more logical way, based on the type of activity that consumes it. Once this has been done, ABC attempts to identify how much of these activity centers' allocation is consumed by specific products. This is accomplished in the second stage of ABC by defining metrics, known as *cost drivers,* that are in some way proportional to the amount of an activity that is consumed by a given product.

Again, let us part the waters of confusion with a simple example. Product A described above is a simple product with very few part numbers, whereas Product B is complex, with many more part numbers. It is logical to assume that Product A uses less "parts-administration overhead," which is to say that the inventory handling and procurement people spend less time on A than they do on B. So why not use "number of part numbers" as a cost driver to determine how much of parts-administration overhead should be allocated to A versus B?

This is all well and good if you're a cost accountant, but we are designers gosh darn it, and we shouldn't have to worry about such arcane (and frankly boring) stuff. Instead, we will leave ABC to the accountants, and establish a more qualitative approach for allocating overhead to products. To do this, we must first identify the most important factors that typically cause disparities in the actual consumption of overhead. Some of these factors are illustrated in Figure 1.15. Rather than trying to precisely calculate the impact on operational overhead of one product versus another, we are going to estimate whether a proposed new product *uses more or less overhead than the average for the factory*. How much more or less will be somewhat subjective, but the scoring system proposed in Figure

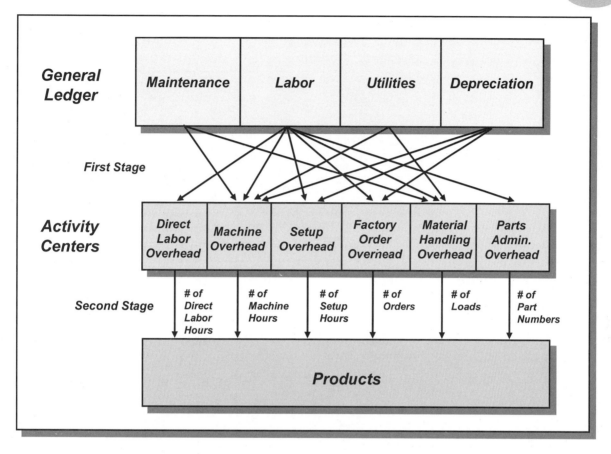

Figure 1.14 – The Activity-Based Costing (ABC) system uses two stages of metric to allocate the "peanut butter" of operational overhead to specific products.

1.16 can allow a design team to perform tradeoffs, recognize gross disparities, and over time, drive down overhead costs for all products produced. You will see how this rating scheme is integrated into a comprehensive scoring system in Section 1.6. For now, you can simply rejoice in the knowledge that your team can positively impact the "overhead knob" of product cost without knowing a general ledger from a laundry list.

Turn up the Volume, Turn down the Cost

You've probably heard the old saying, "It doesn't matter that we're losing money now – we can make it up in volume." Despite the distinct smell of rationalization in this statement, there is also some truth in it. In almost every case, the unit cost of a product decreases with increasing volume. This is not just a "bulk-purchase" effect either; each of our five cost knobs is turned downward by an increase in production quantity.

A qualitative look at how the five cost knobs are impacted by volume is shown in Figure 1.17. The most obvious effect is a decrease in direct material cost. Ordering larger quantities of parts gives buyers leverage in negotiating lower unit costs, and the bulk cost of raw materials is always on a sliding scale with volume. Although these quantity dis-

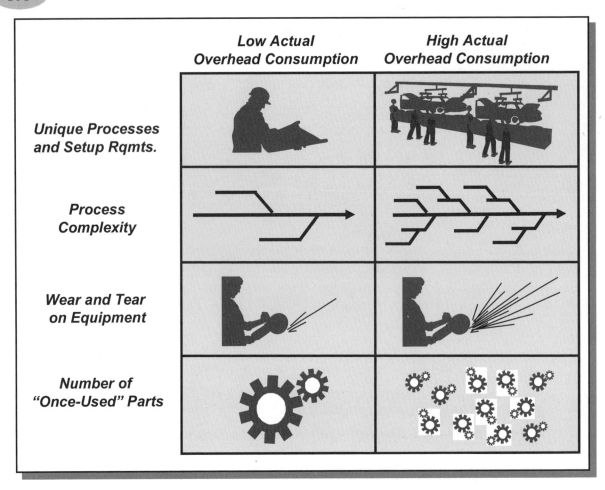

Figure 1.15 – Some of the factors that can significantly impact operational overhead, thereby creating a disparity between the *actual* overhead consumed by a product and its peanut-butter-spread overhead.

counts are often fairly linear with increasing number of units ordered, there can be major spikes caused by the realities of distribution and logistics. If you need to order three-quarters of a shipping container filled with a certain raw material, for example, it may cost very little more to just order a full container load.

Direct labor also displays a volume effect, although the primary benefits are harvested during the early rampup of production. There is a well-established "learning-curve" effect associated with increasing the production volume of any product. The direct labor required to produce unit number one might be a factor of two higher than the labor required to produce unit number one thousand and one. Unfortunately, this effect exponentially decays with higher quantities, so you get the most dramatic labor savings upfront.

Now on to the more subtle effects. Since the fixed cost of non-recurring design is spread over the total manufactured quantity, each additional unit produced helps defray these initial costs. Likewise, the cost of assignable capital (tooling, etc.) can become insignificant if the production quantities are high enough. While the allocated cost of non-recurring design will continually decrease as production volumes grow (assuming you get a handle on those pesky engineering change orders), the allocated per-unit cost of capital will decrease to a plateau and then flatten. The reason for this behavior is that capital equipment requires periodic replacement due to wear and tear. This may occur on a very long cycle for heavy equipment, but delicate tooling and fixturing can wear out in painfully short order. Hence, a continuous capital outlay for replacement of equipment must be planned if the wear-out threshold will be surpassed by a product over its production lifecycle.

Finally, even that nasty little dumpster of costs that we call operational overhead is positively impacted by higher production volumes. Many of the costs embedded in the overhead rate are actually fixed costs. Hence, the higher the volume, the larger the base over which the "peanut butter" can be spread. Variable costs buried in the overhead rate may also improve due to quantity-discount effects and even learning-curve effects (e.g., the labor cost of machine maintenance may decrease with increasing repetition of service and repairs). Indeed, all things related to cost get rosier as the production volume goes up.

	Floor Space Required	Consumables Used	Number of Part Numbers	Unique Processes	Unique Materials	Equipment Capacity Used	Total Score
Factory Average	0	0	0	0	0	0	0
Product Version A	+2	+3	+1	0	+4	+1	+11
Product Version B	+2	-1	0	-2	+2	-3	-2

- A +5 to -5 scoring system is used to determine the relative impact on operational overhead of two different versions of the same product. The factory average is set to zero for comparison.
- Scoring should be done as a team effort; be sure that manufacturing is represented.
- The design version with the lowest score will tend to have the lowest overhead cost impact. A design with a negative score will actually tend to bring down the overhead rate for the entire factory.

Figure 1.16 – A simple scoring system that can allow designers to make a qualitative assessment of how a new product will impact operational overhead. This scorecard tool highlights gross disparities in overhead consumption among product alternatives and helps designers make tradeoffs to better optimize the "overhead knob" of product cost.

Take heart, those of you with low-volume, high-mix product lines. There is very good news about the cost benefits of higher volumes: *they don't have to come from a single product.* If several totally unrelated products share a common part, then the cost of that part will be lower for all products that use it. Likewise, if processes, touch labor, capital equipment, floor space, etc., can be shared across multiple products, all of those products will receive the cost benefit of the *combined volume*. This theme should be at the forefront of any integrated cost-reduction methodology – as long as value is maintained, anything that can be done to standardize, commonize, reuse, combine, etc., to achieve higher effective volumes will yield significant cost benefits. So be of good cheer; you too can achieve mass-production cost advantages...all it takes is a little ingenuity.

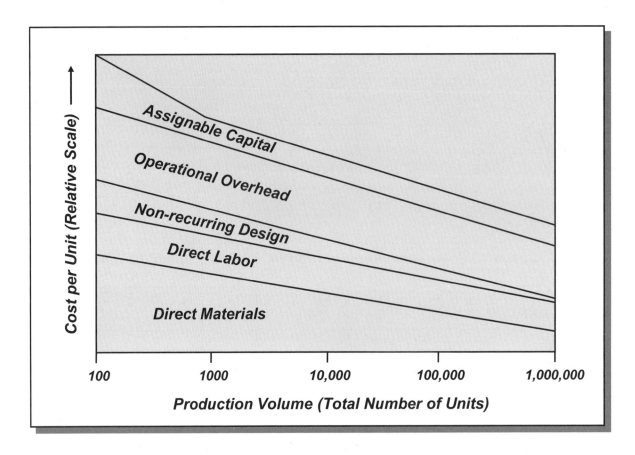

Figure 1.17 – The behavior of the five "cost knobs" as a function of production volume. Note that these curves are qualitative in nature; actual behavior will depend on the specific product and manufacturing operation involved.

Section 1.4 — Screening for Profitable Projects

Before we delve into the many lean design tools available to reduce product cost, it is worthwhile spending a few moments considering how best to screen and prioritize new product development opportunities. It does us little good, after all, to waste precious resources trying to squeeze profits out of a poor product opportunity, when there are far better candidates waiting in the wings. To this end, the following section will describe how opportunities can be evaluated, rank-ordered, and staged for execution, with relatively high accuracy and in minimal time.

The Fascinating World of Product Economics

Ok, so the title of this subsection is a bit of a stretch. If you find watching paint dry fascinating, then understanding how best to evaluate product opportunities will be a real high point for you. That being said, *there is no single activity in your business that is more critical to long-term success than setting accurate new-product priorities*. So fire up your attention span and let's get started.

One of the conundrums of new product development is that you must make major decisions regarding investment of talent and money long before you have any solid information about the product. How big will the market really be? What price will the marketplace accept? Will the production cost of the product allow for acceptable profits at that price? How much capital and non-recurring design cost will be required? And so on. None of these critical questions can be accurately answered until late in the development process (or in some cases, not until the product is in full-rate production). The best we can do is estimate what these data will look like in the future and use the estimates to guide our initial decisions.

A useful product prioritization process must consider the following factors to determine which opportunities will yield the most profits for the company:

- Market forecast for all years of anticipated production
- Manufacturing cost (including direct materials, direct labor, and operational overhead) over the life of the product
- Market price for the product
- Assignable (direct) capital equipment required
- Non-recurring design cost
- Economic, technical, and market risks

One would think that there is but a single way to manipulate these factors to achieve an assessment of a product's "goodness," but of course, things are never that easy. Our financial friends have invented a whole pantheon of metrics that ostensibly represent a goodness rating, as shown in Figure 1.18. Depending on where your interest lies (e.g., are you more concerned with utilization of capital, long-term profits, short-term profits, etc.) it appears there is a metric designed just for you. As thrilling as this may be for the financial types, we're designers, so let's just cut to the chase. The most widely accepted (and in my opinion for good reason) tool for evaluating the benefits of a product opportunity is something called the net present value (NPV). It is comprehensive (i.e., it considers all of the factors listed above), it is relatively simple to calculate (particularly if you are not the one doing the calculating), and it yields a single number that can serve as a ranking metric for projects...after a bit of interpretation. So without further ado, let's see what this little gem of a metric looks like.

The One Thing We Know About Market Forecasts Is…?

Answer: They are always wrong! Any product evaluation tool must have at its core a market forecast, which means that the above "joke" is really not very funny. We are working in a world of uncertainty and risk, regardless of which prioritization method we choose, and net present value is no different. If you ask a financial person what NPV means, they will tell you that it represents, "the total discounted future cash flows from the proposed product, minus the initial investment." If we eliminate the jargon, here is what that statement really means:

> *NPV is an estimate of how much total profit your firm will generate from a new product over its entire market life, after assignable costs and risk factors are taken into account.*

Clearly, the market forecast is deeply embedded in even this lay definition. How much profit? How long a market life? But wait. Let's consider a simple example before I frighten you with any more details.

We are back to running our thingamajig company, and have just identified a possible killer application for our thingamajig core competency. It turns out (who would have guessed it?) that thingamajigs have therapeutic value; they can be used to relieve muscle strain and stress. The size of the market for such a product, which our firm has cleverly named "Wonderjig," depends heavily on the price. Two possible options seem to be the most promising: a high-performance "doctor's version" and a low-cost home model that would no doubt be a hot seller on the Home Shopping Network. But which version should we develop? There are only enough funds and people available in our firm to complete one of these designs during the next fiscal year. Evidently a tough decision must be made.

To make the right choice of which product to pursue, we first need to estimate the size of each market for as many years out as we think makes sense, as shown in Figure

Profitability Metric	Formula	Advantages	Disadvantages

Net Present Value (NPV)	$= \dfrac{\text{Sum}_{t=0,n}(\text{Avg. After-Tax Cashflow})_t}{(1+\text{Discount Rate})^t}$
	t = time in years since product launch
	n = last year of market life
		• Fairly comprehensive
		• Widely used
		• Enables easy decisions:
		  NPV > 0 Profitable
		  NPV < 0 Cancel Project
			• Depends on soft data such as market forecasts
			• Some complexity involved
			• Needs enhancements to accommodate risk

Internal Rate of Return (IRR)	= Discount Rate at which NPV=0	• Easily understood and has intuitive meaning • Considers time value of money, but ignores other risks	• Tedious to calculate, but no harder than NPV • Fails to recognize the varying size of investments in competing projects
Profitability Index (PI)	$= \dfrac{\text{Net Present Value}}{\text{Initial Investment}}$	• A nice concise number for project ranking • Optimizes utilization of capital; important if cash is scarce	• Not intuitive – can only be used for ranking • Puts weight on available cash, rather than available resources
Expected Commercial Value (ECV)	$= ((NPV \times P_{cs} - C) \times P_{ts} - D)$ P_{ts} = Probability of Technical Success P_{cs} = Probability of Commercial Success D = Development Costs Remaining on Project C = Commercialization (Launch) Costs	• Has at least the potential to be highly accurate • Captures risks better than any other approach • Provides job security for your finance department	• Gives the impression of accuracy and validity, but is still dependant on the same risky data • Far too complex for most organizations

Figure 1.18 – Various financial metrics that can help determine the economic value of a new product development project. Each approach has its benefits and drawbacks, but for our purposes the net present value (NPV) is the most useful and universally accepted metric. Note that for firms that are *very* sophisticated financially, there is a more advanced profitability measure called expected commercial value (ECV). It is included here for completeness, but should only be used after some considerable experience has been gained with the more basic NPV.

1.4

1.19. The expected life of a product is a strong function of its application and technology (refrigerators have a much longer market life without redesign than do cellular phones, for example). A word to the wise: *be conservative here.* As much as we'd like to think that our designs will live on into the next millennium, it is a rare product that warrants looking beyond a five-year horizon when calculating NPV. After much soul-searching, we decide that the high-end product should sell ten thousand units per year for the next five years, and the low-end product would likely sell fifty thousand units per year during the same time period. (Note that I am assuming that sales are flat for the five-year period – an actual NPV calculation would look at each year's forecast individually and then sum them up.)

Now what about profits? We estimate that the high-end unit would have an average production cost of $100, while the lower-end unit would benefit from both less-expensive materials and higher production volumes, resulting in a $30 cost. A market price of $200 for the doctor's version seems reasonable, based on surveys of potential customers. Our friends at the shopping network have indicated that they "can sell a bunch of the cheaper ones" for three easy payments of only $25. From the above information, we can calculate the total profit dollars that would be generated by each product over its expected market life. End of story, right?

We still have the little matter of assignable capital and non-recurring design costs to deal with. If a product requires more initial investment dollars than it will generate in profit dollars over its market life, *that product is a net money-loser.* Hence, we should rightfully subtract the initial investment in capital and design from total profits. (Again, note that for clarity I am simplifying how this is actually done – your financial guru can explain the details.) The profit dollars don't look so hefty anymore, do they? In fact, the high-end model looks like it will barely make money, based on our initial estimates. Given the inherent inaccuracy of our numbers, it would be entirely possible that the doctor's version could actually *lose* money, whereas it appears that the cheaper model is a solid winner, even if we were a bit optimistic in our forecasts. Therefore, we go with *el cheapo* and set aside the gold-plated version for reevaluation in the future. Now all we need to do is pick a spokesmodel.

Product Development Is Risky Business

The above example shows how to determine which new product opportunities have the highest potential for profitability. Now if we lived in a world in which price was well-known in advance, costs were clear and obvious, market demand was etched in stone, new technologies were well-behaved and predictable, and economic conditions were stable and benign...well, there's no point in wishing for the impossible. All of these factors can have high uncertainty, and each can render a promising new product profitless if it goes horribly wrong. Hence, to get an accurate prioritization of new product opportunities, *we must consider risk.* In fact, we should actually *discount* the potential profitability of a product by the level of risk involved: economic risk, technical risk, and last but not least, market risk.

Product Opportunity	Estimates	Y1	Y2	Y3	Y4	Y5	Total Profit	Total Profit Less Non-recurring Costs
"Low-Cost" Wonderjig	Volume	50,000	50,000	50,000	50,000	50,000	$11,250,000	$10,050,000
	Price	$75	$75	$75	$75	$75		
	Fully-Burdened Mfg. Cost	$30	$30	$30	$30	$30		
	Capital	$500,000						
	Design	$700,000						
"Professional" Wonderjig	Volume	10,000	10,000	10,000	10,000	10,000	$5,000,000	$2,000,000
	Price	$200	$200	$200	$200	$200		
	Fully-Burdened Mfg. Cost	$100	$100	$100	$100	$100		
	Capital	$1.5 M						
	Design	$1.3 M						

Figure 1.19 – An example of how the total profits of two different product opportunities can be compared. Nothat the above calculations do not tell the whole story, however. We must factor in risk before we can use this data to rank-order our development projects.

The economic risk is perhaps the easiest to handle. We all know that a dollar today is worth more than a dollar in the future, since a dollar today can be earning interest from now until that future date. If we reverse the process, we can say that dollars earned in the future should be discounted based on how much interest we could have earned had we kept our initial investment in the bank (so to speak). For this reason, the standard net present value calculation includes a discount rate that takes into account the future value of money. If we believe that we could have earned 5% interest on our initial investment if we didn't develop a new product, for example, then we would use a 5% discount rate in our NPV calculation.

Here is where I tend to depart from the standard approach to the NPV calculation. Often, the discount rate is used as a catchall for risk; more risky investments take on a higher discount rate. This makes sense when comparing financial investment opportunities, but I believe it is clumsy to use this approach to account for technical and market risk. Instead, I like to include a percentage multiplier that reflects a best relative estimate of these product-specific risks. Let's continue with the Wonderjig example to illustrate how risk can be incorporated into our NPV calculation.

The economic risk for both the high- and low-cost versions of the Wonderjig is the same, since they would enter the market at the same time and have the same market life. We will use a 5% discount rate to account for the future value of money, but we will use an alternative approach to correct for technical and market risk, as shown in Figure 1.20. Let's assume that the doctor's version of the product will require very challenging materials technology to achieve higher performance and reliability levels, whereas the cheaper version will use low-risk materials. Likewise, the doctor's version has a high risk of market failure, since your firm has little background in pricing or selling into the medical market. Home Shopping Network, on the other hand, has a wealth of experience in selling products such as the low-cost Wonderjig, so the market risk is minimal.

We can factor in these risks by using two simple multipliers. We guesstimate the technical risk for the low-end product to be about 20% less than the high-end version. Therefore, we set the low-end product's risk multiplier to one (meaning essentially zero risk) and we multiply the high-end product's NPV by 80%. Similarly, we estimate that the market-failure risk for the doctor's version will be twice that of the low-cost model, so a 50% multiplier is applied. Between the two multipliers, we have reduced the projected profits of the doctor's version by 60% (i.e., 1.0 − (1.0 x 80% x 50%)). This calculation reflects the probability that we will actually realize the profits that we originally estimated, given the uncertainties involved. Our choice is now even more clear; *el cheapo* is the hands-down winner.

It's likely that you are feeling a bit uncomfortable with the "estimates" in the above example. How did we come up with those numbers? Well, we can try to quantify risk, analyze risk, and machinate over risk. Ultimately, however, I feel that getting a smart group of people together to reach a consensus on relative risk is probably as accurate as a more sophisticated approach. Remember, the purpose of generating these numbers is simply to rank-order your opportunities; the actual numbers will not be used in any truly

Product Opportunity	Estimates	Y1	Y2	Y3	Y4	Y5	Standard NPV	Risk-Corrected NPV
"Low-Cost" Wonderjig	Total Profit per Year	$2.25 M	$2.25 M	$2.25 M	$2.25 M	$2.25 M		
	Discount Rate	5%	5%	5%	5%	5%		
	Discounted Profits	$2.14 M	$2.04 M	$1.94 M	$1.85 M	$1.76 M	$8,530,000	$8,530,000
	Technical Risk	100%						
	Market Risk	100%	Risk Multipliers = 1.0					
"Professional" Wonderjig	Total Profit per Year	$1.0 M	$1.0 M	$1.0 M	$1.0 M	$1.0 M		
	Discount Rate	5%	5%	5%	5%	5%		
	Discounted Profits	$952,000	$907,000	$864,000	$823,000	$784,000	$1,530,000	$612,000
	Technical Risk	80%						
	Market Risk	50%	Risk Multipliers Reduce Projected Profits					

Figure 1.20 – Continuation of the Wonderjig example, taking into account economic, technical, and market risks. The economic risk is accounted for in the traditional way, by using a "discount rate," whereas the technical and market risks are reflected as percent probabilities of success.

quantitative way. So relax, generate your priority ranking, and allocate your precious design resources to those opportunities that will pave your path ahead with gold.

Too Many Projects, Too Few Designers

A priority list is all well and good, but how many of those promising products can we reasonably expect to develop? One of the greatest mistakes that firms make is failing to recognize that they have *finite design capacity*. Overloading designers with three or more projects causes tremendous waste due to multitasking turbulence, and ultimately will yield fewer new products getting out the door. Hence, any truly useful prioritization approach must take into account the finite resources available.

A simple way to achieve this is to divide the risk-corrected NPV for each potential new product by the estimated number of non-recurring hours required to complete the design, as shown in Figure 1.21. This end result is what we have been seeking all along: a ranking that maximizes the profits generated per hour worked by a designer (i.e., maximizes the designer's *productivity*). If you have far more opportunities than you have designers, this is the metric to use for priority ranking.

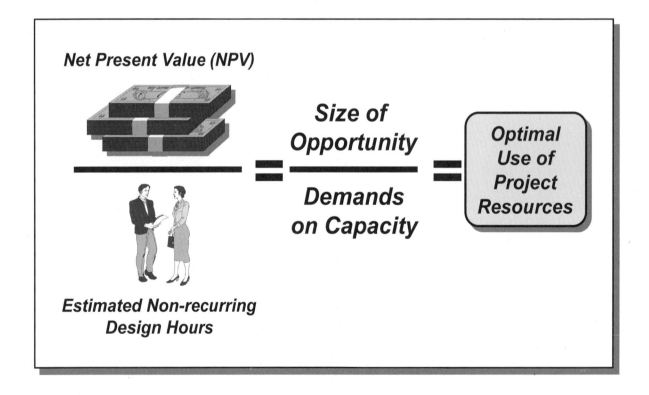

Figure 1.21 – An enhancement of our priority-ranking metric that takes into account the finite number of designers available to execute new product development.

A Final Word – Strategic Products or Just Plain Money-Losers?

I have to laugh when I hear executives talk about their portfolio of "strategic products." Somehow, I can't help feeling that this is just a way of justifying their firm's burgeoning stable of money-losers. Yet, there are some categories of products that are legitimately strategic, and there are even (dare I say it) some situations in which a product should be developed even if it will never be profitable. Some of these reasons include:

- The product will fill a conspicuous hole in your product-line offerings.
- The product will create customer awareness in a new market segment.
- The product will create pull-through sales of more profitable products.
- The product will educate the market and pave the way for future profitable offerings.
- The product will counteract the erosion of market share caused by a competitor's new offering.

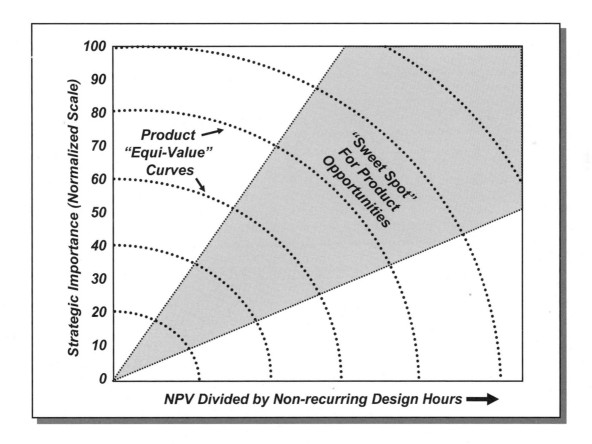

Figure 1.22 – A two-dimensional mapping of new product opportunities based on their profit potential and their strategic importance. The "sweet spot" includes products that are both nicely profitable and have significant strategic value.

1.4

No doubt there are other good reasons to lose money, but I would be careful not to use this "strategic product" euphemism too often. After all, if you are losing money on every unit you sell, you can't make it up in volume.

A good way to think about the prioritization of new product development projects is to picture a two-dimensional space, as shown in Figure 1.22. Along the x-axis is our risk-corrected, finite-resource NPV metric. Along the y-axis is a numerical rating of how "strategic" a new offering might be. This metric can be created by adding together a set of four or five subjective "scores," each rated on a 1-10 scale and normalized to 100. These scores might reflect how well the proposed offering supports strategic goals, such as: 1) market-share increase, 2) pull-through effects, 3) building new markets, 4) undermining competition, and perhaps, 5) completing a product-line portfolio. As you can see in the Figure, there is a logical "sweet spot" on this two-dimensional graph. Products that have good profit potential and also support one or more strategic goals are the real winners. Be careful not to jump at money-losers until you've exhausted all potential opportunities that can give you the best of both worlds.

Section 1.5 — Defining a Target Cost

We're now going to take our point of view into a steep nosedive, leaving the stratospheric world of project portfolio management in favor of a more pragmatic, treetop perspective. Suppose that we have a promising product to develop and our management has committed funds and human resources to kick off the project. What is the first thing that our design team must do to ensure optimal profitability for our new product? Since profits are our primary goal, it seems reasonable that we should start by determining a desired profit margin.

If You Don't Know Where the Target Is, You Can't Hit a Bull's Eye

How much profit do we need to make on this new product to justify the commitment of money and time? In other words, *what is our target margin*? The target margin that we select must be defined with care; too high and we risk pricing ourselves out of the market, too low and we squander our firm's future prospects. A good rule-of-thumb to use is that the target margin should be slightly (perhaps five percentage points) higher than your firm's current average gross margin. This provides you with some protection against cost growth during development, and ensures that you will at least maintain your current level of profitability. Obviously, if we have somehow found a pot-of-gold product that can far exceed our average gross margins, we should go for it. The purpose of a target margin is to establish a *minimum threshold*, below which a new product can never go without risk of cancellation.

We will use this idea of a target margin to establish a clear cost mandate for our design team. At the beginning of product development, a target margin is established, and an estimated market price is divined. Using these two numbers, we can calculate the *target cost* for our new product, as shown here:

Target Cost = Projected Price – Target (Desired) Margin

Note that you should *never* do this calculation the other way: Price = Cost + Margin. Why? *Because you don't control the price!* The marketplace is the final arbiter of price, and although you should try to maximize your remuneration, there are clear limits for a given type of product. Since we can't freely control price, we must insist that the target cost always be maintained as the development process progresses. If the target cost cannot be met, and if there can be no recovery, *the project should be canceled*. This decision process is illustrated in Figure 1.23.

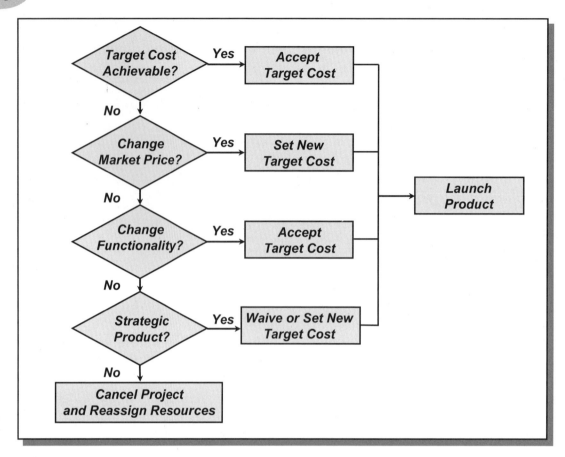

Figure 1.23 – The target cost serves as both a clear mandate for the product design team, and a decision tool for determining if a project is worth the investment of precious resources.

The design process shown in the figure is inherently logical. At several points during the development process (usually synchronized with other "gate" activities such as design reviews and project reviews), the target cost is updated and scrutinized. The first question that should be asked is, "Can the target cost be achieved, based on our best current understanding of the design?" If the answer is yes, we move smartly onward toward launch. A nay response forces us to dig deeper. We might subsequently ask, "Can we somehow change the market price upon which the target cost is based?" This is *not* a call for irrational optimism, however. The market price can *legitimately* be changed, for example, by refocusing the product on a higher-end segment. Sometimes in our efforts to maximize the sales forecast, however, we expand our market segment a bit too broadly. Although the product may be dead on the money for the most demanding users in the segment, there are many customers who might fail to appreciate the majesty of the new offering. Overshooting the needs of these customers means that you just won't get the price you desire or deserve. By narrowing the segment down to just those erudite few who appreciate your product's deeper meaning, you may achieve a significantly higher price and profit (albeit at lower total sales).

If the market price cannot be raised, our next option is a change in the product's functionality. We might ask the question, "Is there something we can add to the product that would justify a higher price?" Please note that while this is often possible, it doesn't help the situation if the cost of the added performance is disproportionately higher than the increase in price. If a functionality change appears to be viable, then by all means proceed. If not, we are into the short hairs of reasonable options.

We must finally ask the question I loath to hear: "Can we justify missing the target cost on this product because it is just so darn strategic that it glows in the dark?" This is a perfectly legitimate question, and if the answer given is objective and the person giving it is strategically prescient, then it deserves inclusion. If, on the other hand, a "yes" answer is the result of organizational denial, then your decision-makers need to buck up. It is hard for firms to face the reality that much time and money may have been wasted chasing a pipe-dream product. Sunk costs weigh heavily on managers as they consider the future of a questionable product. Yet we must all be brave, *because sunk costs should never be honored*. If a product's cost exceeds its target-cost threshold, we must strongly consider cancellation, regardless of how much money and time have already been spent. The reason for this is opportunity cost, as discussed in Section 1.4. Opportunity for your tied-up designers to work on more valuable projects, opportunity for better utilization of scarce capital, and opportunity to optimize the output from your factory's finite capacity. A weak-sister product wastes opportunities that can never be recovered, so develop a hard carapace to deflect criticism and make the tough calls when they become necessary.

How to Build a Basic Cost Model

The target cost represents a touchstone for all cost-reduction initiatives during product development. But wait a minute. How on earth will the design team know whether their work-in-progress is heading for the bull's eye? Clearly some feedback process is needed to allow the team to make course corrections as a new product design matures. The feedback of which I speak will come from a product "cost model," as shown in Figure 1.24. No, I am not referring to some arcane cost-accounting application that generates something called a "standard cost" (a ridiculous concept on the face of it – a product costs what it costs, and any attempt to "standardize" it will obfuscate its true cost structure). A product cost model is one of the critical tools that a design team utilizes iteratively throughout product development. Hence, it must be intuitive, non-threatening, and should easily capture the steadily increasing cost knowledge of the design team as a product design approaches reality.

At its simplest, a cost model is just a list of the stuff that it takes to manufacture a product, including cost estimates for both materials and labor, as shown in Figure 1.25. A basic spreadsheet is all that's needed; perhaps a flexible template that each design team can tailor to the nature of their specific product. At first, the model will build upon wild guesses and numbers pulled from thin air. *This is perfectly fine.* We are not aiming for accuracy, at least in the early stages of development. Our goal is to generate an initial

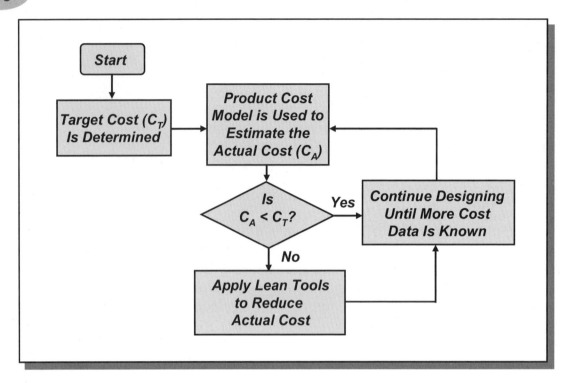

Figure 1.24 – A flow diagram showing how a product cost model is embedded in a feedback loop that must be exercised iteratively throughout the product development process.

sanity-check, and establish an envelop within which the final cost should lie. You might run some scenarios, for example, that rail the possible costs to the highest and lowest levels that are realistically possible. How does the product fare against the target cost when pessimistic assumptions are input? What critical cost items must be nailed down early to ensure that the product can meet its profit goals? What are the tradeoffs between non-recurring capital investment (in tooling, automation, etc.) and direct material and labor costs? To move forward in the design process without a well-worn cost model *is to ignore cost as a requirement of your product.* After all, how many of your hotshot designers would even consider working without CAD / CAM, Monte Carlo simulators, finite-element analysis, and all the other whiz-bang design tools your firm's invested in? Giving your product's cost requirements the same stature doesn't seem to be an unreasonable mandate.

Cost Partitioning (and a First Hint of Systems Thinking)

If your product is relatively simple, the basic cost model suggested above will do the trick. But what if your firm develops jet fighters, or MRI machines, or...you get the picture. That "simple" spreadsheet could morph into an unwieldy monster that provides little useful insight into detailed cost tradeoffs. Is there a way to structure a cost model that delivers both ease of use and deep insight, even for complex system products? I just gave

1.5

	Labor Rate	Labor Burden (%)	# Hours	Material Burden (%)	Scrap Rate (%)	Qty.	Unit Cost @ Production Volume			Totals
							5000 / yr.	10,000 / yr.	20,000 / yr.	
I. Direct Materials										
1. Raw Material A										
2. Raw Material B, etc.										
3. Part A										
4. Part B, etc.										
5. Scrap										
6. Other										
II. Direct Labor										
1. Rough Assy.										
2. Final Assy.										
3. Inspection										
4. Test										
5. Packaging										
6. External Services										
7. Other										
III. Assignable Capital										
1. Dedicated Equipment										
2. Tooling										
3. Fixturing										
4. Other										
IV. Non-recurring Design Costs										
1. Development										
2. Launch Transition										
3. Other										
V. Warrantee Cost										
									Total Cost Buildup =	

Figure 1.25 – A basic cost model need not be complex or even accurate during the early stages of product development. Its purpose is to provide the feedback necessary for a design team to optimize cost in the same rigorous manner as all other product requirements are addressed.

away the answer: *system* products. Every product is actually a problem-solving system. For our purposes in this guidebook, a system can be defined as a set of components or elements that work together toward a common purpose, with feedback. Relatively simple products are what we might call "single-level systems." Hence a simplistic, single-level cost model will suffice. For more complex, multifunctional products, your cost model should be partitioned into logical subsystems, each of which will receive an allocated target cost, as shown in Figure 1.26.

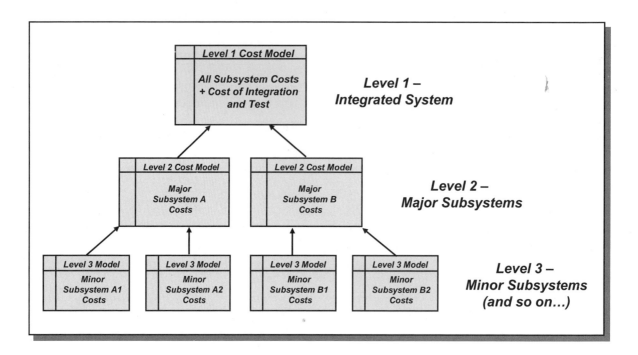

Figure 1.26 – A multilevel product cost model can capture the cost buildup of complex system products in a clear and useful way. At the lowest level in the system, each model would look like the example shown in Figure 1.25. Higher-level models are roll-ups of lower-level ones, but must also include any integration and testing costs.

To partition your product into sensible chunks, look for simple interfaces, grouped functionality, logical subassemblies, or any other natural subdivision of the product. Complex products are usually developed in a tiered structure anyway, so your cost model can simply follow the functional partitioning of software and hardware. If your system product has three levels of subassembly, for example, then you would have a three-level cost model. This way, each component or subassembly has its own simple model. Note that for multilevel cost models you must be careful when rolling up costs to the next highest level. At each level of roll-up, there will be additional costs not included in lower-level models. The cost of integrating and testing the final system product, for example, would appear only on the highest level cost model.

I will have much more to say about systems thinking and its critical role in enterprise-level cost reduction. For now, I'll address just one important aspect that directly impacts cost modeling. In an earlier paragraph, I glibly mentioned that we must allocate the total target cost among each partitioned element of a system product. How should this vital activity be performed? To understand the answer, we must first consider a theorem from system engineering:

"Optimizing the function of any single component or element of a system makes it impossible to optimize the function of the entire system."

Read that theorem again. This is powerful stuff! You can't optimize the function of a sports team, for example, if each player tries to optimize their own individual performance. You can't optimize the performance of a racing engine if each component isn't perfectly matched to every other. Finally, you can't optimize the cost of a product by simply reducing the cost of each item on its bill-of-materials in a vacuum. Functionality is what the customer is paying for, and there may be many ways of reducing the cost of a *function* that would never be considered if cost-reduction efforts are focused only at the level of individual parts.

Now to answer my earlier question: How should the target cost be allocated among partitioned elements of a system? *Based on their estimated importance in achieving the functions and performance needed to satisfy the intended customer.* Critical elements of the design that are dead center on the customer's radar screen should receive a relatively large

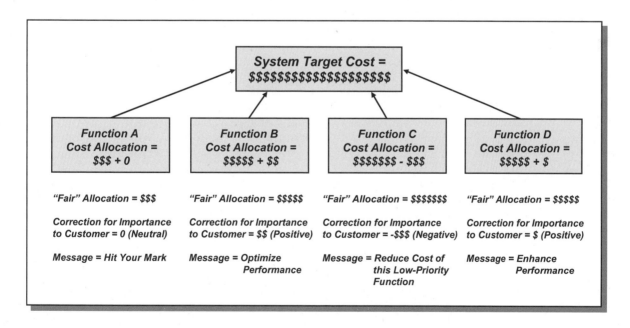

Figure 1.27 – One way in which the target cost for an entire system product can be partitioned and allocated to the various levels of the system. Note that the allocation is strongly influenced by the criticality of the functions performed by various subsystems.

1.5

allocation of target cost, while minor features and niceties can be allotted a much tighter budget. An example of how this allocation process can be performed is shown in Figure 1.27. Note that it is the responsibility of the lead designer for each higher level of subassembly to balance cost and performance for their subsystem; in this way the cost of the entire system can be optimized in a "flow-up" process. There are many other ways of performing cost partitioning, but however you approach it, be sure to flow down cost targets to a level that allows designers to easily understand their models, and can therefore utilize them in a money-saving way.

Section 1.6 — Twenty Levers for Product Cost

We're finally approaching a reasonably complete understanding of product cost. With a target cost established and an appropriate cost model in place, our design team is well-prepared for the challenges ahead. Now all that remains (and this will take the remainder of this guidebook) is to identify tools and methods that can enable dramatic cost reduction consistent with the preservation of quality and value. Before we press ahead, however, there is one more step that we can take to fully illuminate the mysteries of product cost. We know there are five cost "knobs" that a designer can turn to reduce a product's manufacturing cost: 1) we can reduce *direct labor*, 2) we can reduce *material costs*, 3) we can decrease the amount of *assignable capital* required, 4) we can reduce the *non-recurring cost of product design*, and 5) we can try to influence the *factory's overhead* downward. In this final section, I will identify twenty key "cost levers" that impact one or more of the knobs on our control panel. Each lever represents a possible tradeoff that designers might consider when attempting to meet their target cost. These levers are then incorporated into a simple tradeoff evaluation tool that can allow rapid and reasonably accurate decisions on how best to squeeze the last nickel of waste from your new product.

Like Archimedes Said…It's All About Leverage

To paraphrase the illustrious Greek mathematician, Archimedes, "If you give me a cost lever strong enough, I can move the balance sheet." Cost levers are simply aspects of a product's design that can have a significant impact on its manufacturing cost. Before I share with you my choices for the twenty most important cost levers, I must put forward a caveat. The cost levers for your specific products and markets may well be different from the ones that I suggest. This is not a comprehensive list, and depending on your situation, some important levers may not be present. *Please do a sanity-check.* Hopefully my suggestions will illustrate the types of considerations that are critical, and enable you to modify the list to suit your needs. Much more will be said about the opportunities described below, but for now, the following discussion should serve to get your mental gears turning.

Now, in no particular order, are my top-twenty picks for factors that can lever product cost.

1.6

I. Cost Levers for Direct Labor

A. Simplify Manufacturing Processes – Can the production process be simplified by reducing the complexity of assembly, eliminating fasteners or interconnects, designing for top-down assembly, or using standard tools, etc.? Can machine setup and changeover times be reduced? How about the elimination of time-consuming surface finishes, or difficult alignments and adjustments? This is the area in which Design for Manufacture and Assembly (DFMA) really shines (see Section 6.3).

B. Reduce Required Skill Level – It's not just the number of direct labor hours that determines total labor cost; the skill level required can also have a major impact. By designing a product to be simple to assemble and test, and relatively easy to adjust or customize, the per-hour cost of labor can be significantly reduced.

C. Automate Manufacturing Processes – Automation is a wonderful thing, but it should be implemented only after careful consideration of the cost tradeoffs. If the automation will be dedicated to a single new product, then a direct payback analysis should be performed. If the equipment will be shared over several products, however, the justification gets more complicated. It is all too common for firms to just wave their hands and say, "we'll get tons of cost savings from this automation, so let's just commit the capital and reap the benefits." Because capital depreciation costs are buried in the overhead rate, automation may seem like an easy route to lower labor costs and higher profits. In reality, a major capital investment taxes the profits of every product within a profit center, and depletes a firm's reserve of available funds. Automation should be used intelligently, and only with a solid justification behind it.

D. Reduce Test / Inspection Requirements – Here's a ripe opportunity for direct-labor reduction. In the strictest sense, test and inspection are non-value-added activities. If we can ensure that quality is maintained, then any reduction in this area is just free money. Designing products to be easily testable is a good start, but ultimately the elimination of test and inspection should be the goal. Using Six-Sigma Design principles, combined with Statistical Process Control and Design-for-Testability techniques, can yield impressive cost savings (see Section 6.2).

II. Cost Levers for Direct Materials

A. Reduce Scrap – In some industries, such as semiconductor processing or high-precision die-casting, the cost of scrap can be significant. In general, the scrap rate is driven by both the capability of the process (its ability to achieve the required tolerances) and by the robustness of the product design (its ability to accommodate process variability without loss of quality). Again, Six-Sigma Design tools can help optimize these two critical drivers to achieve high first-pass yields and minimal scrap.

B. Reduce Parts Count – One of the guiding principles of lean design is "eliminate or standardize." Can a part be combined with another and thereby be eliminated? Perhaps the way in which a function is performed can be altered to reduce the number of parts required. If a part cannot be eliminated, can it be designed to be common with other parts in the product (e.g., can all fasteners in a product use the same part number)? DFMA principles can assist in achieving parts-count reduction on a single product basis. Using platform design concepts and modular / scalable design principles can have a dramatic impact on parts count across all products within a business unit.

C. Use Cheaper Raw Materials / Parts – The opportunities here fall into two categories: 1) the material selected is an overshoot for the given application (e.g., using stainless steel when painted metal would do, or 2) expensive materials are being specified as a substitute for a more clever design (e.g., using high-precision electronic components instead of taking extra time to design a more tolerant circuit). Obviously, cheapening raw materials must be done with care, but if a part or raw material stands out as being excessively expensive, some soul-searching should be done to determine if there is a lower-cost alternative.

D. Use High-Volume Parts – This opportunity is related to parts-count reduction. If we can commonize on a small set of frequently used parts, then we save in two ways. First, the cost of material handling, purchasing, inventory management, etc., will be reduced (a favorable impact on operational overhead). Second, the common parts will have a larger order quantity, resulting in volume discounts from suppliers. The best application of this cost driver is in the domain of "penny parts," which seem to proliferate like rabbits on Viagra in discrete manufacturing firms.

III. *Cost Levers for Assignable Capital*

A. Eliminate Batch Processes – Oh, it's a vicious cycle. First, we decide that a production line will need some new capital equipment. Then someone looks at cost versus capacity and decides that bigger is better, and huge is better still. Now, of course, the hulking new piece of equipment requires long setup times, and has five times the capacity currently needed, and requires a tower crane to move it, but no matter. We'll just batch up our products until we can fill the darn thing, and look at all the money we'll save! Logic like this is enough to make me weep. Although there are exceptions (which should be carefully justified), small, rapid-throughput equipment that is compatible with one-piece or few-piece flow is generally more economical, flexible, movable, etc.

B. Outsource Capital-Intensive Processes – Purchasing capital equipment is like getting a tattoo; it seems like such a good idea at the time, but the enthusiasm wears off a long time before the tattoo does. Acquiring your own capital equipment means: a) you must keep it utilized, thereby constraining many of your future design decisions, b) much hidden overhead will be spent maintaining it, c) you must employ people trained to use it,

d) you must continue using it until it has paid for itself, even if it has become woefully obsolete, e) you've paid a high price to enter a new market...one which must be recouped before you see your first dollar of real profit. Why not plan to outsource capital-intensive operations for new products, at least until you have solid market data and production experience to justify a capital investment?

C. Optimize Tooling Cost – One of the most powerful cost-saving techniques to come out of Japan, Inc. in recent years is the Toyota "Production Process Preparation (3P)" methodology (see Section 5.2). Within this toolset is a real gem: the "Seven-Alternatives" Process (see Section 5.4). The idea is that for every significant cost item in a product, designers should consider the advantages and disadvantages of seven alternative processes. This can be a mind-expanding experience, particularly if your designers tend to use the same few processes over and over again. As you will see later in this guidebook, the choice of appropriate processes can have a huge impact on profitability, particularly with respect to tooling costs. For lower-volume products, optimizing tooling costs can mean the difference between healthy profitability and cancellation of a development project.

D. Avoid Dedicated Equipment – It's scary enough investing in capital equipment, but if that equipment will be dedicated to a single product, the risks are even greater. What if the product bombs? What if the equipment turns out to be more costly than expected to operate? Don't fall into the trap of euphemizing dedicated equipment by claiming it will be used on multiple products. Capital equipment should only be purchased in support of a *core process capability*; something your firm will be doing regardless of whether any single product thrives or dies. Non-core processes should be outsourced.

IV. Cost Levers for Non-recurring Design

A. Reuse Existing Designs / Processes – Design reuse is just like printing money. You save non-recurring design cost, and get the product to market quicker besides. The problem lies in developing the infrastructure required to implement broad-based design reuse. There is a high potential for wasted effort here; if a reuse library or database is generally ignored by designers of new products, its creation was a money pit.

B. Eliminate Unnecessary Complexity – One of the most exalted compliments one can pay a designer is to tell her that her design is "elegant." Elegance of design means that high performance, quality, and customer satisfaction is achieved in a remarkably simple way. This requires innovation, insight, an artful touch...along with a desire to save money. Elegant designs are often low-cost designs. Resist the voice of that bad little devil on your left shoulder who's whispering, "more parts, more features, more gimmicks, more fluff." Instead, listen to that good angel on your right shoulder (who speaks to the right side of your brain) and strive for simplicity of form and function.

C. Avoid Gold-Plating of Designs – Gold plating means overshooting the customer's needs. If a car with four wheels is good, wouldn't a car with six wheels be better? If a VCR with a simple remote control is good, why not clog it up with a hundred meaningless buttons? Customers will not pay for performance or features that overshoot their needs, but your firm will pay for the cost of including them. Better is the enemy of good enough, so focus on solving the customer's problem, and keep the gold in your firm's pockets.

D. Optimize Make vs. Buy – If you decide to buy a part rather than make it, you may not need to design it. Suppliers have smart engineers waiting by the phone to help you tailor their products to your needs. Typically, if the customization is within reason, their non-recurring design is free. In fact, many suppliers (particularly in mature, commoditized industries) will do a complete set of drawings for you before you even commit to an order. Make the stuff that only your firm can make, or the stuff that has so much profit built into it that you just can't resist, and outsource the rest. Make vs. buy should be considered at the very earliest stages of concept design, with suppliers brought in as team members whenever possible (see Section 5.4).

V. Cost Levers for Factory Overhead

A. Avoid Major Changes to Factory Layout – I like to say that the most competitive companies in the world have products that look like they're customized for every buyer, yet the factory can't tell the difference between them. We want products that capture the market's fancy and often this implies uniqueness. However, if existing workcells, flowlines, capital equipment, material-handling equipment, storage locations, and logistics support can be used, what a savings will result! You can try to fix all this stuff once the new product is in the factory, but why not consider it up front? There may be easy opportunities to reduce the impact on the factory, and it will give your manufacturing engineer something valuable to do during concept development.

B. Reduce Raw Material / Work-in-Process Inventory – Inventory carrying costs can be a significant contributor to operational overhead. Using Just-in-Time (JIT) inventory management is the key, but product designers must be thinking about JIT during the design process to make it work. Are all suppliers onboard to provide frequent small deliveries of materials? Can you use a value-added distributor to provide miscellaneous parts using a self-stocking arrangement (in which the distributor sets up a mini-warehouse in your factory, monitors material use and performs restocking for you)? Can you eliminate long-lead-time parts that might require large safety stocks? Can you design the product to be built-to-order with a short cycle-time, rather than requiring many stages of subassembly and partially-finished-goods inventories?

C. Reduce Material-Handling Requirements – Material handling demands labor hours, floor space, and in some cases, very expensive capital equipment. Think about how the parts and raw materials for your new product will be handled. Are heavy subassemblies designed to be easily maneuvered? Are there crane hooks, handles, or other such features needed to reduce handling labor? Can large and cumbersome structures be designed in a modular fashion? Can any special material-handling requirements be eliminated (such as for hazardous materials)? Are parts designed to avoid jamming of handling equipment, or becoming hooked onto each other in storage bins?

D. Reduce Use of Consumables – In some industries, consumables (those materials that are used up as part of the manufacturing process) can be quite expensive. Examples include: wear on tools and cutting devices, lubricants, abrasives, glues, paints and finishes, etc. This lever is particularly important if your new product would be the only one in the factory to require a specific consumable. As with all of the above cost drivers, uniqueness is a bad thing in lean manufacturing; if your new product is an exception to the rule, then it is almost certainly causing more than its share of added overhead cost.

The Twenty-Cost-Lever Tradeoff Tool

At this point you might be thinking that this cost-reduction stuff is just too complicated. After all, it's hard enough to get a product's performance and features right. Now you are being asked to consider an entirely different (and admittedly complex) set of tradeoffs. Well, I can't let you off the hook on cost reduction, but I will provide you with a tool that will help during the evaluation of design options.

The twenty cost levers described above can be graphically represented, as shown in Figure 1.28. Five knobs, each with four levers. Move one of the levers in the right direction and presumably the product's cost will go down...*unless there is some nasty negative effect on the other cost levers.* Herein lies the challenge. We are working in a twenty-variable space with potentially high degrees of interaction between the variables. Fortunately, the Twenty-Cost-Lever tradeoff tool shown in Figure 1.29 provides a relatively easy means to evaluate these interactions, albeit in a semi-quantitative way.

The twenty cost levers are shown along the left-hand column. Each lever is provided with a space in the adjacent column for a "weighting factor." This is simply a multiplicative factor that captures the difference in importance among the levers for your specific situation. For example, if you have a low-volume, high-value, complex product, your set of weighting factors would be very different from those of a simple, high-volume commodity. I typically limit my weighting-factor range to integers between 1 and 5. Any larger range and the tool's output may be unrealistically skewed. For a first easy cut, set all the weighting factors to one and use the tool to give you qualitative (but still useful) insights.

I've provided space in the sample template for three design options; you can, of course, expand the tool to accommodate as many options as you wish. Normally the way I would use this tool is to begin with a "default" design option. Perhaps this is a concept that is most like your previous product designs. It might also be a "performance-optimized" design that has all the horsepower, but at an unacceptably high cost. Set the

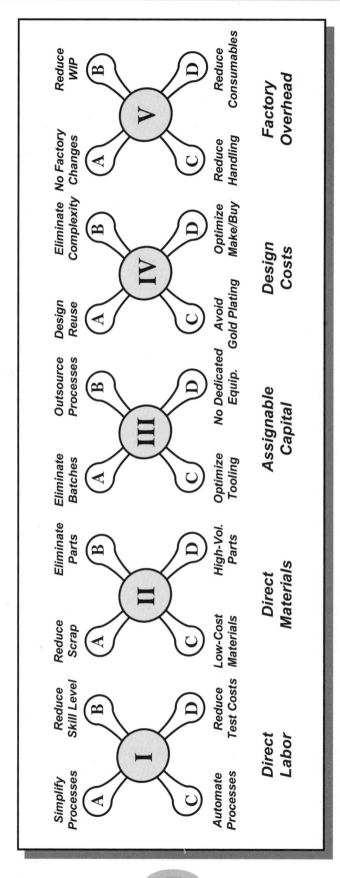

Figure 1.28 – The twenty cost levers and their associated "knobs" for product cost reduction.

"scores" for the Option 1 column that represents this default all to zero. Now get your team together and conceptualize some alternative designs that will move one or more of the cost levers in a beneficial direction. Spend enough time discussing these options to gain a rough understanding of how they would look, what materials would be needed, how much capital equipment would be required, etc. Go through the list of twenty levers and decide how the new design option would compare to Option 1, the default option. If the new design is more favorable from a cost standpoint, give it a positive score (using a range of integers from -5 to +5). If the impact on a given cost lever would be negative, give it a negative score. The magnitude of the scores should be roughly proportional to the estimated impact. Naturally, pulling numbers out of the air is not nearly as accurate as gathering some real cost estimates for all options under consideration. Try at the very least to reach an agreement with your design team on the meaning of a -5 score or a + 5 score, and be as consistent as possible. Note that a score of zero means that the new design option is not significantly different from the default design for that particular cost lever.

Once you've completed your scoring, multiply the weighting factors by the scores in each column to generate a total weighted score for each design option. A positive total score (relative to the default design option set to zero) indicates that the new alternative should have cost advantages over the default. A negative total score says that you are better off with the default design. Given the subjective nature of this tool, total scores that are close to each other (say, a difference of five points or less) are essentially a tie. If all weighting factors are set to one, the highest possible total score would be 100 and the lowest would be -100.

As you might have come to expect by now, an example is in order. Before we disband the thingamajig team from our previous example, let's see how they might use this tool to optimize the cost of the "Home Shopping Network" version of their product. Being the awesome designers that they are, the team immediately realizes that the best way to use the tradeoff tool is to consider different design "scenarios." These are not fully realized design options, but rather they are highly skewed possibilities that take one or more of the cost levers to a dramatic extreme. In this way, the interactions among the cost levers can be illuminated without spending lots of time detailing each option. When a promising direction is identified, more study can be initiated to put a finer point on it.

The thingamajig team selects two alternative design scenarios: Option 1 will be their current default design, Option 2 will assume that the maximum amount of automation will be used to manufacture the product, and Option 3 will consider the possibility that all production will be outsourced (i.e., through contract manufacturing). Extremes to be sure, but much insight can be gained from these high-contrast tradeoffs. The result of their analysis is shown in Figure 1.30. Weighting factors were selected based on the specific circumstances surrounding the high-volume, low-cost thingamajig. The default option is set to all zeros so that the differences in cost behavior of the two alternatives can be clearly observed.

The Twenty-Cost-Lever Tradeoff Tool			
Cost Levers	Weighting	Option 1	Option 2	Option 3
I. Direct Labor				
A. Simplify Processes				
B. Reduce Skill Level				
C. Automate Processes				
D. Reduce Test Costs				
Subtotal =				
II. Direct Materials				
A. Reduce Scrap				
B. Eliminate Parts				
C. Low-Cost Materials				
D. High-Volume Parts				
Subtotal =				
III. Assignable Capital				
A. Eliminate Batches				
B. Outsource Processes				
C. Optimize Tooling				
D. No Dedicated Equipment				
Subtotal =				
IV. Design Costs				
A. Design Reuse				
B. Eliminate Complexity				
C. Avoid Gold Plating				
D. Optimize Make vs. Buy				
Subtotal =				
V. Factory Overhead				
A. No Factory Changes				
B. Reduce WIP				
C. Reduce Handling				
D. Reduce Consumables				
Subtotal =				
Total Scores =				

Figure 1.29 – The Twenty-Cost-Lever tradeoff tool allows design teams to quickly (but, of course, approximately) evaluate possible cost improvement ideas. The primary benefit of this tool is to identify the impact of a design change across all five of our "cost knobs." Often an idea that positively impacts one cost knob will have a negative impact on one or more of the others. With the weighting factors all set to one, a score of 100 is the best possible, and a score of -100 says that you enjoy bankruptcy court.

1.6

Cost Levers	Weighting	Option 1	Option 2	Option 3
I. Direct Labor				
A. Simplify Processes	1	0	3	5
B. Reduce Skill Level	2	0	4	5
C. Automate Processes	1	0	5	0
D. Reduce Test Costs	4	0	0	2
Subtotal =		0	16	23
II. Direct Materials				
A. Reduce Scrap	3	0	1	-3
B. Eliminate Parts	1	0	0	0
C. Low-Cost Materials	1	0	0	0
D. High-Volume Parts	1	0	0	0
Subtotal =		0	3	-9
III. Assignable Capital				
A. Eliminate Batches	1	0	-3	0
B. Outsource Processes	1	0	-5	5
C. Optimize Tooling	3	0	-3	0
D. No Dedicated Equipment	4	0	-5	5
Subtotal =		0	-37	25
IV. Design Costs				
A. Design Reuse	2	0	0	0
B. Eliminate Complexity	1	0	0	0
C. Avoid Gold Plating	1	0	0	0
D. Optimize Make vs. Buy	1	0	0	0
Subtotal =		0	0	0
V. Factory Overhead				
A. No Factory Changes	1	0	-3	5
B. Reduce WIP	2	0	-1	-3
C. Reduce Handling	1	0	3	3
D. Reduce Consumables	1	0	0	0
Subtotal =		0	-2	2
Total Scores =		0	-20	41

Figure 1.30 – An example of how the Twenty-Cost-Lever tradeoff tool can be used to select which of two or more design options for the thingamajig product would result in a lower manufacturing cost. In this case, Option 1 is the current design (hence, set to zero), Option 2 considers the impact of extensive automation of the process, and Option 3 considers the benefits of complete outsourcing of the product. Naturally, these results are qualitative; excellent for performing quick tradeoffs and gaining early insight, but no substitute for detailed cost modeling once a preferred approach is selected.

First they consider the highly automated Option 2. The manufacturing processes will be significantly simplified and will require a lower-skilled operator (but they are probably neglecting the highly skilled maintenance people that will be hovering over that automation to keep it working). Obviously, Option 2 receives a high score for the automation cost lever, but testing costs will not be significantly effected. Under direct materials, there is only a minor impact on scrap, presumably in a positive direction. Lots of action under assignable capital, however, with strong negative scores across the board due to the huge amount of product-specific capital equipment required. Design costs will not be changed significantly (remember to keep your high-altitude perspective...minor second- and third-order effects should be ignored). Factory overhead, however, will also receive a chunk of added costs, particularly with respect to changes in factory layout, maintenance, etc. Work-in-process inventory (WIP) will increase slightly due to the larger batch sizes required by the automation under consideration.

Well, Option 2 turned out to be a loser with a significantly negative total score, but what about Option 3, the outsourced design approach? Option 3 starts off well, with high positive marks for impact on direct labor. There is a small hit due to the potential for a higher scrap rate using a contract manufacturer, but the elimination of dedicated capital equipment makes the world bright again. Factory overhead will actually benefit from Option 3 since more capacity will be available for the next generation of products. Work-in-process inventory goes up, however, due to the batching that will no doubt take place in shipments to and from the contract manufacturer. In total, contract manufacturing appears to be a very promising option. Will the ultimate design be completely outsourced? Almost certainly not. It may turn out that many of the cost advantages can be captured by simply outsourcing a percentage of the product's assembly work. Again, *this is an indicator of promising new directions and a tradeoff tool for evaluating various possibilities*. Give it a try on your next design. This tool is the product-cost equivalent of Lasik surgery; your eyesight for cost-reduction opportunities will be much improved through its use.

Notes

Part I

Recommendations for Further Learning

References

The following books will give you a more detailed insight into the topics covered in Part I. At the end of each major section of this guidebook, I will provide some suggestions on how you can dig in more deeply if your situation warrants it. Rather than just giving you a list of references, I've taken the liberty of providing a brief "review" of each book, along with a value rating, on a one-to-five-star scale. Note that additional references are provided in the Bibliography.

Activity-Based Costing

***** *The Complete Guide to Activity-Based Costing,*
O'Guin, M. C., 1991

This is the seminal book on the subject, and a very useful one at that. Practical and easy to understand for the financially challenged, it is really the only book you need on the subject, unless you are planning a career change from designer to bean counter.

***** *Activity-Based Cost Management: Making it Work,*
Cokins, G., 1996

Another great reference on the subject, but from the perspective of the implementer. The author tries to show that ABC must be embedded in an enterprise-wide management system (Activity-Based Management, ABM) to be an effective tool. Lots of good material, but optimistic in its view of ABC acceptance and deployment.

*** *Cost & Effect,* Kaplan, R. S., and R. Cooper, 1998

Well, they can't all be winners. This book adds little to the references above, but since it's published by Harvard Business School Press, I was concerned that you might go to this one first. It does include some excellent case examples and some good practical tips, so if you just can't get enough of ABC, this might be a good third choice.

Net Present Value, Etc.

**** *Portfolio Management for New Products,* Cooper, R. G., Edgett, S. J., and E. J. Kleinschmidt, 1998

This is a very useful book, but from an unfailingly strategic perspective. Most designers or team leaders would find the air a bit rarified throughout most of the book, but it includes a very good discussion of Expected Commercial Value (ECV) and other metrics.

***** *Fundamentals of Engineering Design,* Hyman, B., 1998

This book is such a rarity in the professional book world that I can't really think of a parallel. It is a design book, for designers, by a designer, that actually describes how to design *products*, not overpriced and unproducible prototypes. Great practical discussion of project ranking and metrics, along with some excellent words to live by on the design side.

Target Costing and Cost Modeling

**** *Target Costing and Value Engineering,* Cooper, R., and R. Slagmulder, 1997

A nearly seminal book (whatever that means) on target costing. A good practical discussion with lots of detail and an excellent linkage to another critical topic; value engineering. My only quibble is the book's thinly veiled academic flavor. I'm sure these guys have industry experience, but they don't exactly speak to that audience.

***** *Target Costing and Kaizen Costing,* Monden, Y., 1995

A truly excellent book by one of the great thinkers of Japanese industry. An Asian flavor to be sure, but you just can't beat the commonsense, practical advice from someone who has really been there. *Kaizen* costing is an added bonus; an excellent methodology for continuous cost reduction.

*** *Integrated Cost Management,* Sakurai, M., 1996

If you are deeply interested in how Japanese firms calculate factory overhead (certainly better than we do), then this is your book. Otherwise, skip it.

**** *Office Kaizen,* Lareau, W., 2003

A very good book, but not really on the subject. I've included it because it has a nice (but somewhat cursory) discussion of "Kobayashi's 20 Keys," a practical multivariable assessment tool not unlike my "Twenty-Cost-Lever" tradeoff tool.

Consider Cost From the Very Beginning

2.1 - Capturing the Voice of the Customer

2.2 - Prioritizing Customer Requirements

Part II

"No one wearies of benefits received."

Marcus Aurelius Antoninus

"If you mean to profit, learn to please."

Winston Churchill

"Nothing is cheap which is superfluous,
for what one does not need,
is dear at a penny."

Plutarch

Section 2.1 — Capturing the Voice of the Customer

As I've said before, your team's greatest opportunity (and challenge) in new product design is to solve your customer's problem completely, *and then stop*. An incomplete solution will receive a poor market response, and typically a poor price to match. A gold-plated product, on the other hand, will overshoot your customer's needs at the expense of profit margin. There is an optimal design for every problem, and depending on how well-defined your customer or market segment is, you can home in on an ideal product solution that will maximize *value*; performance delivered at a given price.

Unfortunately, unless you are psychic (or have Vulcan blood), it is impossible to read the minds of potential customers. Moreover, customers are not homogeneous, are notoriously fickle, and often don't have a clue what a good product solution would look like until it is sitting in front of them. This section provides some ideas on how to gather and rank-order customer feedback, both at the beginning of the development process and also iteratively as the product design matures.

What Do Customers Really Pay For?

There is a critical distinction between what customers will pay for and what a design team actually creates. Customers have a *problem* that they need solved, and they will pay for anything that *benefits* them in that regard. The amount they are willing to pay is directly related to both how important the problem is to them and how much benefit they receive from the product solution. Now here is the critical part: *Benefits are not the same thing as requirements!* Benefits are perceived by the customer, in their own language, and are independent of the specifics of a product's features, performance, configuration, materials, etc. All of the latter items are *requirements* of the product that will presumably deliver the benefits that the customer is hungry for. Hence, it can be said that *requirements should and must be derived from benefits* to be close to the mark in your customer's mind.

All of this is not simply a formality, nor are these distinctions semantic. Product development is like playing that old grade-school game of "telephone." Recall that during rainy days, your trapped and desperate teacher would have a student think up a phrase and whisper it into the ear of the person next to them. That person would then whisper what they thought to be exactly the same phrase to their neighbor, and so on throughout the rest of the room. What came out of the other end of this fascinating activity (at least

2.1

for third-graders) was something that sounded nothing like the phrase that started the process. Lesson learned: Much can be lost in the translation of information between individuals.

Here's how "telephone" is played in today's business world. A customer is willing to pay for some benefit. This willingness is detected by a sales or marketing person within your firm. This is the first time that the "message" is transferred. Assuming that your firm has the competencies necessary to proceed, a "product description" is created by marketing that suggests what the product solution might look like (the second translation of the message). Your design group reviews the product description and generates a detailed engineering requirements document (i.e., a product specification...the third translation). We're just getting started in the development process and our customer's needs have already been filtered through three layers of interpretation. As the project moves forward, the message can continue to drift, unless constant customer feedback is solicited. The product that results from this game of telephone may be very different from what the customer imagined, and often not in a good way.

A systematic process for the translation of customer needs and benefits into the language of product design is needed. Unfortunately, any such approach will be subject to the vagarities of human communication. Yet we can do much to improve the fidelity of each translation by following the process described in Figure 2.1. We begin by attempting to understand the problem that our potential customer faces and the benefits that they would be willing to pay for. From these benefits, a list of *functions* is defined that are essential to solving the customer's problem. In subsequent sections of this book, the definition of a function will be thoroughly discussed. For now, we'll describe a function with simply a verb and a noun (e.g., the function of a car's engine is to "power car"). From the list of functions, the design team will derive the requirements that must be met (or alternatively, the specifications that must be achieved). These requirements will then become the basis for development of our new product.

How can we best ensure that our product delivers the benefits that our customer desires? Back in third grade, how could you have made certain that the message you received was as close as possible to the original? That's right: *Go back to the source!* The source of all truly useful information about a future product is the customer. Yet most product design teams have zero contact with end users, being effectively shielded from the "real world" by the marketing function. Even marketing may have, at best, anecdotal information about customer needs which can rapidly become out-of-date in highly dynamic markets. What we need is a way for our design team to become "intimate" with the customer. The first step toward achieving this goal is for designers to learn how to *listen*.

If You're Not Hearing Voices, There's Something Wrong With You

There are a number of ways in which a design team can harvest fresh-off-the-vine customer information. All of them have their advantages and disadvantages, as shown in Figure 2.2. The ultimate goal is to achieve customer intimacy: the ability to empathically

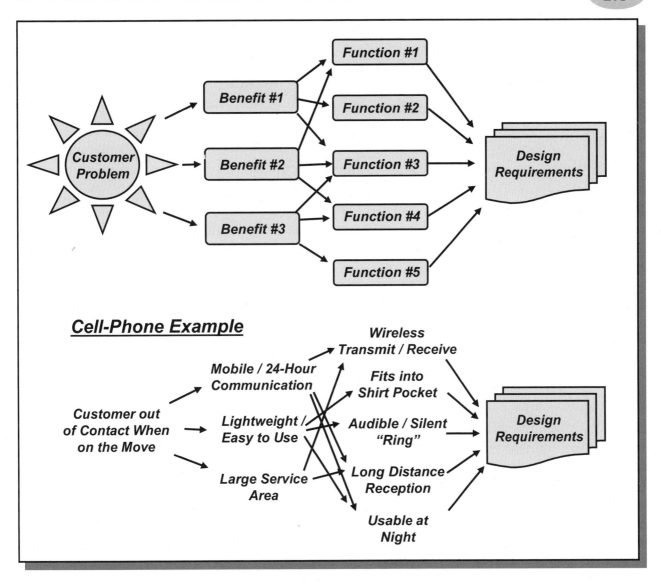

Figure 2.1 – There is a systematic progression of information that will yield the highest fidelity when translating customer benefits into product requirements. Several tools provided within this guidebook will help your team follow this progression, thereby avoiding overshoot or undershoot of market needs.

understand your customer's problems and see possible solutions as though you are looking though their eyes. The marketing representative within your design team (yes, marketing *must* be a part of your core product development team) should be responsible for arranging customer contacts. If you have a single, well-defined customer (such as a major OEM), then frequent visits with their technical representatives should be planned. For open-market products (which target a segment of presumably similar customers) a more sophisticated approach will be necessary.

2.1

How frequently should customer feedback be solicited? Suppose you were driving from your home to Las Vegas for the weekend (I'm making the fairly safe assumption here that few product designers actually *live* in Las Vegas). If you had been there many times before and were familiar with the route, you might quickly check a map at the beginning of the trip, and only open it again if something unexpected comes along. On the other hand, if you had never been west of the Rockies, you might find yourself referring to your map on an almost continuous basis, particularly if you can't afford to make a wrong turn. Product development is no different. If you understand the customer's problem precisely and the possible solutions are fairly obvious, only a solid initial dialog may be required. For unique and innovative products that may have little precedent in the marketplace, however, the design team should be chasing customers down on the street to get feedback at every critical juncture. The model for this iterative feedback approach is shown in Figure 2.3.

At the early stages of concept development, rough prototypes are created by the design team to help gather customer feedback. Iterative prototyping is critical to gaining maximum insight, since customers are often ill-equipped to understand technical specifications and solid-model CAD outputs. A physical prototype (or a mocked-up graphical user interface (GUI) for software) can serve as a *boundary-spanning object* that allows customers and designers to speak a common language. As the design process proceeds, the prototypes become more "real," eventually embodying functionality, look and feel, etc. Near the end of development, alpha and beta users can be of tremendous assistance in assuring that the new product will be all that it can be. If you think that iterative prototyping is a waste of time, just consider all of those products out there that have failed to capture the market's affection. Without allowing customers to show you the way, your new product could become part of that unfortunate group.

Prioritizing Product Requirements Using the Lean QFD

If we had all the time and money in the world, the systematic feedback approach described above would be a great way to capture the voice of the customer. Unfortunately, with all that customer contact, we may find ourselves with an embarrassment of riches. Product improvement suggestions of all kinds will come through the floodgates, without any prioritization. Why is it important to establish priorities? Because "value" is not just performance delivered; it is *performance delivered at a given price.* Taking this further (and assuming that you are not a charitable organization), your team must deliver performance at a *target cost.* Hence, some critical tradeoffs must be made regarding which functions and features should be included in your product and which should be left on the drawing board.

The necessity for prioritizing customer needs and design requirements brings us to our first lean design tool for product cost reduction. Since this is your first cost-reduction tool, you will notice that an overview of its application and benefits is provided in a standard format, as shown in Figure 2.4. Every important lean tool will receive this treat-

Achieving Customer Intimacy

	Description	Advantages	Disadvantages
Focus Groups	• Potential customers are gathered and asked questions about product	• Captures demographics • Can yield many new ideas for improvements	• Can be influenced by facilitator; results often inaccurate
Customer Surveys	• Several questions are sent to potential customers for statistical feedback	• Easy to create and distribute • Large statistical basis	• Somewhat distant, and "digital" in results
Indwelling	• Employees are paid to spend time at customer's facilities and on teams	• Best source of direct feedback • Can help develop alpha customer relationships	• Can be an expensive drain on resources
Probe-and-Learn	• Several versions of a product are test marketed in semi-prototype form	• Reduces risk in new or unfamiliar markets • Yields direct market data	• Can be costly if there is no inexpensive way to prototype product
Alpha Customers	• A real-world customer is asked to participate in product design and testing	• Almost assures early orders • High-value feedback from real-world users	• Product design may be "wired" for just the alpha customer
Iterative Prototyping	• Prototypes are created at several points in process to gain customer inputs	• Helps span the gap between designers and customers • Reduces risk of major errors	• Can take time and create waste if not used judiciously
Internal "Surrogates"	• Employees are encouraged to participate in activities that use firm's products	• Convenient, once developed • Designers become their own customers	• Great if you can find them, but developing them takes time
Polling the Sales Force	• Sales force is asked for new product ideas	• Quick and easy • Many new, but anecdotal, ideas	• "Shotgun" list of ideas, without clear priorities

Figure 2.2 – There are many ways to gather firsthand information from your potential customers. Each approach has advantages and disadvantages; often it makes sense to use two or more techniques and compare the results for a sanity-check.

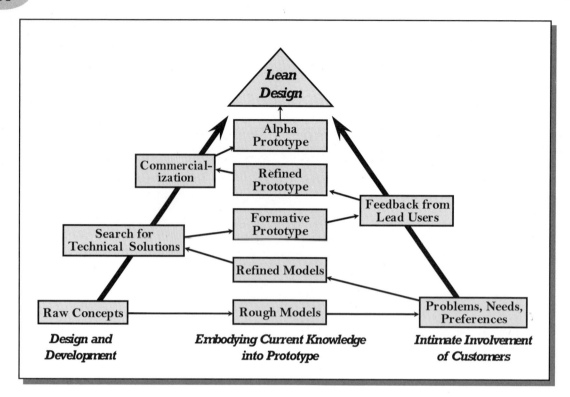

Figure 2.3 – A model for the gathering of customer feedback throughout the product development process. Note that iterative prototyping is used to provide potential customers with something tangible to consider and comment on.

ment, with the goal of helping you choose only those tools that will work best for you. At the bottom of the figure is a "meatball" chart that lists the Twenty Cost Levers described in Section 1.6. The darkness of the meatball indicates how strongly the tool impacts that particular cost lever. Based on your specific product type, you can use this as a guide for selecting the tools that strongly affect areas of high cost impact for your firm.

Now on to the tool. Those of you with a few grey hairs will likely remember the granddaddy of all corporate improvement programs: the Total Quality Management (TQM) movement. Oh, there are other initiatives that predated TQM, but this was the first truly global improvement religion. Where is Total Quality today? Hopefully burned into the very souls of every employee in the manufacturing world. Where are all of those nifty tools that TQM promulgated? What nifty tools, you say? Frankly, many of the tools of TQM proved to be far too arcane and time-consuming for most companies. Improvement philosophies usually start out sensibly, but over time there is a tendency to turn practical and useful tools into complex and jargon-laden clunkers. A classic example of this is Quality Function Deployment (QFD, aka House of Quality). What began life as a very effective method for capturing the voice of the customer grew to become what we jokingly used to call the "Mansion of Quality." Instead of an hour or two of activity, the process came to require days or weeks. Rather than being applied on an as-needed basis, it became a mandatory tax on every phase of every project.

In the lean world, we have no patience for misapplied tools, nor do we tolerate unnecessary complexity. I have therefore retooled the QFD tool into what I call the Lean QFD: A simple, easy to use decision and prioritization tool that can be applied judiciously at the beginning of a project, and as needed throughout the product development process. Earlier I discussed the "translation" of a product's description from customer problem, to customer benefits, to product functions, and finally to detailed requirements. We will use

---

"At a Glance" – The Lean QFD

Overview –
  A simplified version of a classic Total Quality Management tool. The Lean QFD captures the voice of the customer by mapping customer needs and benefits into possible product functions and requirements. A subjective scoring system is used to aid in making difficult decisions and to allow prioritization of requirements.

Primary Benefits –
  Enables design teams to verify that features and performance levels will satisfy customer needs without overshoot or undershoot. Avoids "feature creep" by forcing designers and marketers to justify design enhancements. Yields a priority listing that can aid in meeting target cost.

Best Suited Products –
  This tool can be used for any product type, and in fact is useful in developing service products.

Advantages –
  Better than just guessing at requirements and priorities. Can be a real eye-opener if used properly. An excellent discussion and negotiation tool for entire team.

Disadvantages –
  May be difficult to define customer benefits and appropriate scores if your firm does not have intimate contact with its customers.

Impact on the Twenty Cost Levers –

I. Direct Labor				II. Direct Materials				III. Capital				IV. Design Cost				V. Overhead			
1a	1b	1c	1d	2a	2b	2c	2d	3a	3b	3c	3d	4a	4b	4c	4d	5a	5b	5c	5d
○		○			◉	◉				○		◉	●	●	◉				

Figure 2.4 – "At-a-glance" description of the Lean QFD decision and prioritization tool.

the Lean QFD to help improve the fidelity of these translations, and to prioritize the outcomes. Hence, two levels of application are recommended: one to take us from benefits (which can be gleaned from customer contact) to functions, and a second application to convert prioritized functions into design requirements. Note that it would be a waste of time to use such a systematic tool for simple and obvious product solutions. When the fog rolls in, however, and everything looks pretty fuzzy, this methodology can be invaluable.

The first-level application will help us translate customer benefits into prioritized functions, as shown in Figure 2.5. I have continued the cell-phone product example from Figure 2.1 to illustrate how this tool is applied. (Please don't take my inputs and results

2.1

"Function" Lean QFD

		Key Customer Benefits				
		A) Mobile / 24-Hr. Comm	B) Lightweight / Easy to Use	C) Large Service Area	Customer Ranking of Functions	Function Priority No.
Weighting Factors for Key Benefits →		2	1	1.5		
Possible Functions that Could Deliver Desired Benefits	1) Wireless Transmit / Receive	5	0	5	17.5	1
	2) Fits into Shirt Pocket	0	5	0	5	5
	3) Audible / Silent "Ring"	2	3	0	7	4
	4) Long Distance Reception	4	0	5	15.5	2
	5) Usable at Night	3	3	0	9	3
	6) Voice and Data Capability	1	1	0	3	6
	7) Color Display	0	1	0	1	7
	8) Games	0	0	0	0	--
	9) Text Messaging	3	1	0	7	4
	10) Digital Camera	0	0	0	0	--

Figure 2.5 – The first-level application of Lean QFD is to convert customer benefits into prioritized functions. The example of a cell-phone product is used to illustrate how the tool works.

in this example too seriously; this is clearly an incomplete set of functions.) The first thing to observe about the tool is that it takes the form of a two-dimensional matrix. Along one dimension (the horizontal axis), we capture the key benefits that our potential customers demand from the new product. These benefits should be derived directly from customer discussions whenever possible. In fact, ideally we would have real-time customer participation during our first-level application of Lean QFD. Remember, benefits are always viewed from the customer's perspective and in their own language, so who better to help you fill out this matrix?

Note that space has been provided for only three "key benefits." This is because in my experience with the original version of QFD, teams would list every possible customer benefit, sometimes *dozens* of them. This tool only works if clear decisions can be made, and limiting the list of benefits to just those that are central in the minds of customers helps increase the utility of its outputs. As with every tool in this guidebook, you are free to "enhance" it in anyway you wish, including adding space for a few more benefits. Just don't get carried away or you'll be back to building the "mansion" that I spoke derisively about a moment ago.

Once the key customer benefits are selected (and this may prove to be an iterative process), a weighting factor is identified for each benefit. The weighting factor is simply a multiplier that captures the reality of customer perception; not all benefits are equal. I try to keep the range of weighting factors narrow, perhaps from 1 to 3. If you allow larger weighting factors to be used, it is easy for a strong-willed team member to skew the results by insisting on a huge multiplier (e.g., "This is certainly ten times more important than that!"). Now you and your team are ready to brainstorm on the possible functions that might be needed to deliver the key benefits desired by your customer.

Don't be afraid to cast a big net on functions. It doesn't take long to sort out the wheat from the chaff, and a comprehensive list may capture some innovative mix of functions that might otherwise have been missed. Once all of the candidate functions are listed, your design team should begin the scoring process. I suggest a subjective (but hopefully somewhat consistent) scoring range from -5 to +5. A positive score indicates that the function under review positively impacts a key benefit; a negative score implies that the function actually degrades that benefit. A zero score means that the function has no impact on that particular benefit. Conduct the scoring as a team (with customers present, if possible) and try to obtain a consensus. Again, this may be an iterative process: the first time through, you may find that you didn't get the benefits right, or perhaps the weighting factors were just not realistic. Be careful not to cheat, however. It is all too easy to get any answer you want from subjective scoring tools like this one; *objectivity is critical to obtaining useful results*. The best way to avoid the subjectivity trap is to designate one or more people as "customer surrogates" and have them defend the customer's position during your discussions (assuming that you don't have real live customers in the room).

Next, total the scores and see what your priorities will be. Multiply the score in each box by the appropriate weighting factor and add up each row. The higher the positive score, the more critical that function will be to the ultimate product. Functions that receive low or negative scores should be considered for elimination. Once you have a priority list that both your team and your customer (or surrogate thereof) are comfortable with, you can move on to deriving design requirements for each function, as shown in Figure 2.6.

You will note that the second-level Lean QFD tool looks slightly different from the first-level version. The most important change, from a process perspective, is that *we don't really want an external customer present during these discussions*. The reason is that two additional columns have been included in the second-level tool that are highly sensitive: unit manufacturing cost and time-to-market. Whenever we make decisions about design requirements, it is critical that we consider their impact on cost and time. By including these two columns, we create a "balanced scorecard" for our requirements choices. As a

"Requirements" Lean QFD

First-Priority Function Requirements – Wireless Transmit / Receive

Possible Performance Requirements or Design Tradeoffs

Weighting Factors for Key Benefits →

	Key Customer Benefits			Unit Manufacturing Cost	Time-to-Market	Selected Requirements
	A) Mobile / 24-Hr. Comm	B) Lightweight / Easy to Use	C) Large Service Area			
	2	1	1.5	2	1	
1) Type of Cell-Phone Chip Used						
Option 1 - 1st Generation	0	0	0	0	0	0
Option 2 - 2nd Generation	2	1	2	-1	0	(6)
Option 3 - 3rd Generation	3	1	3	-5	-3	-1.5
2) Power Utilization						
Option 1 - Low	0	0	0	0	0	(0)
Option 2 - Moderate	0	-2	2	-2	0	-3
3) Communications Standard						
Option 1 - GMT	0	0	0	0	0	0
Option 2 - CDMA	0	1	3	-1	0	(3.5)

Figure 2.6 – The second-level application of Lean QFD. In this case, we are translating our prioritized product functions into design requirements. Note that a separate matrix like the one above should be created for each critical function. Again, the cell-phone example has been used purely for illustration; please don't go out and design a cell-phone based on these results.

side note, if price is a critical factor for the product under consideration, it should be included as a *key benefit*, not as a substitute for unit cost. Also note that we will use exactly the same benefits and weighting factors that were agreed upon during the first-level application of this tool.

Begin your analysis with the highest priority function. You will use an entire matrix to derive requirements for this function, a second matrix for the next priority, and so on. How far do you need to go? Generally, the top three-to-five functions deserve this highhanded treatment, provided that the rest are minor, both from a customer satisfaction and cost standpoint. For each function, list possible design tradeoffs, or alternatively, several levels of performance. Your goal is to compare apples with apples for each design requirement and select the performance level that best balances customer needs with the practical constraints of cost and schedule. The design requirements that receive the highest positive scores are the logical choices as your team moves forward with product design.

Just a few hints and we'll put this tool to bed. First, you will notice that I have "normalized" one of the choices for each design requirement to zero. Since the Lean QFD tool is comparative in nature, all that matters is the difference in scores among the options being considered. In most cases there will be some "baseline" or default choice for each requirement which will be compared to possible alternatives. Usually the baseline is the low-risk, low-tech choice; something that your firm has had experience with in previous products. By setting the default option to all zeros, the other alternatives can be determined to be "better" (a positive total score relative to zero) or "worse" (a negative total score relative to zero).

One final point. Since this tool is quite subjective, a small difference in total scores between options is really a non-decision. If there are just a few points separating two alternatives, more study is needed to make that call. Another approach would be to add one or more additional benefits to your matrix that might help make the choice more clear. Whatever you do, try to avoid cluttering up the process. Like our friend Pareto always says: You get 80% of the benefit from the first 20% of the time and energy spent. Keep it simple and someone else won't have to come along in twenty years to slice the fat off of this powerful tool.

Notes

Section 2.2

Prioritizing Customer Requirements

We've gone through a lot of trouble in the previous section to prioritize our product's functions and subsequently its requirements. It would be a shame not to use that prioritization to help us manage product cost, right? But how do we integrate target costs, cost models, functions, requirements, and so on? Clearly there must be a pony in here somewhere. In this section I will tie all of these pieces together into a logical and systematic framework for product requirements management.

All Requirements Are Not Created Equal

When it comes to product requirements, this ain't no democracy. Your team has a finite cost target that must be met to achieve your desired profit margins. That meager sum must be divided among every requirement in your specification in such a way that your customer's satisfaction (or its surrogate, the product's price) is maximized. Getting this right will mean financial success, while getting it wrong will mean...well, you know. I'll give you a quick example to drive "home" my point.

If you have recently walked through a model home, you have seen what can only be described as an optical illusion. Successful housing developers are magicians; they lead buyers to believe that they are purchasing their dream home at a bargain price, while still making a comfortable profit on each property sold. How is this sleight of hand accomplished? Developers carefully set priorities among construction requirements to create the *illusion* of quality, exclusivity, luxury, and comfort. You see polished brass fixtures in the bathrooms, but don't notice the barely-to-code PVC piping that has been used as a poor substitute for copper. You see a beautiful oak spiral staircase, but the treads are actually veneered plywood that will look dreadful after a year or two of use. Marble floors hide a thin and poorly reinforced concrete-slab foundation. Lovely wallpaper masks clumsy drywall seams, and you dare not lean against those walls for fear of falling through the paper-thin sheetrock.

Certainly an educated buyer will be aware of these tradeoffs and not be fooled by unscrupulous "magicians." In fact, reputable developers work hard to educate their customers on the benefits of quality construction. This allows them to capture a higher price for their properties, and thereby retain acceptable margins. But make no mistake; you aren't going to see extra steel in your foundation or extra nails in your stud walls unless you hire your own contractor or do the work yourself. If the target cost is fixed, only a fool of a developer would add extra nails when they could add extra closet space instead.

2.2

But First a Word from Our Competition

Out of left field comes a topic we have yet to address; our competition. What do those characters have to do with prioritizing your product's requirements? Potentially, a great deal. Each of your competitors has had to go through the same tradeoffs that you are struggling with (although they probably haven't read this guidebook yet, so you've got a leg up on them). It would be criminal for your design team to miss such a great opportunity to learn from the successes and failures of others. How did they allocate their target cost? What functions received the most attention? Which were neglected or given short shrift? What tricks did they use to reduce production cost? What are the unique attributes of similar products offered by different competitors? It's all gold, folks.

Learning from Competitors

Learning Opportunity	Advantages	Disadvantages
Benchmarking	Excellent way to establish basic requirements for a product category. Can also provide useful thresholds for "must-have" rqmts.	Assumes competitors actually know their customers. Can result in overshoot if benchmarking leads to insecurity.
Reverse Engineering	One of the best ways to ensure cost competitiveness is to analyze how your competition designs and manufactures their product.	Can be very time-consuming. Also assumes that competition has some sophistication in using lean design tools.
Position Analysis	Identifies opportunities within a specific product category and market segment. Can dramatically increase profit margins.	Again, can be very time-consuming. Hard to understand the customer's perspective on the position of some "glamour" products.
SWOT Analysis	Strengths / Weaknesses / Opportunities / Threats – a classic treatment of market strategy.	Great for overall vision, but doesn't usually yield enough hard data to support a specific product design.
Network Effects	Is there an industry standard that could increase the acceptance of your product? Can you link your product to others?	The standards game is not for the weak of heart, especially in the high-tech world. Don't get caught on the wrong side of a standards debate!

Figure 2.7 – Several ways to use competitors' products to help establish priorities for your new product requirements. One thing to keep in mind, however; just because a competitor does something a certain way, doesn't mean that they are *right*. Think about all the blunders your firm has made. There's a good chance that your competition has just as many mistakes buried in their products. Steal with pride, but only steal the good stuff!

Several ways of using competitors' products to your advantage are described in Figure 2.7. Before we leave this tangent, however, I will define for you the most important word in requirements management – *positioning*. If you lay out all of your competitors' products on a table next to your own (assuming your firm doesn't build steam shovels), you should be able to identify each product's unique position in the marketplace. For commodity products (ones for which there are many equivalent substitutes), positioning means only one thing; who's got the lowest price. Differentiated products, however, must each find their own identity in the marketplace to achieve elevated margins. The real art in product development is figuring out where the gaps are in that table-full of products. Is there space between the high- and low-priced models to squeeze in a mid-range offering? Is there a sizable niche in the market that isn't being addressed? Most important, is the product you are about to develop clearly positioned in a "sweet spot" relative to the other guys? Me-too products get me-too margins, so if you can find a hole that needs filling, you are halfway to market success.

Better Is the Enemy of Good Enough…Sometimes

Enough chitchat. It's time for another tool; please refer to Figure 2.8 for an overview. One of the more valuable outgrowths of the Total Quality Management movement was a model for product requirements first proposed by Noriaki Kano. The aptly named "Kano Model" illuminates a critical factor in customer perception; that it isn't 20/20. Customers tend to focus on certain attributes of a product and ignore others, based on a number of psychological and market factors. Specifically, Kano observed that many of the attributes of a given product may not even be on the customer's radar screen…*unless they fail to perform*. These attributes were *assumed* by customers to be adequate in both performance and quality, based on past experience. Any violation of that assumption will trigger immediate dissatisfaction with the product.

To illustrate this point, let's consider the purchase of a new car. When you go car shopping, what are the attributes that you are most focused on? Price to be sure, but within a given price range, what requirements are most important? Styling? Performance? Safety? Cargo space? How about the muffler? The muffler is not on your priority list, you say? How about the U-joints? Hopefully you're starting to get Kano's point. A substantial subset of the design requirements for a car are not of much interest to the buying public. Over years of car purchase and use, these attributes have become table stakes in customers' minds. Any *decent* car should have an acceptable muffler, U-joint, radiator, etc. These items are not even worth comparison shopping, since they are presumed to be adequate, and are far outweighed in importance by comfortable leather seating and extra horsepower.

Getting back to Kano's model, one can consider the requirements for any product as being divided into three categories: must-haves, should-haves, and could-haves, as shown graphically in Figure 2.9 and described in Figure 2.10. (Note that this is not Kano's original terminology; I've taken the liberty of modifying the original to be more intuitively relevant to product requirements management.) The two-dimensional plane described by Kano can be thought of as a "customer-sensitivity map." As the performance of a given product attribute increases, how sensitive is the market to that improvement? Does it

2.2

"At a Glance" – The Must / Should / Could Tool

Overview –
It is critical that the customer-driven ranking of functions be captured at the level of the design specification. This tool categorizes product requirements into three bins: must-haves, should-haves, and could-haves. This prioritization allows the design team to focus its efforts on those aspects of the product that will have the greatest impact on customer satisfaction.

Primary Benefits –
Enables control over target cost and time-to-market by setting clear priorities among product requirements. Lower-priority features can be downscoped if the development effort is behind schedule or if the target cost will be exceeded by the current design.

Best Suited Products –
This tool can be used for any product type, but is best suited to more complex, multifunction products.

Advantages –
Quick and easy tool that provides significant improvement in customer value and satisfaction.

Disadvantages –
Forces team to make some tough decisions upfront; it is often hard to subordinate "could-haves", knowing that they may be eliminated as a result.

Impact on the Twenty Cost Levers –

I. Direct Labor				II. Direct Materials				III. Capital				IV. Design Cost				V. Overhead			
1a	1b	1c	1d	2a	2b	2c	2d	3a	3b	3c	3d	4a	4b	4c	4d	5a	5b	5c	5d
			○		⊙			○	○	○	○	⊙	●	●	⊙				

Figure 2.8 – "At-a-glance" overview of the Must / Should / Could requirements prioritization tool.

excite customers, interest them, or is the increased performance completely ignored? Obviously, heightened customer interest often translates into increased price, market share, or both. Hence, we need to move beyond the must-haves (which really are only on the customer's radar screen if they fail to perform), to the should-haves and could-haves, which determine the lion's share of price.

This concept of Must / Should / Could prioritization offers design teams an effective and straightforward way to organize several different categories of product requirements, as shown in Figure 2.11. We begin with the must-haves, setting tough limits on performance so that we don't overshoot market expectations and thereby flush some profits down the drain. The most common source of waste in product design, in my opinion, is the gold plating of must-have requirements. Certainly we need to be careful not to undershoot; we don't want to ruin our product's reputation by allowing our must-haves to become noticeable in a bad way. On the other hand, anything that we can do to reduce the cost invested in must-have requirements will yield a bounty when it comes time to attack the more valuable shoulds and coulds.

Ideally, the Lean QFD will provide us with sufficient visibility into customer priorities to enable categorization of requirements into musts, shoulds, and coulds. As a fallback, we can use the following criteria to help us make a determination. A must-have requirement will typically display one or more of the following indicators:

Must-Have Indicators:

1) Little or no customer interest – assumed to be acceptable.
2) Doubling the performance or quality of the requirement will yield a zero price increase.
3) A tendency toward a standardized level of performance – an entire industry uses the same requirement.

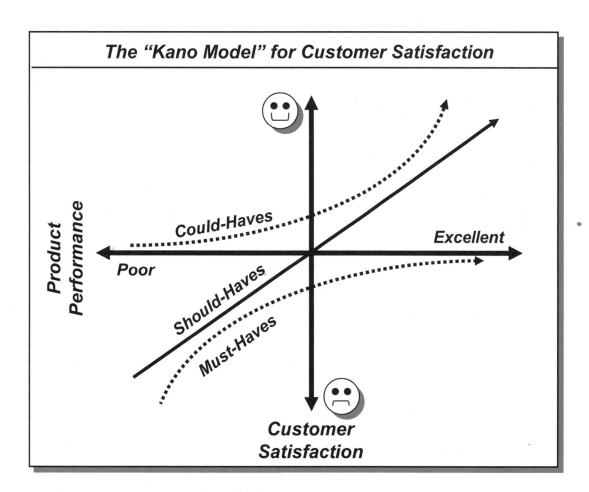

Figure 2.9 – Graphical representation of the Kano Model, showing the impact of increasing performance on customer satisfaction for several categories of product requirement.

	Must-Haves	**Should-Haves**	**Could-Haves**
Automotive	• Adequate Safety • Free of Defects	• Horsepower • Handling	• DVD Video • Sports Package
Software	• No Bugs • Adequate Speed	• Compatibility • Security	• Exciting GUI • WEB Features
Cell-Phone	• Adequate Range • Acceptable Noise	• Small Size • Color Display	• GPS • Digital Photos
Airline Service	• Attendants • No Overbooking	• Legroom • Carryon Space	• Decent Food • TV in Coach
Digital Camera	• Basic Memory • Good Optics	• Lots of Pixels • Zoom Features	• Miniature Size • Streaming Video

Figure 2.10 – Some examples of Must / Should / Could requirements. Must-haves are essential to customer satisfaction, but are not of direct interest to customers during the purchasing process. Should-haves determine price and market share. Could-haves are the "wow-factor" enhancements that *might* be great, but are optional, risky, or unproven in the marketplace.

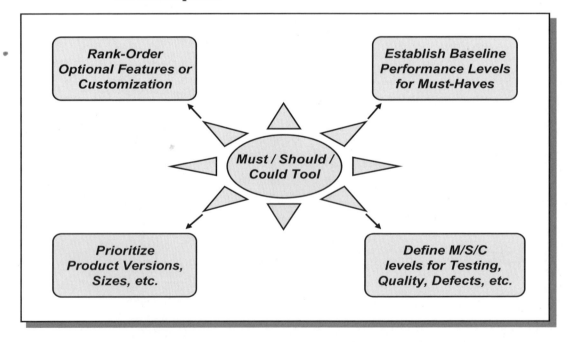

Figure 2.11 – Some examples of the prioritization of product requirements using the Must / Should / Could tool. The priority of each product requirement is explicitly indicated in the design specification (see Figure 2.12). Note that this method can be used to rank several sets of attributes, including feature set, performance levels, versions, customization, etc.

Should-have requirements are where we want to focus most of our time and allocated cost. A should-have requirement will typically display one or more of the following indicators:

Should-Have Indicators:

1) Customers directly ask for or demand this requirement.
2) An improvement in the performance or quality of this requirement would yield an increase in price.
3) There are multiple levels of this type of requirement, based on the specific needs of each market segment (i.e., it is a *differentiating* requirement).
4) The pricing power of the requirement is directly related to its customer priority or importance.

I suppose the could-haves will be whatever is left over, but just in case, use these indicators to identify those risky but exciting "wow-factor" requirements:

Could-Have Indicators:

1) The feature or performance level is not currently on the market in the form you are considering.
2) Customers are not asking for it, but if they are told about it, they are interested (and hopefully excited).
3) There is some significant risk involved: market risk, technical risk, or both.
4) Could-have features tend to appeal only to a subsegment of your product's customers.

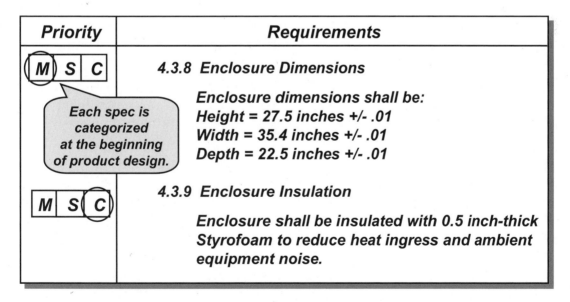

Figure 2.12 – An example of how Must / Should / Could requirements can be explicitly identified in a product design specification. Note that the status of a requirement might change throughout the development process, based on new customer inputs or a changing competitive landscape.

Now that we have filled our three bins with must, should, and could requirements, the resulting prioritization is explicitly indicated on our product specification, as shown in Figure 2.12. As your development project moves forward, work should be prioritized to first deal with the must-haves, using a "good-enough" strategy to keep cost and design time to a minimum. (Note that must-haves are prime candidates for commercial-off-the-shelf components or other outsourcing strategies.) The should-haves come next, receiving the lion's share of allocated target cost and development time. Finally, if we are on schedule and within our target cost, we attack the could-haves, being careful to weigh risks and benefits as we proceed. This general strategy is shown graphically in Figure 2.13. Remember, if you can't squeeze the could-haves into the current product design, they can be carried over into a future version of the product.

Once this technique has been applied, we will have completed the preliminary steps necessary to achieving cost optimization in our product design. All we need to do now is execute the design to our prioritized requirements.

Let's Pause to Catch Our Breath

We have reached something of a milestone in this guidebook (and in our journey toward dramatic product cost reduction). We now have at our disposal a methodology which will help ensure that every product your firm launches will meet your profit goals, as shown in Figure 2.14. Obviously, as time progresses, your objective should be to push

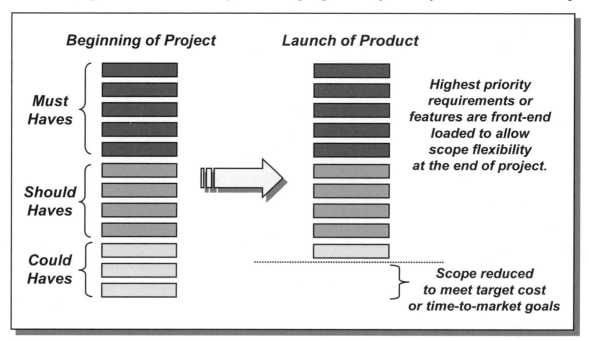

Figure 2.13 – The Must / Should / Could prioritization tool can be used to ensure that a development project is completed on schedule and that the target cost is met. Note that any could-have functionality or feature that is downscoped from an initial development project is ripe for inclusion in subsequent versions of the product.

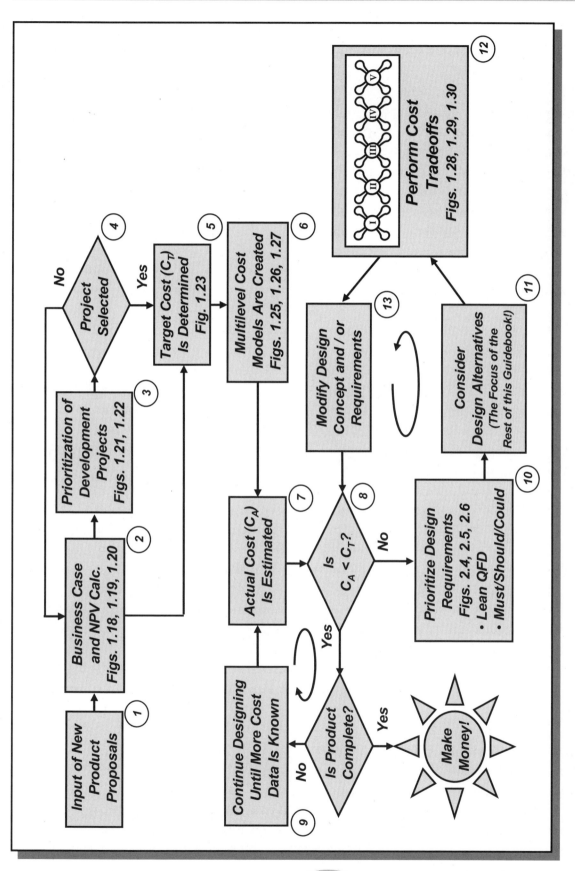

Figure 2.14 – Pulling it all together from Parts I and II. The methodology described above is comprehensive, but may be too cumbersome for simple line-extension-type products. Scale your use of the above tools to the size of the opportunity. For minor projects, a more qualitative approach is reasonable, whereas for major new product initiatives, the entire methodology should be employed.

toward ever-increasing margins in a cycle of continuous cost improvement. For now, let's walk through the process so that you have a clear picture of how this approach really works.

The start of the product development process is always the same; ideas for new products come into the firm from various sources (1) (note that the numbers shown in parenthesis in the following paragraphs refer to the process steps in Figure 2.14). Hopefully, your firm has a simple, one-page template for new product proposals that allows prescreening of ideas before they are placed into the formal ranking process. Each acceptable proposal is then evaluated for its business potential by calculating a net present value (NPV), perhaps spanning several possible market scenarios (2). The NPV gives an indication of viability, and by using the strategic ranking tool shown in Figure 1.22, a prioritized list can be generated (3). As design resources become available, products are selected for development based on this prioritization (4). If a product is rejected for development, it goes back into the hopper for reevaluation at a future time (or killed entirely if the market window has passed).

The first step in managing cost for a new product initiative is to determine its target cost (C_T). This must be done using the same business-case data that was used to calculate its NPV (5). The target cost is then allocated to various subsystems, assemblies, and even components, based on their relative importance. A cost model is created for each level of subsystem in tandem with the allocation of target cost (6). Now we can calculate an initial estimate of the actual cost (C_A) of our future product and sanity-check it against the target cost (7). If $C_A < C_T$ everything is cool so far and we can begin the design process. However, if $C_A > C_T$, we'd better stop in our tracks and consider our options (8).

During development, the cost-reduction process consists of two operating feedback loops. On the higher loop (middle-left of the figure), we are designing a product that is meeting its target cost, based on our current best estimates. We continue in this loop until product launch, provided that we stay on track with respect to cost (9). If at any point during development our current estimate rises above the target cost, we exit the "we're cool" loop and enter the "cost-reduction" loop (lower-right of the figure). The first step in the cost-reduction loop is to reestablish our prioritization of design requirements (10). Once the musts, shoulds, and coulds have been redefined, we begin considering design alternatives (11). (Note that this will be the primary focus of much of this guidebook.) After several design alternatives have been proposed, we perform a qualitative cost trade-off, using our Twenty-Cost-Lever evaluation tool and our cost model (12). If a promising alternative is identified, we modify our design concept and / or our design requirements, and reenter the design loop (13). If we stay the course and stick to our target, we will launch a product that will be a good little moneymaker.

Now all that remains is to give you a few hints about the use of this process and we can move on to new tools that will help generate low-cost design alternatives. First hint: the process steps I described above assume that *both cost and time-to-market are important to the product's business case.* If development time is not hypercritical (e.g., you are performing a cost-reduction redesign on an already successful product), you might want to take a more aggressive stance in setting the target cost. In fact, you might want to establish some blue-sky cost goal and spend time early in development evaluating as many different low-cost alternatives as possible. In a sense, this approach would begin the design process in the "cost-reduction" loop, and may never exit unless dramatic cost improvement can be attained.

One final point is worth mentioning. As with every tool in this guidebook, you and your team *need to scale the tool to the size and complexity of the product being developed.* If your team is tasked with developing the "next big thing" for your firm, the entire methodology should be utilized, at some reasonable level of rigor. On the other hand, if your product is relatively simple, you should eliminate the more formal and time-consuming elements of the process. For example, a trimmed-down methodology might utilize a simple, one-level cost model, and only a qualitative prioritization of customer requirements. Whatever you do, however, *don't abandon the logic of the process.* The steps of setting a target cost, creating a cost model, iterating the model, and verifying that the target cost can be achieved, is absolutely essential to slashing product costs and achieving the profit margins that are rightfully yours.

Notes

Part II

Recommendations for Further Learning

The following books will give you more detail on the topics covered in Part II. Again, you get the "benefit" of my personal opinion regarding which references to focus on; additional resources are listed in the Bibliography.

Lean QFD

***** *Step-by-Step QFD, 2nd Edition,* Terninko, J., 1997

A very nice, practical "guidebook" to the traditional QFD methodology. Tons of detail in an easily understood format. Also provides a useful linkage between QFD and other important innovation and quality management tools.

**** *Quality Function Deployment: How to Make QFD Work for You,* Cohen, L., 1995

Also a very well-organized and useful book. The only reason for subtracting a star relative to the book mentioned above is that this is more of a traditional textbook, and requires slightly more effort to get to the practical stuff. If you like background and context, then this book may be your preferred choice.

Kano Model & Must/Should/Could

***** *A New American TQM,* Shiba, S., Graham, A., and D. Walden, 1993

One of the best books available on the Total Quality Management improvement philosophy. Only a very small section of the book is dedicated to the Kano Model, however, so if you are only interested in that topic, you might want to consider digging up the article that is mentioned below.

***** *"Make Kano Analysis part of your new product requirements,"* Goodpasture, J. C., 2001

This is a fine article, both from the standpoint of providing a good overview of the Kano approach, and also for the implementation suggestions of the author. The article can be found in *PM Network* magazine, May issue, pgs. 42-45.

Notes

Reduce Cost Through Cross-Product Synergy

3.1 - The Product Line as a "System"

3.2 - Platforms Come in All Sizes

3.3 - Modular, Scalable, and Mass Customizable

Part III

> *"Beware of little expenses; a small leak will sink a great ship."*
>
> Benjamin Franklin

> *"Everything should be made as simple as possible, but not simpler."*
>
> Albert Einstein

> *"Nothing is more simple than greatness: indeed, to be simple is to be great."*
>
> Ralph Waldo Emerson

Section 3.1 — The Product Line as a "System"

You've volunteered to coach a youth soccer team and you're determined to lead your kids to victory. What should your training strategy be? Should you focus on each team member's individual skills, or emphasize teamwork and cooperation? Is it best for one or two superstars to carry the team, or should you try to balance each member's abilities so that no one person dominates the game? The problem with sports analogies like this one (for which I refuse to apologize) is that the reality of competition rarely supports the great "lessons" we are supposed to learn from them. Clearly, I am trying to build a case for teamwork and cooperation. Yet plenty of successful sports franchises have been built around a single superstar player, and teams that are loaded with talent often win championships without much teamwork.

The same is true in business (see, there was a reason for the analogy after all). There are many firms that have been supported for years by one or two "superstar" products. Pharmaceutical manufacturers are an excellent example. One breakthrough drug can sustain a firm through years of failed new product attempts. Likewise, businesses that are well-positioned in a hot market have little need for "cooperation" among their products. If margins are high enough and demand is strong enough, a bit of inefficiency can easily be absorbed. Many high-tech firms fall into this category, including telecoms, semiconductor fabricators, software designers, and so on.

Now, here's my long awaited point. You *might* win at sports with one or two superstars, and you *might* win with a bunch of talented but uncooperative individual contributors, but you *will* win if you have *both talent and cooperation*. In business, you can manage to keep the doors open with one or two profitable products, but why not thrive and flourish by embedding cooperation and synergy into your product design strategy? The most dramatic opportunities for your firm to boost overall profits require that you treat your entire line of products as a *profit-maximizing system*. To accomplish this, however, you must first learn the art of systems thinking.

A Holistic Approach to Design

There are some words in the English language that we use every day but have no idea what they really mean. The word "system" is an excellent example. There are laundry-cleaning systems, and computer systems, and sewer systems, and even shaving systems, so evidently these things are everywhere. But what makes a system a system? Well, there are, in fact, several specific criteria that must be met for something to truly be a system (despite what some advertisements might lead you to believe). First of all, a system must consist of more than one element or component. Second, a system must perform at least one function that cannot be accomplished without cooperation among its elements. Finally, the system must receive some form of feedback, meaning that the way in which the world interacts with the system must in some way influence how the system behaves, as shown in Figure 3.1. If these three criteria are met, then you've got a system on your hands. Hence, for a laundry detergent to be a *real* system, it must: a) consist of more than one type of cleaning agent, b) be able to clean certain types of laundry only if these multiple cleaning agents work together synergistically, and c) react in some way to the type of dirt being removed.

Somehow I can't picture a group of advertising executives sitting around a table ticking off these three criteria before approving an advertisement that uses the word "system." Yet for our purposes, these criteria are critical, because true systems have some predictable behaviors *that can help us make more money*. Picture in your mind every product that your firm produces (or at least all products within a business unit). If managed properly, this suite of products can constitute a *system for profit maximization*, or they can remain a bunch of isolated loaners that gain no benefit from their brethren.

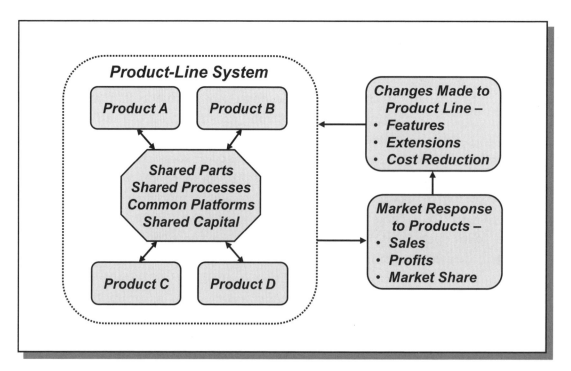

Figure 3.1 – The general definition of a system requires that three criteria be met: 1) more than one element or component must be involved, 2) these elements must work together cooperatively toward a common purpose, and 3) there must be some feedback process that enables the system to adapt or change based on its interaction with the outside world. A closed-loop feedback system for profit maximization within a manufacturing firm is shown.

For a product line to behave like a system, it must meet our three criteria. First, there must be more than one product in the line. Ok, that one is probably fairly easy. Next, the various products within the product line must work together synergistically to accomplish the function of the system. Since the function that we have defined for our system is to make maximum profits, *the products within your firm must somehow be working together to increase profitability.* This one is a bit harder, *n'est pas*? Luckily, the final criterion is also relatively easy. The feedback for a product-line system comes from the sales and profit dollars generated in the marketplace. A negative or positive response from the market is detectable almost immediately, and provided that the system reacts to this feedback (such as by changing the type of products offered), we are in good shape.

So how do we meet criterion number two? Suppose, for example, that our current products each use their own unique set of fasteners. If we could define a common fastener that would work for all of our products, we would increase our profits across the board. Why, you ask? Because we could purchase the common fastener in higher volumes (thereby gaining quantity discounts), and we would have fewer parts in our inventory that need to be purchased, received, inspected, counted, stored, moved, etc. As trivial as this example may seem, the cost savings that can be derived from parts-count-reduction initiatives can be dramatic.

There are a number of other ways in which multi-product synergies can help maximize profits, as shown in Figure 3.2. In almost every case, some form of commonality is involved. Common parts, as mentioned above, are only the beginning. How about common capital equipment, shared workcells, common raw-material stock, standardized testing and inspection, and so on? In fact, an ideal product line would consist of products that are virtually indistinguishable from a manufacturing standpoint. The problems they solve might be very different, but there are huge economies of scope among them. To accomplish this, however, we must do some things that may seem counterintuitive.

For example, we may need to actually *increase* the cost of one product to capture significant savings across our entire product line. Suppose we have ten products within a product line and eight of them require enclosures made of stainless steel. The other two products are lower-priced models that can be sold with just a painted metal enclosure. It would increase the cost of the low-priced models to use stainless steel instead, but overall it might be cheaper than maintaining an inventory of plain sheet metal and a painting facility that would otherwise be unnecessary. We have to look beyond the superficial to see the network of synergies that lies below the surface of any product family.

Designing Product Lines Instead of Products

If your firm is well down the road toward a lean enterprise, you may have considered abandoning those stogy old functional departments in favor of "value-stream teams." A value-stream team sounds fancier than it really is; it is simply a cross-functional team that includes all skills needed to design, develop, launch, manufacture, and support an entire product line. These value-stream teams take the place of traditional functional

3.1

Capturing Product-Line Synergy	
Opportunities for Cooperation	Primary Cost Benefits
Shared Parts	• Reduces overhead charges for inventory management, purchasing, inspection, storage, handling, etc. Can enable lower per-part cost due to higher volumes.
Shared Raw Materials	• Same as above, plus added cost savings due to reduced wastage and scrap.
Shared Processes	• Reduces overhead costs of factory re-layout, process development and prove-in, training, test and inspection, etc.
Common Capital	• Spreads the cost of capital equipment over several products, thereby shortening payback period. Reduces floor-space requirements, maintenance costs, etc.
"Second-Order" Effects	• There are many less obvious costs that will decline due to product-line synergy. Examples include packaging, warrantee, service, and repair costs, qualification testing costs, agency approval costs, and so on.

Figure 3.2 – Ways in which a multi-product family can act as a profit-maximizing system. Note that it may be necessary to actually *increase* the cost of a single product slightly in order to capture cost synergies across all products within a business unit.

departments and can improve operating efficiency considerably...provided that you survive the transition. Although there is merit to the BIG-THINK approach of reorganizing entire business units, this is a practical, little-think kind of guidebook. Hence, we will find a way to get some of the benefit of value-stream teams without the cultural and organizational turmoil.

Before I describe how this can be accomplished, a few definitions are in order:

Product Line – A product line is any collection of products that have a common configuration, market segment, technology, or some other logical similarity.

Product Platform – A subset or portion of a product that is common to multiple models (or versions) within a product line. Traditionally, platforms have been thought of as nearly finished products that have not yet received the customization that differentiates the various models. In the sections that follow, I will demonstrate how taking a much broader view of platforms can yield substantial cost savings.

Product Family – Similar to a product line, but often the commonality involved is in how the products are manufactured.

Line Extensions – These are models within a product line that have been added to capture new subsegments of the target market. Often a line extension is a relatively minor modification of an existing product within the line, such as offering a new color, size, or other superficial change.

Product-Line Roadmap – A strategic guide to the future of a product line. The horizontal axis represents time (typically in years), while the vertical axis represents the segments of the market that will be targeted. A product-line roadmap helps designers see opportunities to merge functions, provide for future extensions, implement low-cost customization, and other cost-saving measures that require some visibility into a product-line's future.

Armed with these definitions, we can introduce a new lean design tool; the Product-Line Optimization Team (PLOT), as described in Figure 3.3. The PLOT (god I love that acronym) is an ad hoc team that comes together for a specific purpose; to advise design teams on ways to capture multi-product cost savings. The PLOT consists of representatives from each critical design area, along with manufacturing, marketing, and possibly others. The goal is to establish a group that can visualize cross-product-line opportunities, so use your own judgment.

"At a Glance" – The Product-Line Optimization Team

Overview –
An easy-to-implement approach to capturing cost synergy across multiple products within a product line. The team consists of representatives from all critical functions (i.e., marketing, design, manufacturing, and possibly others) who have a strategic perspective on the future direction of the product line. The purpose of the team is to establish product-line roadmaps, identify possible commonality, define platforms, innovate ways to reduce capital investment, etc.

Primary Benefits –
A straightforward way to begin merging distinct products into a system for maximizing profits. Reduction of overhead is a major benefit, since this approach can uncover and eliminate waste that would typically be buried in overhead burden rates.

Best Suited Products –
This tool can be used for any product type, provided that synergy among products can offer some potential cost savings.

Advantages –
Not disruptive to organization or culture. Can be integrated into your firm's strategic planning process. Takes very little time when compared to its potential benefits.

Disadvantages –
Requires that members have at least a basic understanding of the firm's long-term strategy. It may be hard to get volunteers for this, at least until the groundwork is in place.

Impact on the Twenty Cost Levers –

I. Direct Labor				II. Direct Materials				III. Capital				IV. Design Cost				V. Overhead			
1a	1b	1c	1d	2a	2b	2c	2d	3a	3b	3c	3d	4a	4b	4c	4d	5a	5b	5c	5d
○	○	○	⊙		●	⊙	⊙	○	○	⊙	●	●	○	○	⊙	●	●		

Figure 3.3 – "At-a-glance" description of the Product-Line Optimization Team (PLOT) cost-saving tool.

3.1

Keep the membership relatively low (five to ten people is a good range) so that consensus is at least a possibility. Members should be explicitly identified, notified, and given basic instructions in the process that I will describe below. The team should come together whenever a new product design project is initiated, and will typically exist for only one day on each project. Just a quick infusion of great cost-saving ideas, without any muss, fuss, or waste.

Upon the invitation of the project leader, a PLOT meeting is called at the beginning of each new product development project. A sample agenda and invitee list for such a meeting is shown in Figure 3.4. The duration of the meeting should scale to the complexity of the product; for single-function products a few hours should be plenty, whereas for major systems products, such as aircraft and automobiles, a week or more might be warranted. A standardized process is followed, based on a checklist such as the example provided in Figure 3.5. After pleasantries, the PLOT works its way through the checklist. For each cost-improvement opportunity, a brief brainstorming session is held to harvest ideas for cross-product-line cost savings. These suggestions are then rank-ordered by the team, based on two factors: potential *impact* on product-line profitability and *ease* of implementation on the current project. The entire team performs the ranking, using a 1-5 subjective scoring system. A "1" score for impact implies insignificant cost-saving potential, while a "5" score represents a major cost-improvement opportunity. For ease of imple-

---

Meeting Notice

Time: Wednesday, March 23, 2010   8:00 am – 12:00 noon
Place: Conference Room 3
Purpose: Product-Line Optimization Team Review Meeting
Deliverable: Prioritized list of recommendations to the A-35 core design team for product-line cost reduction.
Attendees: PLOT team, A-35 core design team, and if available: engineering manager, manufacturing manager, marketing manager, materials manager, purchasing manager, chief financial officer (or controller), business-unit / product-line managers.

Agenda:

8:00 – 8:15	Introduction and Description of Process
8:15 – 9:00	Question and Answer Session with A-35 Core Design Team
9:00 – 11:00	Brainstorming Sessions Based on PLOT Checklist
11:00 – 11:45	Group Priority Ranking of Cost Improvement Ideas
11:45 – 12:00	Summary of Recommendations to A-35 Core Design Team

Figure 3.4 – A sample agenda and invitee list for a Product-Line Optimization Team meeting. This meeting is typically held very early in a new product development project and provides non-binding cost-saving recommendations to the design team.

Cost Improvement Opportunities	Ideas for Cross-Product-Line Cost Savings	Ratings (1-5)		Priority Ranking
		Impact	Ease	
1. Shared Parts	1.			
	2.			
	3.			
	4.			
2. Shared Raw Mtls.	1.			
	2.			
	3.			
	4.			
3. Shared Processes	1.			
	2.			
	3.			
	4.			
4. Common Capital	1.			
	2.			
	3.			
	4.			
5. Other Opportunities	1.			
	2.			
	3.			
	4.			

Figure 3.5 – An example of a PLOT meeting checklist. The opportunities included on your list should be derived from your specific business situation. I've identified several categories that are almost always important to product-line optimization.

mentation, a "1" score implies the idea is difficult to incorporate, while a "5" score indicates that the opportunity will require minimal time and effort. The two scores are then multiplied together (twenty-five is the highest possible total and one is the lowest) and recorded next to the appropriate idea.

After a set period of brainstorming (which should scale to the size of the cost-saving opportunity), the PLOT moves on to the next item on the checklist until it is completed. The opportunities that receive the highest total scores are gathered up and provided to the new product design team *as recommendations for action*. It should be left to the design team to evaluate the practicality of each high-ranking suggestion and to validate its potential cost savings. It is *not* a good idea to require that PLOT-team recommendations be mandatory for design teams. The design team has a much more detailed knowledge of what is and is not possible for their specific product. Mandatory actions from a PLOT meeting would likely result in lots of wasted time chasing down rabbit trails just to prove that an idea is a turkey (sorry for the mixed metaphor). It is, however, entirely reasonable to consider incentivizing a design team to incorporate one or more product-line cost improvements into their product. What these incentives consist of depends on your culture, but I've found that money works quite well.

3.1

Visualizing Your Future With a Product-Line Roadmap

Since we've already made the effort to set up a Product-Line Optimization Team, we might as well give them something else important to do. A Product-Line Roadmap is a tool that graphically illustrates the future development of a given product line, as described in Figure 3.6. Whether you use a complex template or just a simple fishbone diagram, it makes sense that the PLOT for your business unit be responsible for the initial creation and ongoing maintenance of the roadmap. At the kickoff of each new product development project, the PLOT comes together to discuss cost-improvement opportunities and to update the Product-Line Roadmap. In this way, the roadmap is kept relatively current, and can be used for strategic planning, resource and capital allocation, capacity planning, and so on. Its main purpose, however, remains eminently practical: A tool to help the PLOT identify cross-product synergies and plan for cost-saving opportunities across all products within the business unit.

The format of a Product-Line Roadmap can be anything your heart desires, but I'll share with you one possible implementation; a medium-complexity version that can work for the smallest of firms and still be useful for firms with complex products and multi-segment markets. Some potential elements of a Product-Line Roadmap include:

Time Base – This one is essential. The time base for a Product-Line Roadmap typically runs horizontally across a landscaped page, with a scale suited to the type of products and markets involved. For very fast moving markets (e.g., the fashion industry, some high-tech sectors), a one- or two-year horizon may be sufficient. For products that require a long time to mature (e.g., pharmaceuticals, aerospace), a significantly longer time base may make sense. I generally use a three-year horizon unless there is a dramatic need for longer or shorter. Remember this is not intended to be a prognostication tool; it simply captures your firm's best thinking about what the future of a product line might hold.

Top-Level View – It is critical that your roadmap show a top-level view of the product line. A whole sheaf of individual product-level roadmaps won't do the job (although you certainly might consider developing such detail after a top-level map has been formed and agreed upon). Climb to 40,000 feet and show everything on one page, then you can drill down to lower levels in a nice logical way. Obviously, if the roadmap is too high level, it won't provide enough insight into cross-product synergies, so use a tiered approach if the top-level view proves to be a bit too rarified.

Market Segmentation – The vertical axis of a typical Product-Line Roadmap lists several market segments. The goal is to understand how products (and the parts that comprise them) can bridge segment boundaries and enable higher production volumes and greater levels of commonality. Again, start with high-level segmentation (e.g., military vs. commercial, or East Coast vs. West Coast), and then consider adding more detailed roadmaps if they are needed to capture reality.

> ### "At a Glance" – The Product-Line Roadmap
>
> *Overview* –
> A visual representation of the "future" of a product line. A time base is provided that typically spans three to five years. Each major product platform is presented, along with any important versions or models of each platform. New product development projects are shown in outlying years, along with terminations of current models. The goal is to capture your firm's best current understanding of the evolution of a product line.
>
> *Primary Benefits* –
> An outstanding tool for identifying cross-product-line cost-saving opportunities. Which models could share parts, processes, suppliers, workcells, capital equipment, etc.? Also provides a critical feed into the strategic planning and portfolio management processes for your firm.
>
> *Best Suited Products* –
> This tool can be used for any product type, provided that synergy among products within a product line can offer some potential cost savings.
>
> *Advantages* –
> Excellent visual management and communications tool. Allows a team (such as a PLOT) to discuss cross-product-line opportunities and can support the strategic planning process.
>
> *Disadvantages* –
> Insight and future visualization skills are hard to come by. Don't set too high an expectation for the roadmap; it's really just a strawman to help your teams identify opportunities.
>
> *Impact on the Twenty Cost Levers* –
>
> | I. Direct Labor | | | | II. Direct Materials | | | | III. Capital | | | | IV. Design Cost | | | | V. Overhead | | | |
> |---|---|---|---|---|---|---|---|---|---|---|---|---|---|---|---|---|---|---|---|
> | 1a | 1b | 1c | 1d | 2a | 2b | 2c | 2d | 3a | 3b | 3c | 3d | 4a | 4b | 4c | 4d | 5a | 5b | 5c | 5d |
> | ○ | ○ | ○ | ◉ | ● | ◉ | ◉ | ○ | ○ | ◉ | ● | ● | ● | ○ | ○ | ◉ | ● | ● | | |

Figure 3.6 – "At-a-glance" overview of the Product-Line Roadmap visualization tool.

Platforms – Platforms are those portions of a product that are shared across multiple models within a product line. A platform can be a large subset of the final product (as is the case with automobiles, for example), or it might be something as innocuous as a package, software module, or enclosure. Capturing opportunities to merge non-synergistic products into common platforms is one of the most useful and powerful applications of a Product-Line Roadmap.

Extensions – If you strive for a bit more detail in your roadmap, adding potential product-line extensions is a great idea. These branches can be placed at the approximate times in the future that make sense to your team. A solid line can be used to indicate a "sure thing" (as if anything on this roadmap is really a sure thing), whereas a dotted line would indicate a potential avenue of growth that will need further validation before being addressed.

3.1

New Technologies – At the risk of cluttering up your roadmap with too much junk, including an indication of when new technologies will impact your product line can be critical for fast-moving industries. You may also consider creating a "multi-view" roadmap in which the same fishbone-style plan is used to illustrate market segments in one view, technological change in a second view, competitive landscape in a third, and so on. Please strive to keep it simple, however. These tools can take on a virulent life of their own, and soon they'll be sucking valuable resources into a bureaucratic black hole.

Competitive Factors – This is another example of a valuable perspective that might represent too much detail for a useful and practical roadmap. How do competitors' anticipated product introductions impact your market strategy? Are you "me tooing" the competition as a "fast second," or are you the market leader, with your introductions timed to keep that lead intact? This roadmap addition can help you visualize your priorities and recognize threats before they are upon you.

 An example of a Product-Line Roadmap is shown in Figure 3.7. In this version, a three-year time base is used for the horizontal axis, while the vertical axis serves multiple purposes. Above the timeline, the current and planned products offered by XYZ Corp. are represented. Either a Gantt or fishbone format can work well for this type of roadmap, but I prefer the latter approach because I feel it gives a clearer picture of interconnections and dependencies. Current product lines die and new products are born as your firm's future unfolds. Opportunities to consolidate products into platforms, or to redesign them to enable low-cost customization, are indicated by simple notations. Remember that the purpose of the roadmap is *not* to show explicitly every idea for cross-product-line cost savings. It is simply a tool to help visualize various opportunities; specific recommendations should be documented separately for each new design opportunity.

 Below the time base are two of many possible "feeds" that could be included in your roadmap. If your firm has an R&D activity that is distinct from new product development, a section can be provided to show when new product and process technologies might be ready to feed into new product development projects. Likewise, if competitors' actions are of concern, a few milestones can be included that represent your best guess as to when new and troublesome products will enter the market. Market segments could be shown on either the top or bottom half of the roadmap, depending on how fractionated your markets are. As with all of the tools in this guidebook, there are no dogmatic rules here; feel free to innovate and modify my example in any way that you deem beneficial.

 Now that we have some "procedural" tools in place to help your firm identify cross-product-line cost savings, I'll spend the remainder of Part III describing several detailed strategies with which to arm your design teams. Keep in mind that these synergy-enhancing tools must be considered early in the development process, since they may affect the fundamental architecture of the product. Once we've embedded as much product-line-level optimization as we can into our new product design, we will narrow our focus in Parts IV, V, and VI to consider powerful tools for slashing the manufacturing cost of an individual product.

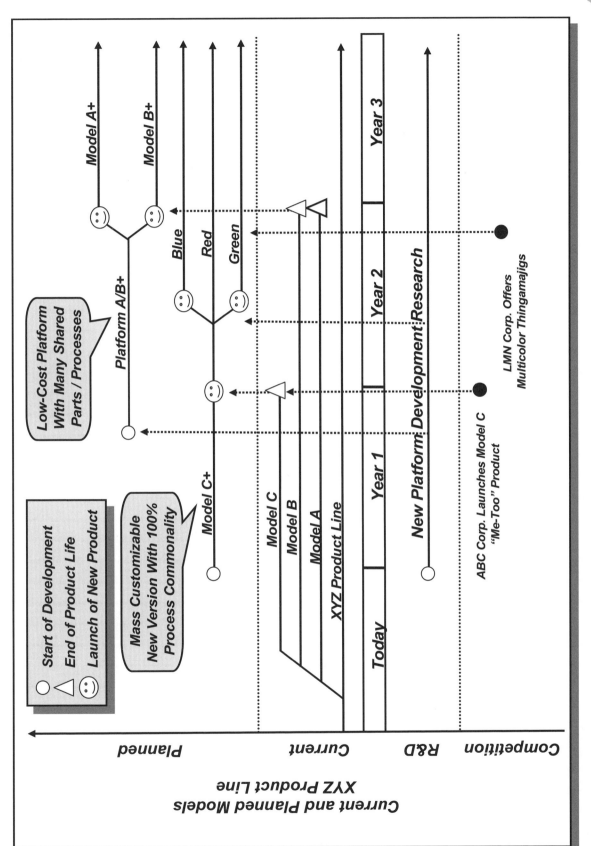

Figure 3.7 – A basic Product-Line Roadmap, showing time in the future along the horizontal axis and various current and planned products along the vertical axis. Note that either a fishbone-diagram format (shown) or a Gantt-chart format can be used.

Notes

Section 3.2 — Platforms Come in All Sizes

In the context of product design, what does the word "platform" mean to you? The most common perception of product platforms comes from the auto industry. When I was young, my friend and I would argue for hours over whether my Pontiac Firebird was a better car than his Chevy Camero. To us, the differences between them were dramatic; I would never own a Chevy and he wouldn't be caught dead in a Pontiac. Only later did I realize that the Firebird and the Camero *were essentially the same car*. Some minor cosmetics here and there, but really they could have been twins. An assembly line that produced the Camero could have easily produced a Firebird, since the chassis and many of the structural members and body panels were identical. Even the engines were generally interchangeable (something that any teenager with a set of Craftsman tools and too much time on their hands could tell you from experience).

Automobile manufacturers have recognized for years that production economies are driven not by the number of car models offered, but rather by the number of platforms required. When Daimler Benz took over (oops, I mean "merged with") Chrysler, one of their key strategic goals was to reduce the total number of platforms required to produce the combined models of the two companies. So it seems that a platform can be thought of as a "core" upon which several different finished-goods models can be based.

Now let's broaden our thinking a bit. What if our product is software instead of SUVs. Can we still apply this concept? Absolutely! It is common for software designers to define a core application as a platform, with multiple versions or customizations being built upon that core. A basic searchable database platform, for example, might be adapted for use as an inventory-management package, a sales-contact directory, a literature archive, and even a recipe minder for the kitchen. Although the user interface may look totally different, the number of common lines of code could easily be greater than ninety-five percent.

Once we start to think about it, platforms are everywhere. An Intel Pentium processor serves as a CPU platform for many different configurations of Dell computers. Ah, but wait a minute. Isn't Microsoft Windows the operating-system platform for those same Dell computers? It seems that a product can embody *multiple platforms*; evidently the auto-industry example given above is too restrictive. That is, in fact, the central point of this section. A product can include an unlimited number of "platforms" provided that we expand our notion of a platform beyond the traditional definition. To capture true economies of scope across multiple product lines, we need to get past "Mister Potato Head" thinking (i.e., some product core that can be customized by sticking on different stuff). Instead, platforms should be thought of as any aspect of a product, large or small, that can be shared in common by multiple models within a product line.

A Hierarchy of Platforms

Platform strategies are driven to a great extent by the specific architecture of your products. Hence, it is difficult to come up with a lean design tool that will provide equal benefit to computer makers, toy producers, drug manufacturers, and software designers. Nonetheless, by using systems thinking I can propose a common general approach, and then provide you with some flexible techniques for capturing platform-based cost savings.

The first insight that systems thinking offers us about platform strategy is that products embody a hierarchy of complexity, as shown in Figure 3.8. Core functionality is

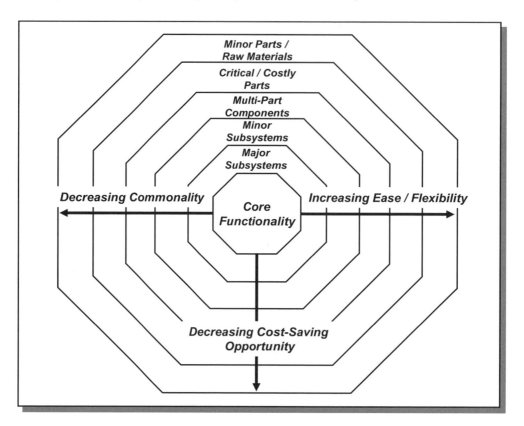

Figure 3.8 – The typical hierarchy of platform opportunities for a complex system product. At the center of the hierarchy is a core functionality that can be customized for multiple market segments. The steps of the hierarchy represent a logical flow: major subsystems, minor subsystems, and so on down to inexpensive parts and raw material stock. As we move outward from the center, the cost-saving opportunities decline in proportion to the reduction in commonality between models. Both the ease of standardization and the flexibility retained in the product line increase, however, as we approach the outer limits of the hierarchy.

"central" to any system – the primary task that the product is expected to perform. Models of a product that share core functionality have a very high degree of *commonality*, and hence offer the highest levels of cost savings. Although this is a great (and traditional) approach to platform architecture, it places severe limits on how *distinct* the models within a product line can be. (As much as General Motors might have wanted to make my Firebird look different from the Camero, it would not have been cost effective to make it look like a Lamborghini.) If we move outward in our hierarchy to standardizing on major subsystems, however, we can still gain considerable commonality benefits while increasing product-line flexibility. So it goes through minor subsystems, assembled components, and finally to raw materials and minor parts. At each level, the cost benefit declines in proportion to increased flexibility and ease of standardization.

A few examples that illustrate the hierarchical structure of platforms are provided in Figure 3.9. First, let's consider a complex mechanical system such as a hydraulic actuator. Its core functionality is to convert fluid pressure into linear movement. To achieve the greatest commonality among models, we would want all three major subsystems (controls, pump, and drive cylinder) to be common to all models within the product line. Distinctive models would result from relatively minor changes to one or more design parameters, such as increasing the length of the drive cylinder, or perhaps tailoring the accuracy of motion control. But what if the market demands more significant differences? Then our next option would be to define one of our major subsystems as a platform, such as standardizing the control system, while offering a large variety of cylinder lengths, capacities, and operating pressures. If this level of commonality is still too restrictive to satisfy market needs, we can continue down the hierarchy to minor subsystems, components, and finally discrete parts. Defining an oil-seal platform for our actuator line, for example, certainly won't yield as great a cost savings as defining the entire drive cylinder as a platform. It may be quite easy to standardize on a common seal configuration, however.

The story is remarkably similar for a shampoo / conditioner product line, a software application product line, or even an information / media product line. The power of systems thinking is its ability to partition any type of system into logical chunks that can be evaluated for their platform potential. Changing the packaging of a shampoo / conditioner product can create variety in the marketplace at minimal cost (since the core functionality is the same for both). If the market should desire shampoos that are optimized for dry or oily hair, perhaps the conditioner "subsystem" can still remain a common platform for both products. If even that level of standardization is too restrictive, at least the fragrance "component" might serve as a platform. For any category of product, the process is the same; consider the demands of the marketplace, then look to the highest level of the system hierarchy that can be commonized while still completely satisfying your customers.

At the lowest level of benefit, but the highest level of ease, are "microplatforms." A microplatform is a part, process, component, material, or other low-level element of a product design that can be standardized across several (if not all) models within a product line. Although you may feel that every product you produce is necessarily distinct, there are always opportunities to define microplatforms: fasteners, fittings, passive electronic

Core Product Example	Platform Hierarchy		
	Major Subsystem	Minor Subsystem	Part
Hydraulic Cylinder	Control Electronics	Pump Motor	Oil Seal
Pocket Digital Assistant	User Interface HW/SW	Digital Camera	Battery
Automobile	Chassis	Sound System	Brake Pads
Shampoo / Conditioner	Shampoo Formulation	Fragrance	Bottle
Database Software	Database Engine	Report-Writing Module	Printer Driver
Consulting Report	Generic Boilerplate	Canned Statistical Graphs	Consultant Biographies

Figure 3.9 – Some examples of how a system hierarchy can be used to identify platform opportunities among products within a product line. The greatest cost savings are achieved with high-levels of commonality, but standardization of even minor parts can yield measurable cost benefits.

components, seals, bearings, wiring harnesses, connectors...the list is endless. So repeat after me, "There is no excuse for me not to save money by defining at least a few micro-platforms within my product line." See, that didn't hurt a bit.

The Platform Plan

Now that we have liberated our perspective on platforms, how can we exploit this knowledge to change the world? I'll be quite honest with you; it requires a special kind of organizational leadership and discipline to capture all but the most rudimentary benefits from platform-based commonality. Why? Because organizations are remarkably short-sighted, and achieving a breakthrough in platform synergy *takes time*. In fact, it is most typically accomplished as a generational process, wherein each new generation of a product line has a higher degree of commonality than the last. Certainly a major product-line renovation can move the agenda forward a long way in a short time. Typically, however, the definition and integration of platforms is evolutionary and incremental, which brings us back to that attention-span thing.

In the remainder of this section, I'll describe a lean design tool that can help keep your organization on track toward a platform-based future. If you've elected to form a Product-Line Optimization Team (PLOT), then this tool will be integral to their efforts. Even if you decide not to do any PLOTing, at least do some planning (acronym abuse should be a crime, don't you think?). The Platform Plan is a two-part tool that can allow an organization to identify, execute, and track the status of a platform-based cost-reduction effort, as summarized in Figure 3.10. The Platform Plan is derived from a Product-Line Roadmap, and provides an organization with detailed steps and measurable milestones. If a PLOT exists, they should be the owners of the Platform Plan, with each new product design team receiving specific recommendations based on the Plan. If there is no

"At a Glance" – The Platform Plan

Overview –
>Provides the details, definitions, milestones and actions required to implement a platform-based cost-reduction strategy. This tool serves as the executable output of the Product-Line Roadmap described previously. Can be used either by a PLOT (if one has been formed) or by individual product design teams as opportunities surface.

Primary Benefits –
>Advances product platforms from the domain of strategic planning to the actionable world of specific opportunities, timing, responsibilities, etc. Provides clear cross-design-team connections and avoids duplication of effort and missed opportunities.

Best Suited Products –
>This tool can be used for any product type, provided that synergy among products within a product line can offer some potential cost savings.

Advantages –
>Excellent visual management and communications tool. Allows a team to execute specific opportunities early in the design process by making plans available in advance.

Disadvantages –
>Requires that an organization have both the vision and the discipline to set up the plan and take the time to consider it for every new product development opportunity.

Impact on the Twenty Cost Levers –

I. Direct Labor				II. Direct Materials				III. Capital				IV. Design Cost				V. Overhead			
1a	1b	1c	1d	2a	2b	2c	2d	3a	3b	3c	3d	4a	4b	4c	4d	5a	5b	5c	5d
○	○	○	◉	○	●	◉	◉	○	○	◉	◉	●	○	○	◉	●	●	○	○

Figure 3.10 – "At-a-glance" overview of the Platform Plan lean design tool.

PLOT, the Plan should be owned either by the director of engineering, or on a rotating basis by whichever design team is most actively involved in platform development.

There are two components of a Platform Plan: the Platform Matrix, shown in Figure 3.11, and the Platform Integration Schedule, shown in Figure 3.12. The Platform Matrix offers a relatively simple way to visually organize potential platform cost-saving opportunities. The various product models within a product line are shown along the horizontal axis, while potential platform opportunities (at all levels of the hierarchy, but with emphasis on higher-level opportunities) are defined along the vertical axis. A platform opportunity is any existing element of a design that has high potential for reuse or standardization across multiple products. Clearly some advanced screening should be performed to eliminate all but the most promising candidates. At the junction between a platform opportunity and a product model are two "scores." The first (upper-left corner of each junction) represents the *potential* that the given platform has for incorporation within the corresponding product model. I've used the classic "meatball" scoring system, in which a darker meatball represents greater potential. You could easily substitute a numerical scoring system if you desire a higher degree of granularity, but the meatballs provide a quick visual cue for identifying high-potential combinations. The other score that appears at each junction (lower-right corner) reflects the *priority* for implementing the platform within that product model. Priority should be based on the junction's "potential" score, along with consideration of the ease of incorporation and the cost benefit if accomplished. Ideally, junctions that display a dark meatball for both potential and priority represent the first actions to be taken in your Platform Plan.

The second component of a Platform Plan, the Platform Integration Schedule, tracks the implementation of high-potential / high-priority opportunities. This is simply a standard project schedule, with "reducing product-line costs through platform standardization" as the project charter. Opportunities that display two reasonably dark meatballs on the Platform Matrix are given a line in the Platform Integration Schedule. Often, several platforms might be incorporated into a product at the same time, usually in concert with a product-model upgrade or other planned improvement. So if, for example, Model A1 is

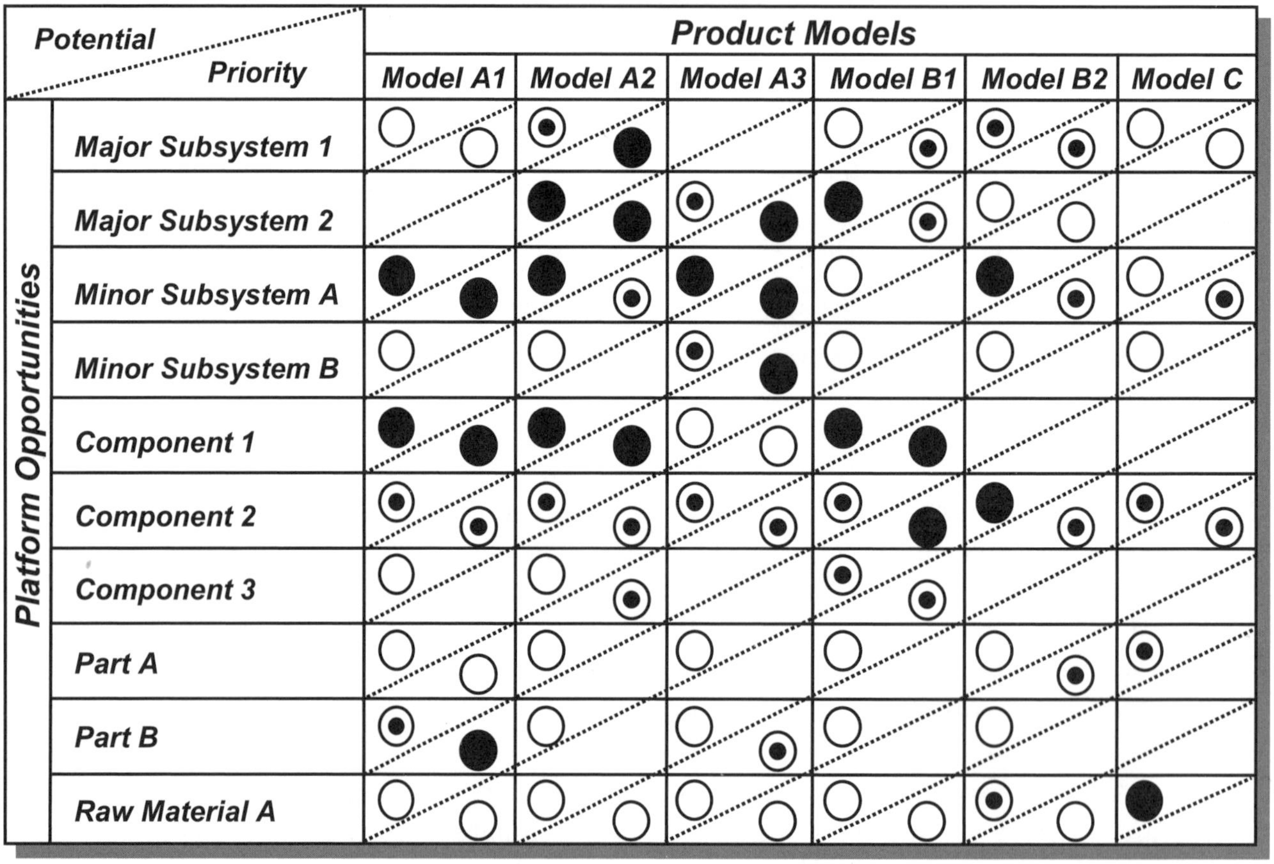

Figure 3.11 – A Platform Matrix aligns platform opportunities with specific product models within a product line. The priority and potential for commonality is indicated by the darkness of the "meatball." The timeframe for these opportunities is established in the second component of the Platform Plan, shown in Figure 3.12.

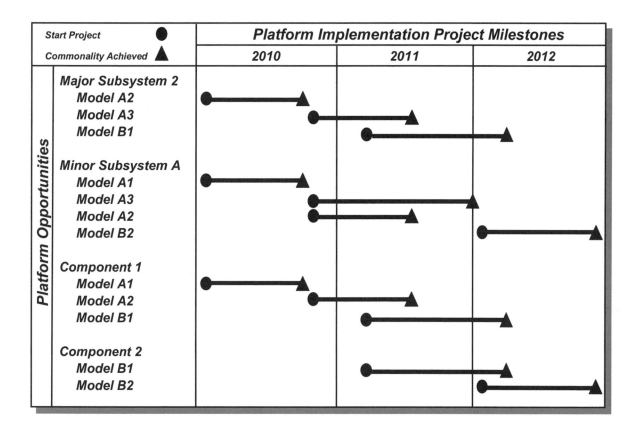

Figure 3.12 – The second component of a Platform Plan is the Platform Integration Schedule. This provides a timeframe for platform implementation and reflects the generational evolution of a product line from low to high levels of commonality. Note that this somewhat simplified example is based upon the sample Platform Matrix provided in Figure 3.11.

scheduled for an upgrade project anyway, why not implement some platform commonality while you're at it? Each time a development project is initiated (either for a new product model or an upgrade to an existing one), the Platform Matrix should be consulted and updated, and a set of tasks should be added to the Platform Integration Schedule (if a high-priority platform opportunity exists). Note that normally more detail would be provided in a real Platform Integration Schedule than I've shown in my example. Don't get carried away, however; the actual planning for integration of platform opportunities should be left to each product design team. The combination of the matrix and schedule components of the Platform Plan should provide your organization with enough guidance to start getting serious about platforms...provided that you've conquered your organization's attention-deficit disorder.

3.2

Platform Efficiency and Effectiveness

To validate the effectiveness of our Platform Plan, we must answer a critical question: How much benefit have we gained from commonizing on a platform? As with most things that are business related, there are a number of possible metrics that we can use to estimate our gains. This final subsection identifies several measures that can be used to evaluate the success of your platform implementation program. The choice of metric (or metrics) is up to you, but *be careful*. Pick the wrong metric and you may either: a) drive your organization to do the wrong things, b) create the impression that your program is not successful, c) underestimate or overestimate the benefits, or d) all of the above. I always use a set of two or more uncorrelated metrics to estimate benefit, since this "balanced-scorecard" approach reduces the risk of doing (a) through (d) considerably.

The first category of metric relates to the savings (in both non-recurring design costs and time-to-market) associated with reuse of a platform design element, as opposed to designing a new element from scratch. Note that there are really two ways in which platforms can be used to optimize a product line. The first way is "proactive," in the sense that a platform is defined during the development of a new strategic product line. In this situation, the time and cost to develop subsequent derivatives or extensions of the core platform should be considerably less than for previous, non-platform-based models. The second approach to platform implementation is more "reactive." The goal here is purely cost savings, and in some cases the development time and cost might actually *increase*, in return for the elimination of part / assembly variety within the product line. Obviously, it is better to be proactive than reactive, but major product-line renovations are few and far between. Hence, most firms find that their platform implementation strategy is a mixture of both proactive and reactive opportunities. In such a case, a mixture of metrics that reflects this reality is highly recommended.

The second category of metric is more central to the goals of this book. These metrics attempt to quantify (at least in relative terms) the actual production cost savings resulting from platform-based initiatives. The possibilities here range from calculating actual cost savings through some form of payback analysis, to using several "figures of merit" for evaluating the cost optimization of a product line. A summary of both categories of metric is provided in Figure 3.13. When it comes to metrics, a little common sense goes a long way. Try to look at the big picture, rather than letting numbers overwhelm you (or cause you to make bad decisions). If I were a pilot, I'd certainly prefer to be flying by direct visual observation then by instrumentation. Check your instruments now and then, but spend most of your time directly observing the improved efficiencies associated with standardization, simplification, and commonality.

Platform Implementation Metrics

Metric Definition	Measured Improvement
Platform Efficiency (Cost) = $\dfrac{\text{Platform Derivative Engineering Costs}}{\text{Platform Engineering Costs}}$	• Cost savings due to reduced design labor for products based on a platform design element.
Platform Efficiency (Time) = $\dfrac{\text{Platform Derivative Time-to-Market}}{\text{Avg. Time-to-Market for Non-Platform Products}}$	• Time saved during development due to use of already existing platform design elements.
Platform Effectiveness = $\dfrac{\text{Net Sales of a Platform Derivative}}{\text{Development Costs of Platform Derivative}}$	• Market acceptance of a platform-based product strategy. Are products sufficiently distinct?
Derivative Commonality = Percentage of a derivative product model that is common to a platform (by either part numbers or cost of materials).	• Relative cost savings resulting from platform implementation.
Platform Flexibility = Number of derivatives (models) supported by a specific platform.	• How large is your cost-saving opportunity? How suitable are your products to a platform strategy?
Product-line Inefficiency = Percentage of unique or "once-used" part numbers of total part numbers within a product line.	• How large is your cost saving opportunity? How distinct are your current products?

Platform-Based Cost Savings –

- Volume purchasing discounts
- Reduction in number of purchase orders
- Reduction in number of parts in inventory
- Reduction in inventory carrying costs
- Reduction in material movement
- Reduction in storage costs
- Reduction in scrap costs
- Reduction in test and inspection costs
- Reduction in field service and repair costs
- Reduction in factory floor space required
- Reduction in direct labor costs
- Learning-curve labor savings
- Reduction in order-to-ship time
- Reduced warrantee costs
- Reduction in production planning costs
- Reduction in engineering change notices
- Reduction in setup and changeover time
- Reduction in capital for unique tooling / processes

Figure 3.13 – An overview of several metrics or "figures of merit" that can be used to evaluate the success of your platform-based cost-saving program. It is highly recommended that several uncorrelated metrics be used in concert to gain a balanced perspective.

Notes

Section 3.3 — Modular, Scalable, and Mass Customizable

Let's take a quick look back at whence we came. Systems thinking shows us that a product line can and should be thought of as a profit-maximizing system. With that new perspective, we can see that there are multiple opportunities to improve profit margins through cross-product-line synergy. The key mandates here are to simplify and commonize at the level of core products, subassemblies, components, and even minor parts and raw materials. One pathway to achieving breakthroughs in commonality is through the use of a platform strategy, as described in Section 3.2. Ah, but are there not many pathways that lead to Rome?

In this final section of Part III, we will dig even deeper into design methodologies that enable high levels of product-line commonality, while still retaining the flexibility needed to satisfy the marketplace. Three powerful approaches will be discussed: modularity, scalability, and mass customization. Although each offers its own unique advantages, they are actually just variations on the platform theme. The specific nature of your product will determine which (if any) strategy will work best for you. And while we're on the subject, I should mention that the following section is really aimed at firms that produce discrete physical products. I don't mean to exclude anyone, but if you don't make hardware, you might find the discussions below a bit arcane. Hence, if you're a food or drug manufacturer (really any process industry), you might consider skipping on to Part IV.

Modules Need Not Look Like Legos

Recall that a system consists of multiple interacting elements that work together to perform a common function. Often this common system function is delivered through the contributions of subsystems that are distinct entities within a product. For example, the common function of an automobile system is to transport its passengers safely. To accomplish this, several subsystems are actually at work. An engine creates rotational energy in proportion to the throttle command. A drive train couples the rotational energy of the engine to the axles. A braking subsystem performs the stopping function, and so on. Normally, these subsystems are so interwoven into the design of the product that we don't think of them as separate entities. We turn the key, hit the gas, and away we go. Yet to optimize the "transport passengers safely" function, we need to optimize the interplay between these (and many other) subsystems within the system product. Furthermore, we'd like to be able to tailor the performance of the product to the specific needs of various market segments. An aggressive driver might want a more powerful engine, a six-speed standard transmission, and four-wheel, high-performance disk brakes. An economy-minded driver would likely prefer a smaller engine, while a convenience-minded driver might choose a four-speed automatic transmission. If each of these preferences demanded the design of an entirely new product, the cost of customization would be astronomical.

The obvious solution to this problem is to design our system to allow the swapping out of engines, drive trains, and braking subsystems based on customer preference. But how can we achieve this? It's really very simple. We design our automobile to be *modular*, by establishing simple, *standardized interfaces* between each subsystem. For example, our engine's interface to the drive train would consist of a standardized coupling plate and engine mounts. Now any engine (within reason) that conforms to that interface can be used in our auto. Our braking subsystem interface with the axle and wheel hubs could also be standardized, thereby allowing several levels of braking performance to be specified without affecting the rest of the car. In this way, modularity enables high levels of flexibility in meeting specific market needs, while still providing the manufacturer with significant platform-based cost savings. The key to modularity is establishing efficient, standardized interfaces.

But do we get all this flexibility for free? Actually, there is a tradeoff to be made. Increased modularity almost always is achieved at the expense of overall system performance. Creating standardized interfaces may add weight, increase friction, consume more power, or cause some other suboptimal situation. Even software products are not immune. High levels of modularity in a software application can often result in slower run times and larger file sizes. Moreover, modularity usually adds at least a small amount of incremental cost, either to the non-recurring design effort, to the production cost, or both. So why do it? *Because the rewards may far outweigh the drawbacks*, as shown in Figure 3.14.

What rewards, you say? First and foremost, we gain flexibility. From a design standpoint, we have the ability to isolate one aspect of our product for enhancement or even breakthrough redesign, with no added risk to the rest of the product. Our development times are shortened due to the reuse of design elements and through the maturity and stability of our interface. Production costs for direct materials and labor may increase slightly, but these added costs may be insignificant when compared to savings in fixed capital, and both fixed and variable overhead. Moreover, we now may have the ability to build "customized" finished goods to order rather than to forecast (simply by piecing together modules), thereby reducing inventory and storage costs. Finally, *the marketplace loves modular products*. Customers are offered the flexibility to adapt the product to their specific needs, and as those needs evolve over time, there is the potential to upgrade without replacing the entire product. It may also make sense to encourage third-party manufacturers to build add-ons or enhancements to your product, based on your specified standard interface. This can create a steamroller effect in the marketplace, driven by what economists call "network externalities" (the tendency for markets to adopt a single standard product whenever there is a dense network of other products available to support it).

Modular Product Architecture

Advantages

- Significant reduction in development time and cost for new line extensions.

- Ability to customize product performance at very low recurring cost.

- Increases value to customer by enabling upgrades or alterations to performance after purchase.

- Allows for third-party development of product enhancements – a major market-share factor.

- Significant reduction of production cycle-time. Can enable build-to-order final assembly.

- Ease of assembly, test, maintenance, service, etc.

- High levels of product-line commonality will drive both fixed and variable production costs downward.

Disadvantages

- By definition, overall product performance will be at least slightly compromised.

- May add time to development cycle, although risk-reduction effects might compensate for this.

- May add incremental direct cost to each model of a modular product line. (Hopefully, reduction of indirect costs will countervail.)

- Increased weight, size, power consumption, run-time, file size, noise, friction, etc. Must be traded off with flexibility benefits to customer.

Figure 3.14 – Advantages and disadvantages of a modular product architecture. Compromises in performance are balanced by achieving high levels of flexibility while still capturing platform-based cost savings.

If modular architecture makes sense in your situation, how might you go about carving up your product? The first step toward modularizing a product is to *partition* it. Partitioning simply means that functionality is grouped in such a way that a simple and standardized interface can be defined between each subsystem. There is a broad spectrum of possibilities here, ranging from a design with no partitioned functionality, referred to as an *integral design*, to a fully modularized product with virtually no unpartitioned functionality. A quick example will help illustrate. Picture a side chair made from pieces of chrome tubing. A curved metal seat is welded to the frame, with only some foam rubber and upholstery breaking up the solid metal architecture. This is an integral design, in that there is no possibility of changing one aspect of the chair, such as the angle of the seat back, without disturbing the entire product's structure. Now consider a typical adjustable office chair. Height, seat tilt, back tilt, lumbar support, arm height, and even seat firmness can be adjusted by the user. If I want to upgrade the back of the chair, I can simply remove the current back from its standardized mounting and replace it with a new design. The same is true for all of the other subsystems: the seat, the base, the arms, and so on. Although the adjustable office chair is not as elegant in appearance (nor as economical to produce) as the simple bent-tube side chair, what a world of difference in the flexibility of design, manufacture, and use.

Here are a few rules to follow when partitioning a product's functionality:

1) The main reason for partitioning a product into modules is to address a market need for flexibility. If you can't justify the partition based on a clear opportunity to extend your product line or to capture some other significant differentiating benefit, don't do it. Remember, you don't have to use modular architecture to employ a platform-based cost-reduction strategy; modularity is just a special case of platform implementation.

2) It may be necessary to significantly change the design of a product to enable a simple interface, but achieving this is crucial. Flexibility and simplicity of interface go hand in hand, so move things physically, electrically, mechanically, or whatever other "ility" your product possesses, to keep that interface simple.

3) In a hardware product, a module is a separate physical entity, so carefully consider the physical boundaries of the newly defined module. Can other planned versions of the module fit into the space allowed? Are there adequate provisions for additional connections, data lines, power, weight, torque, etc.? When you define a module, you are really defining an entire family of modules. Remember that when newlyweds buy a house, they must consider the needs of all those little gleams in daddy's eye that will be coming along in the future.

4) Finally, don't consider just the customer's needs when establishing a partition. The factory may have some important inputs as well. Is it easier on the manufacturing folks to define an interface before or after a weld joint, connector, or other fitting, for example? Will a particular partitioning of electronic functionality put a strain on circuit-board density, noise shielding, or even functional testing? What are the capabilities of current workcells to produce a module, based on different partition points within the product? Is the skill level required for assembly roughly homogeneous throughout the module? It's okay to have a high-skill module and a lower-skill module, but waste abounds if all of your modules require a little bit of high skill and a little bit of lower skill.

Once functionality has been partitioned, we must define an "architecture," including both module and interface designs. There are a number of options to consider when creating a modularized product line, leading us to our next lean design tool: the Module-Optimization Checklist. It is often the case that the cleverness of the interface design determines the financial benefits of a modularization effort. Therefore, I've provided a design-review tool to facilitate the optimization of modules and interfaces, as summarized in Figure 3.15. This tool can be used in a variety of settings, although it works best as a stimulator for group discussion.

Embedded within the Checklist are some non-obvious options for interface design. Using a bit of abstract thinking we can come up with at least six different ways to establish a standardized interface between modules. These alternatives include: 1) slot modu-

"At a Glance" – The Module-Optimization Checklist

Overview –
A brainstorming tool for either individual designers or design teams. Its purpose is to stimulate creativity and ensure thoroughness in defining and designing a modular product-line architecture

Primary Benefits –
Firms that win using modular strategies almost always have come up with some clever ways to reduce the negative impact of modularization, while retaining high levels of flexibility and ease of customization. This tool will help designers consider several alternatives that might prove to be the solution to a specific modular design challenge.

Best Suited Products –
This tool can be used for any product type that lends itself to a modular architecture.

Advantages –
Enables optimization of modules and interfaces with minimal time and effort.

Disadvantages –
Requires that teams or designers have the discipline to follow the guidance of the tool.

Impact on the Twenty Cost Levers –

I. Direct Labor				II. Direct Materials				III. Capital				IV. Design Cost				V. Overhead			
1a	1b	1c	1d	2a	2b	2c	2d	3a	3b	3c	3d	4a	4b	4c	4d	5a	5b	5c	5d
○			◉	●	○	◉		◉	◉	○		●				◉	○	●	

Figure 3.15 – "At-a-glance" overview of the Module-Optimization Checklist.

larity, 2) bus modularity, 3) sectional modularity, 4) component-sharing modularity, 5) component-swapping modularity, and 6) cut-to-fit modularity. These (admittedly overlapping) possibilities are illustrated in Figure 3.16, and described as follows:

Slot Modularity – Even if you lack imagination, this type of modularity should be quite familiar. In this case, each modular function has its own unique and dedicated "slot" in the product. No two functions can share the same interface, so flexibility is somewhat limited. (Note that the term "slot" doesn't necessarily mean that a physical slot is provided.) Examples include the radio "slot" in your car's dashboard, the battery "slot" in your laptop computer, or the "slot" for a bulb in a table lamp. In each case, varying levels of performance can be substituted in the slot, but the same function is always performed: music for your car, power for your laptop, or lighting for your room.

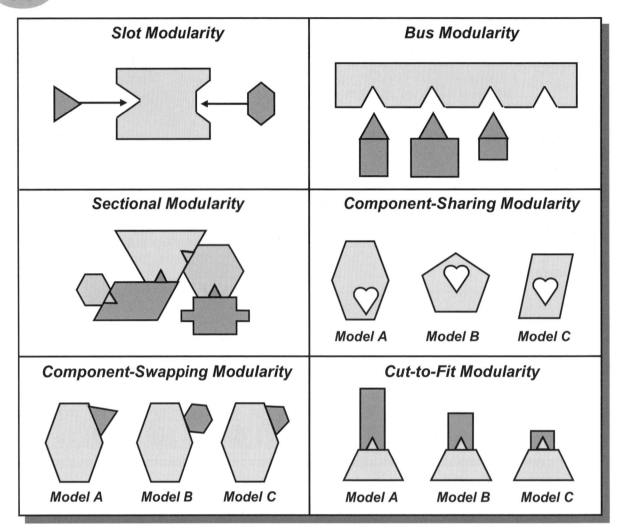

Figure 3.16 – Illustration of the six types of modularity that can enable high levels of commonality and flexibility within a product line. The choice of interface type is critical, since most of the economics of a modular architecture are driven by the efficiency and flexibility of its interfaces.

Bus Modularity – In bus modularity, a common structure is provided that allows variation in the type, number, and location of modules that can "plug" into it. The interface to all modules is the same, and the functionality that can be provided by the modules is only limited by the richness of the bus interface. Familiar examples come from the world of electronics: a computer backplane that accepts expansion cards, the clever interconnect on several brands of PDA that allows those devices to become a cell-phone, a digital camera, a laser weapon, etc. Even track lighting provides a standardized power bus with a high degree of flexibility. Yet bus modularity is certainly not confined to electronic products. A shelving system with a standardized rail used for component attachment is a good example of a mechanical bus structure. A pneumatic (air pressure) system with standardized couplings can perform a multitude of functions, depending on the type of "module" (in this case, a tool or some other powered device) that is plugged into it. The main benefit of the bus-modularity architecture is that it is simple and clean; usually only a few "commons" flow across the interface. The primary disadvantage is that of all of the modular approaches, this one tends to be the most inefficient; the entire bus structure is really waste from a design standpoint. Some products lend themselves to the use of a bus, and in those cases the inefficiencies are not significant. In many cases, however, this architecture would go over like either a performance or economic lead balloon.

Sectional Modularity – So let's just get rid of the bus, if it is so inefficient. Sectional modularity does exactly that. A common interface is provided for all modules, just like in bus modularity, but the modules *attach to each other*, rather than to a common bus structure. Sectional office furniture is a good example of sectional modularity. Often the differences between bus and sectional modularity are subtle (and not really important, as long as the modular strategy works for you). To clarify the distinction (I hope), consider another example. A freight train is a good illustration of sectional modularity, since you can attach any railcar you wish to the train, in any order you wish, through a standard coupling. The cars are hitched to each other, rather than to some external (and ostensibly unnecessary) bus. Now recall your last trip to the carwash. Remember that chain gizmo that the attendant hooks your car onto so that it can be pulled through the wash? That chain thing is a bus, and the cars that are moving through the carwash are being pulled *by it*, not by each other. The advantages of a sectional architecture are obvious; much of the flexibility of a bus architecture, but without the wasteful bus. The disadvantage is a slight limitation in flexibility, particularly with respect to changing the order of its components quickly and easily. A shelving system with a standard attachment rail (a bus) allows the removal and relocation of one shelf without disturbing the other shelves. A stackable shelving system (sectional – each shelf relies on its neighbors for mechanical support) is flexible, but relocating a single shelf might require unstacking and restacking the entire system.

Component-Sharing Modularity – Here we are back to our familiar "standardized-parts" concept. Component-sharing modularity is sort of a last resort from a modularity standpoint; we are capturing economies of scope, but with no real flexibility benefit. Great for incremental cost reduction, of course, but we don't get any kick in the marketplace for our clever modular strategy. For each shared part, we need only standardize its specific interface across multiple products. If we specify that only #12 x 20 screws will be used in our product assembly, all holes for attachments must have the appropriate diameter and thread density. Not very exciting, but every penny counts.

Component-Swapping Modularity – Much like slot modularity, the idea with component-swapping modularity is to create multiple product models from a single base product by swapping one or more components. We have returned to the "Mister Potato Head" concept, wherein the potato is the base product, and the features that we apply create each unique "model." A form letter is a good example of component-swapping modularity. A basic customer service letter can be customized to specific situations by changing the addressee block, the signature block, and maybe a sentence or two within the letter. A Swatch watch is also a fine example; the core product is the basic wristwatch, with the customization provided by a host of different colored bezels that can be selected based on your outfit, mood, etc.

Cut-to-Fit Modularity – By now the distinctions between these various categories of modularity must be blurring together for you. Don't fret; it really doesn't matter which category you select. The goal here is to stimulate your thinking. Cut-to-fit modularity is similar to the previous two categories, but in this case, one or more of the product's components are continuously variable within preset and practical limits. Often this final type of modularity is paired with an automated production system that allows the customization to occur quickly and efficiently. Matsushita, for example, has a division that produces customized bicycles that are tailored to the exact specifications of each rider. Once the measurements are taken, the unique specification is sent to the factory, where an automated cutting and welding system creates the bike frame to match. The "cutting" might even be done by the customer subsequent to purchase. An electrical box for residential wiring is cut-to-fit modular; there are many possible combinations of openings, with each opening covered by a "knockout" panel. The box can be configured to your specific needs by breaking off the knockout wherever you wish to penetrate the box.

    The Module-Optimization Checklist tool helps to focus a modularization project by forcing designers to consider the full breadth of available options, as shown in Figure 3.17. The use of the tool should be self-explanatory, but one might imagine a product design team gathering at the early stages of a project to consider modularity prospects. The team leader would simply go down the checklist, and after some discussion, ask the group to agree on a score of from 1 to 5 for each statement on the list (including both Parts I and II). For this tool, my ubiquitous numerical scoring system relates to how successfully and thoroughly each topic on the Checklist has been addressed. So, for example, Item 1.4 states that "bus modularity has been considered and either accepted or rejected." If this possible interface architecture has been carefully analyzed and dispositioned by the design team, then it should receive a "4" or "5" score. If the possibility of a bus-type interface hasn't been given the time of day, then this statement should receive a "1" or "2" ranking. After each statement has been discussed and scored, the total scores for Parts I and II are calculated and compared to the "interpretation" guide at the bottom of the figure. If your team has done a thorough and comprehensive job of developing a modular architecture, your scores should be in the 40-50 range for both portions of the Checklist. If you're totals are falling below this mark, you might consider additional optimization efforts before firming up your designs. In this way, the Module-Optimization Checklist helps your team formulate a successful plan for developing a modular product family.

Module-Optimization Checklist

Indicators of an Optimized Modular Design	Agreement With Statement
	Low — High

Part I – Overall Modular Architecture

1.1 The decision to modularize was directly based on market demand for higher customization and / or product design flexibility. | 1 | 2 | 3 | 4 | 5 |

1.2 The loss of product "efficiency" (e.g., loss of performance, added weight, added cost, etc.) was considered in your choice of architecture. | 1 | 2 | 3 | 4 | 5 |

1.3 A "slot modularity" approach was evaluated and either accepted or rejected. | 1 | 2 | 3 | 4 | 5 |

1.4 A "bus modularity" architecture was considered and either accepted or rejected. | 1 | 2 | 3 | 4 | 5 |

1.5 The potential for "sectional modularity" was determined and either accepted or rejected. | 1 | 2 | 3 | 4 | 5 |

1.6 The possibility of employing "cut-to-fit modularity" was evaluated and either accepted or rejected. | 1 | 2 | 3 | 4 | 5 |

1.7 The interface(s) between modules were selected based on maximizing simplicity and flexibility. | 1 | 2 | 3 | 4 | 5 |

1.8 Future extensions and enhancements of the product line have been discussed and integrated into your modular strategy. | 1 | 2 | 3 | 4 | 5 |

1.9 Competitors' modular architectures have been analyzed and the best features integrated into your approach. | 1 | 2 | 3 | 4 | 5 |

1.10 The non-recurring and recurring cost impact on the factory have been analyzed and minimized. | 1 | 2 | 3 | 4 | 5 |

Interpretation of Total Score

1 - 10	11 - 20	21 - 30	31 - 40	41 - 50
Abandon Modular Architecture	Major Modifications Required	Iterate Design Until Total Improves	Review Low Scores Before Proceeding	Architecture Is Ready for Primetime

Figure 3.17 – The Module-Optimization Checklist identifies twenty critical factors that should be considered during the development of a modular product line. Part I focuses on the overall architecture of the product line, while Part II addresses the optimization of the modular interface and the modules themselves. The "interpretation guide" at the bottom of each Part offers a guideline for ensuring the success of your team's module design efforts.

Module-Optimization Checklist	
Indicators of an Optimized Modular Design	**Agreement With Statement** Low High

Part II – Modules and Interfaces

   2.1   All possible "commons" have been considered as candidates for sharing across module interfaces (i.e., power, ground, fluids, information, structural strength, etc.). | 1 | 2 | 3 | 4 | 5 |

   2.2   All possibilities for "component sharing" and "component swapping" have been considered in module designs. | 1 | 2 | 3 | 4 | 5 |

   2.3   All applicable industry and commercial standards have been considered when designing module interfaces. | 1 | 2 | 3 | 4 | 5 |

   2.4   The potential for third-party enhancements to the product line have been considered and provided for. | 1 | 2 | 3 | 4 | 5 |

   2.5   The largest and smallest possible modules have been considered (alternatively: lightest and heaviest, fastest and slowest, lowest and highest power, etc.). | 1 | 2 | 3 | 4 | 5 |

   2.6   Excess capacity has been designed into the module interfaces to accommodate future unexpected needs. | 1 | 2 | 3 | 4 | 5 |

   2.7   The production cycle-time of both the product platform and modules have been minimized to enable build-to-order. | 1 | 2 | 3 | 4 | 5 |

   2.8   Customer feedback has been gathered to validate the design. | 1 | 2 | 3 | 4 | 5 |

   2.9   A marketing communications strategy has been developed that highlights the advantages of modular architecture. | 1 | 2 | 3 | 4 | 5 |

   2.10 The impact on distributors, wholesalers, retailers, repair facilities, sales representatives, etc., has been considered. | 1 | 2 | 3 | 4 | 5 |

Interpretation of Total Score

1 - 10	11 - 20	21 - 30	31 - 40	41 - 50
Redesign Modular Architecture	Major Modifications Required	Iterate Design Until Total Improves	Review Low Scores Before Proceeding	Modules Are Ready for Primetime

Figure 3.17 – (Continued)

The Incredible Elastic Product

Suppose you have a standard product on the market; let's call it Model A. Now Model A is a pretty hot seller…except for one annoying problem. Many of the "sales" of Model A products are actually custom-order jobs. Oh, the customization is relatively minor; just a nip here and a tuck there, but the engineering time required is significant. In fact, custom-order design work is taking resources away from new product development – a very bad thing from an opportunity-cost standpoint. How might a platform-based strategy help you retain the high sales from this great product, while reducing the cost and time wasted on order-by-order customization?

The answer lies in the concept of *design scalability*. Suppose you receive an order for a minor modification to Model A. This new product (and make no mistake; this represents a *new product*), which we'll call Model A1, has a fitting that must be an inch longer in one dimension than your standard version. (Please note that this discussion is easily generalized to any design parameter within any product, so don't get hung up on this "inch-longer" example.) The cost associated with creating this new version of the product could be substantial: non-recurring design and drawing release, new tooling or equipment setups, revised work instructions, perhaps even some unique inventory. On the other hand, the cost for this new model could be virtually identical to Model A, margins and all, provided that your product is designed to be scalable.

Scalability simply means that when the initial product is developed, certain parameters that are often the focus of customization requests are identified as *scalable requirements*. Scalable requirements are specified by a range rather than a value. In our example above, the Model A scalable family of products would have a well-defined range of acceptable fitting lengths. As the design process progresses, raw material availability is considered over the entire scalable range, manufacturing process capabilities are established to handle the entire range, and design and manufacturing documentation is modified to accommodate the full range of scalable parameters. It may even be possible to create a CAD parametric design program that can take in a few custom variables for Model A and spit out the new version of drawings, bills of material, routings, and so on. This scalable approach to platform design is illustrated in Figure 3.18, and some common examples of scalable requirements are provided in Figure 3.19.

So now when you get a call for a Model A, "with just a minor tweak," you can tell your customer, "No problem, we've got a team of designers that are at your beck and call." Of course, there is no need for the team of designers. Just one person, part-time, entering custom parameters into your CAD system, and a quick mention at the morning production meeting that a new configuration of Model A will be in the mix. Get really good at this scalability stuff and you can create a powerful differentiating advantage for your firm, even in heavily commoditized markets. There is nothing that customers love more than having it their way.

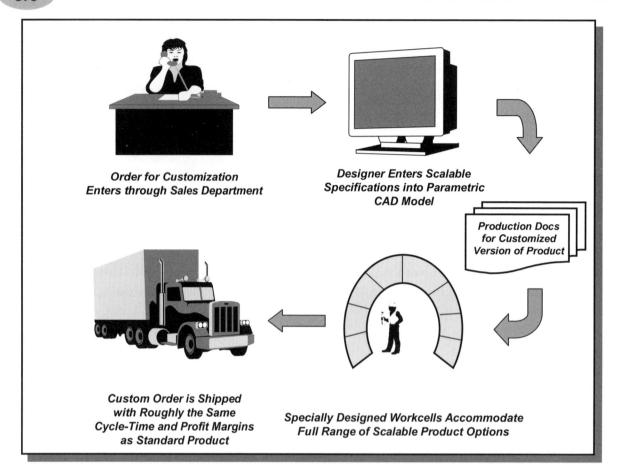

Figure 3.18 – Scalability is a special case of a platform-based product strategy that focuses on easy customization of a standard product. By designing both product and processes to accommodate a range of values for one or more design parameters, the product can be modified within that range at little or no additional cost.

How an Oxymoron Can Save You Big Bucks

Every once in a while, an improvement concept comes along that rises like a skyrocket, bursts with a brilliant flash, and then fades into the background of best practices, all in a matter of a few years. The oxymoronically named *mass customization* is just such a concept; a one-trick pony to be sure, but it's a pretty good trick. You might recall my earlier statement: "The ideal firm has products that customers believe are customized especially for them, while the factory can't tell the difference between them." This assertion captures the essence of mass customization; gain all of the cost benefits of mass production, while also harvesting the price advantages of customized products. How might this be accomplished? The operative word is *postponement*. Our goal in a mass-customizable product line is to delay the customization of our product family as long as possible. In fact, if we can delay customization until the product is actually in the hands of the customer, so much the better.

Typical Candidates for Scalability

Mechanical –
- External dimensions
- Pressure
- Diameter
- Volume / Capacity
- Load
- Rotational Speed
- Linear Speed
- Accuracy of Control
- Torque
- Horsepower

Electrical –
- Wattage
- Voltage
- Data Rate
- Number of Channels
- Memory
- Power
- Digital Bits
- Signal-to-Noise Ratio
- Processor Speed

Optical –
- Resolution
- Number of Pixels
- Zoom Multiplier
- Modulation Transfer Function
- Dynamic Range
- Neutral Density
- Flatness
- Power
- Spherical Aberration

Ergonomic –
- Adjustability
- Physical Dimensions
- Firmness
- Brightness
- Graphical Richness
- Handedness
- Information Volume
- Power Assist Ratio
- Language Compatibility
- Dosage

Figure 3.19 – Some common examples of scalable requirements that can be incorporated into the design of a product.

First the "why" of mass customization, and then we'll explore the "how." If we can postpone customization of a product (or one or more of its modules), we increase the effective volume along that common production line. We gain better utilization of our capital equipment and tooling, while requiring less floor space, less worker training, less work-in-process (WIP) inventory, and so on. Moreover, we can reduce the cycle-time from order to shipment of a custom product by staging up "almost finished goods" based on a combined (and therefore slightly more accurate) forecast. We can then configure each product on a customize-to-order (i.e., pull) basis. Although this semi-pull strategy might increase WIP slightly, in markets that value rapid, build-to-order customization, the advantages can be enormous.

Some of the differences between a mass-customization strategy and traditional manufacturing are described in Figure 3.20. Just to solidify the concept, let's consider some familiar examples. The first and most obvious way to mass customize a product is to have the physical hardware remain completely unchanged for every model within a product family. How then might the products be customized? Through multiple software versions, of course! Software-intensive products enjoy a world of advantages over pure

3.3

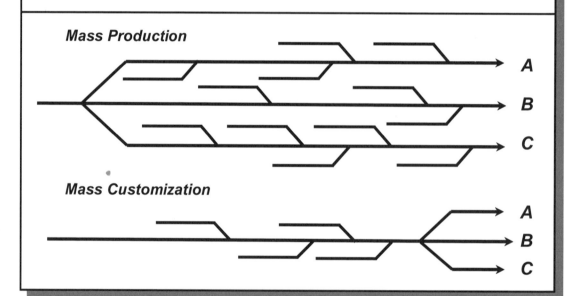

Figure 3.20 – Contrasts between traditional mass production and a "mass-customization" product strategy.

hardware products because the final configuration of the product can be customized by simply downloading the appropriate version of software. Even if your product has no software content, the possibilities remain endless. Both Nokia and Swatch discovered hidden treasure in the form of point-of-use customization of their products. Each company produces their products, cell-phones and wrist watches respectively, at high volumes with little or no customization. They then offer a set of interchangeable bezels that can alter the appearance of the product to suit the taste of the customer. In the case of Nokia, the colorful bezel set is sold as a separate product, thereby generating additional profits.

Another fun example of mass customization is the Select Comfort Mattress. You've probably stayed up late at night and found yourself watching an infomercial for these air-filled, infinitely adjustable beds. Each person (up to a maximum of two) can select their own "comfort number" that corresponds to a desired firmness. Customers perceive this as a differentiating advantage, while Select Comfort pockets the savings associated with offering only one adjustable "firmness" of mattress in each standard size. Examples of mass customization are everywhere, particularly in this information-intensive age. Point-of-purchase color-matching systems for paint, on-line purchase of personally configured computer systems, user-customizable software interfaces, etc.

Fortunately, by embracing a platform-based product architecture you are already most of the way there. To join the ranks of mass customizers, all you need is a little delay. Here are some questions to consider when designing your next product:

- Have you partitioned your product to ensure that those modules that are frequent subjects of customization are assembled as late as possible in the process?

- Would it make sense to allow the customer to customize your product? Can after-purchase adjustments be provided that are straightforward and low-risk?

- Can a design element that is a frequent subject of customization be made adjustable by the final-assembly workcell?

- Can testing and inspection be organized so that product modules are fully testable at the module level, thereby reducing the need for customized final testing?

- Can functionality that is currently provided by hardware be transferred to software? Can the product's hardware be generalized to accommodate software customization over a broad range?

- Can customization be provided as part of a product / service combination? The product portion of the package would be relatively standardized, while the service component would be highly tailorable.

- Can customization be performed somewhere downstream in your distribution system? Can a distributor, retailer, installer, etc., perform customization based on local demand?

Before we leave the topic of mass customization, it is fitting that I give you a quick glimpse of something to come – a portent of future events, as my literature teacher would have called it. There is something called "design rules" that will help your design teams create products that "fit" within a platform family. These design rules are simple, practical guidelines for specific aspects of a design that enable any designer to conform to a desired product-line architecture. I will have much more to say about design rules in Section 6.3, so keep a warm spot in your heart for them.

At last, we have come to the end of our platform-based cost-reduction saga. To bring this all together, consider the diagram in Figure 3.21. The concept of a product platform is fundamental; a shared design element across multiple product models. We

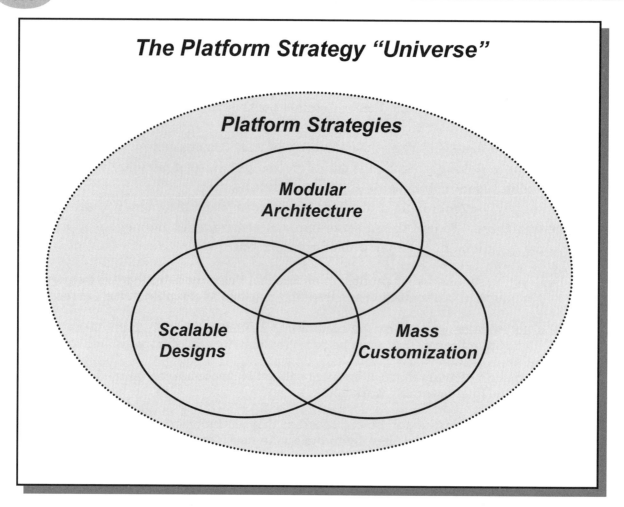

Figure 3.21 – Modular design, scalable design, and design for mass customization are really just special cases of a platform-based cost-reduction strategy. Moreover, it is entirely possible for a single product family to take advantage of several of these powerful concepts.

can expand the benefits of a platform architecture by considering modular design, scalable design, and mass customization. These concepts are all special cases of a platform strategy, and they are not exclusive of each other. It is entirely possible (and more than a little scary) for a product family to have extremely high levels of commonality, a modular architecture, some scalable aspects, and customization that is postponed until very late in production. Just imagine the fear you would strike in the hearts of your pathetic, distinct-product competitors. And oh, the accolades you will enjoy when your customers realize that they can have exactly what they want, and in just the blink of an eye... Sorry, sometimes my enthusiasm gets the better of me.

References

Part III

Recommendations for Further Learning

There are some excellent books available on the topics covered in Part III, so I encourage you to dig deeper if you feel that a platform strategy is right for you.

Systems Thinking

***** ***The Fifth Discipline,*** Senge, P. M., 1990

If you haven't come across this book, stop whatever you're doing and get it in front of you. It will open your eyes to how the world works, how people learn, and how systems govern most of our lives. It will change your life if you are open to such things. If not, you will at least come away a better product designer.

Platform Strategies

***** ***Product Strategy for High-Technology Companies,*** McGrath, M. E., 1995

If all this strategy and differentiation stuff is somewhat new to you, this book is a great place to start. Michael McGrath, one of the principals of the PRTM consultancy, has put together a great primer on market strategy. My only complaint is that some of the thinking is a bit "five minutes ago" in light of more complex global competitive strategies. No matter, it's still the best book available for the neophyte.

**** ***The Power of Product Platforms,*** Meyer, M. H., and A. P. Lehnerd, 1997

Good solid discussion of how platform strategies can make all the difference in achieving "value and cost leadership." Not a how-to book to be sure, but lots of good insights for the practitioner.

*** ***Platform Leadership,*** Gawer, A., and M. A. Cusumano, 2002

I'm a practical guy, and I guess books by scholars that are supposedly for practitioners, but are really for other scholars, just leave me a bit cold. Great case examples, but not a lot that would be useful to designers. If you're in an engineering management position, you should give this book a look.

Part III

***** *"The role of product architecture in the manufacturing firm,"* Ulrich, K., 1995, *Research Policy*, Vol. 24, pgs. 419-440

Okay, so here is a scholarly paper, written by and for scholars, that is just awesome. If you've never seen a truly landmark journal article, try this one. It has lots of practical value, and provides a context that will make your head swim.

Modularity and Scalability

**** *Design Rules: The Power of Modularity,* Baldwin, C. Y., and K. B. Clark, 2000

Within this somewhat overlong and overwrought book is a really good book waiting to be distilled. Scan it for valuable ideas rather than reading it cover to cover. Some real gems buried under a lot of overly complex detail.

***** *"Managing modularity of product architectures: toward an integrated theory,"* Mikkola, J. H., 2003, *IEEE Transactions on Engineering Management*, Vol. 50, No. 2, May Issue, pgs. 204-218

How rare it is to find two great papers that deal with a common subject. This is another one of those, "it's worth it to actually read a journal article because it is so great," papers. As with any journal paper, sift out the stuff that's there for the peer reviewers; you'll find a great deal of valuable information for the rest of us.

Mass Customization

***** *Mass Customization,* Pine, J. B. II, 1993

Joe Pine coined the term "mass customization" in a Harvard Business Review article a year or so before this book came out. There are really only two books on this subject of any worth. This one establishes the competitive context and serves up a helping of useful and practical tidbits. Not really a practitioners manual, however.

***** *Agile Product Development for Mass Customization,* Anderson, D. M., and J. B. Pine II, 1997

This book completes the job that the one above left undone. More for the practitioner and full of useful insights, this is a good read from cover to cover. Note, however, that what the authors call "mass customization" is really platform strategies with a new "buzz-word" name. To fill an entire book, they have gone beyond the narrow definition to be far more inclusive…an approach which I have clearly embraced in my own treatment of the subject.

Cost Leverage Is Greatest During Conceptual Design

4.1 - Value Engineering and Analysis

4.2 - The Quick-Look Value Engineering Event

4.3 - Sponsoring a Design Challenge

Part IV

"Those who speak of diamonds having no use
value and of food as having infinite
use value, must be drawing
their ideas, not from the life of men,
but from the life of cattle."

William Smart

"It ain't what you know that hurts you,
it's what you know for sure that ain't so."

Abe Martin

Section 4.1

Value Engineering and Analysis

We will now leave behind the high-level, cross-product-line world of platforms to focus on the design of a single product. Recall that this guidebook is organized chronologically; the strategic stuff must be considered *before* we commit ourselves to product-specific details. That being said, we know that time-to-market is of the essence, so after a rapid but serious look at product-line-wide cost-saving opportunities, it's time to get on with development. Our next cost-reduction activity should take place during conceptual design (i.e., early in the development process). As was discussed in earlier sections, the first challenge for any design team is to accurately translate customer needs into technical requirements. This section will describe a sophisticated methodology for accomplishing this translation in a way that fosters innovation, ensures value capture, and can dramatically slash your product's manufacturing cost.

A More Precise Definition of Value

Previously, I glibly defined value as "performance delivered at a specified price." Presumably, as "performance" increases, so does the customer's willingness to pay a higher price, up to some point of diminishing return that I have called "design overshoot." Here's the problem with my nice, tidy definition: By what standard do I measure performance? If I'm comparing automobiles, for example, there are some well-established tests and inspections that I can perform to compare various models. But what if I am comparing jewelry? Does performance in this context mean number of carats, or does the beauty of the design and the quality of the workmanship enter into the equation? And while we are digging in this pasture, exactly what customer "problem" does a diamond necklace solve? (Some opportunities for humor are just too easy…fill in your own punch line here.)

Well, as it turns out, Adam Smith, the great economist and author of *The Wealth of Nations,* presented exactly this conundrum in what has been called, "The Value Paradox." Smith notes that water, for example, has extremely high *use value* (particularly if you are parched) but essentially zero market value, whereas diamond jewelry has almost no use value, but has a very high market value. What Smith identified is a fundamental problem for product designers; use value (often referred to as "utility," meaning the ability of a product to solve a specific problem or to provide some needed performance) is only part of the value equation.

4.1

It has been suggested that there are at least four categories of value that can contribute to the price that a product will garner in the marketplace. The utility, or *use value*, is the most obvious. How effective is the product at solving the customer's specific problem? In addition, many products provide *esteem value*, meaning that they somehow increase our sense of well-being or self-worth. Furthermore, if a product embodies labor and / or materials that are known to be in short supply, the *scarcity value* of the product could be significant. Finally, even if the product isn't scarce, doesn't solve your particular problem, and fails to raise your self-esteem, it might be desirable to others, thereby accruing some *exchange value*. These four categories of value are illustrated by example in Figure 4.1. For a product to command a relatively high market price, it must embody a positive combination of all four of these value categories.

Now armed with this deeper understanding of value, we can easily dispense with Adam Smith's paradox. Water clearly has very high use value, but this is undermined by its extreme abundance (i.e., its scarcity value is essentially zero). Hence, your everyday, average water cannot command any price. But wait. What if we package that H_2O in a sexy bottle with a French name and sell it at a fine restaurant? We still have all of our use value, but we've finessed the scarcity problem. Exotic imported water appears to be scarce (or at least exclusive), and that pretentious label and sophisticated-looking bottle might even deliver some esteem value for those customers with a tendency toward superficiality. Diamonds, on the other hand, have almost no use value (at least when incorporated into jewelry), but their esteem value is through the roof. This lofty esteem value is reinforced by a presumed scarcity, resulting in an extremely high price. In reality, of course, diamonds are not scarce at all. In fact, if diamonds were sold as commodities on the open market, rather than being tightly controlled by an international cartel, their price would drop to pennies on the dollar.

Use value, esteem value, and scarcity value are all present to some degree in most products. But how does exchange value enter into this equation? The best way to consider exchange value is to ask the question, "How much of the purchase price of this product could I recover if I were to sell it to someone else?" In other words, exchange value could be thought of as either "value retention" or "resale value." Imported water may have a relatively high initial price tag, but see how much you can get for it at a flea market. Even diamonds have a notoriously poor resale value, despite those inflated "appraisals" that jewelers are happy to provide. In general, products with a high use value tend to have a much higher exchange value than products whose price is driven disproportionately by esteem value. A used power tool in good condition, for example, is worth a large fraction of what it cost when it was new. In fact people often run ads in the newspaper to sell them, implying the existence of a healthy market for used tools. Used clothing, on the other hand, is generally fodder for garage sales and donations, regardless of its condition. The marketplace is much thinner for products that depend heavily on personal taste (i.e., esteem value) as opposed to practical utility.

Product Examples	Elements of Product Value				Relative Market Price
	Use / Utility	Esteem	Scarcity	Exchange	
Paper Clip	▬▬▬	▪	▪	▪	▪
Gold Tie Clasp	▬	▬▬	▬▬	▬	▬▬▬
Tap Water	▬▬▬▬	▪	▪	▪	▪
Imported Bottled Water	▬▬▬	▬	▬	▪	▬▬
Decorative Wall Poster	▪	▪	▪	▪	▪
Original Oil Painting	▪	▬▬	▬▬	▬▬	▬▬
Tickets to Local Movie Theater	▬▬	▪	▪	▪	▪
Tickets to See Bruce Springsteen	▬	▬▬	▬▬▬	▬▬▬	▬▬▬
Magnetic Compass	▬	▪	▪	▪	▪
Portable GPS Locator	▬▬	▪	▬▬	▬▬	▬▬
Generic Office Software	▬	▪	▪	▪	▪
Fully Customized Office Software	▬▬	▪	▬▬▬	▪	▬▬▬
Digital Alarm Clock	▬	▪	▪	▪	▪
Swiss Grandfather Clock	▬	▬	▬▬	▬▬▬	▬▬▬

Figure 4.1 – Some examples of how the four categories of product value manifest themselves in various types of products. Note that a change in just one of the four categories can make a substantial difference in the price of the product.

How do your products fit within this four-dimensional value space? This is more than a rhetorical question. Your design team must understand how each of these four facets will interplay in your new product. The use value is probably fairly well understood, although overshoot or undershoot of performance is still a danger. The esteem value of your product, however, may not be so evident, given the inherently vague nature of "esteem." Would your product attain a higher price point if it were customized to individual taste or made more aesthetically pleasing? What about scarcity? Is your product a commodity that has many equivalent substitutes or is your firm the only one that makes this specific type of product? Is the technology embodied in the product "rare" (e.g., protected by patents, copyrights, licenses, etc.) or is it ubiquitous? Finally, what is the value retention of your product? Will it become obsolete in short order, or can it be designed either to be upgradeable in the future, or at least to have a high trade-in or resale value? Answering these questions and others like them is the goal of Value Engineering; a powerful and flexible approach to optimizing the cost / price ratio for any type of product.

4.1

The Roots of Value Engineering

The Japanese have been given disproportionate credit for "inventing" the lean enterprise. In reality, firms like Toyota Motor Company were masters at seizing and building upon insightful Western concepts and executing them to near perfection. Although many Asian firms have become famous for embracing a value-focused approach to business activities, much of the groundwork for this approach was developed by some unsung heroes of American engineering. Thought leaders such as Lawrence Miles and Arthur Mudge developed a system for analyzing the customer value of product designs back in the late fifties and early sixties (see the reference list at the end of Part IV for more information). This methodology came to be known as *Value Engineering* (VE) or alternatively (and somewhat interchangeably) *Value Analysis*.

The American Management Association has defined Value Engineering as follows:

> *"Value engineering is a functionally oriented scientific method for improving product value by relating the elements of product worth to their corresponding elements of product cost in order to accomplish the required function(s) at the least possible cost in labor and materials."*

What does this mean in English? Recall the requirements-translation process that I described in Section 2.1. Customers pay for solutions to their problems and the way they evaluate possible solutions is through the benefits they believe they will receive, as shown in Figure 4.2. To deliver these benefits, product designers must understand the *functions* that the product is expected to perform. Each function can then be translated into design requirements so that conceptual design can begin. Here is where VE fits in, as is evident from my somewhat more pragmatic definition:

> *"Value engineering is a method for identifying, clarifying, and prioritizing the functions of a product, and subsequently reducing the cost of delivering those functions through systematic brainstorming on lower-cost design alternatives."*

In the next section, I will introduce a new lean design tool called the Quick-Look Value Engineering event. Before we get into the details, however, let's explore how VE works. At the very earliest stages of a product's conceptual design, the team gathers for a "functional review" of the proposed new product. As a group, the team identifies the primary functions (things that the product as a whole is expected to perform), and secondary functions (things that support the performance of the primary functions) of the product. These functions are then prioritized based on their importance to the customer and their relative cost. This activity is enabled in part by the use of the Lean QFD (see Section 2.1) and the Must / Should / Could (see Section 2.2) approaches to prioritization.

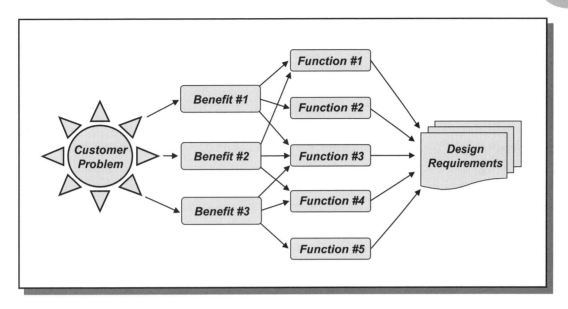

Figure 4.2 – A reprise of the translation process from customer problem, through benefits and functions, and finally to design requirements. Value Engineering enables cost reduction by optimizing the translation from functions to requirements.

Once a list of prioritized primary and secondary functions are in hand, the team will go through each function in rank-order and ask, in a brainstorming format, the five key questions of Value Engineering:

- What is the function?
- How can it be performed?
- What does this approach cost?
- How else can this function be performed?
- Would that alternative be lower cost?

The goal of this process is to break down preconceptions and assumptions about how the product should be designed, and facilitate the discovery of lower-cost design alternatives. In its full-blown form (i.e., as described in the rigorous works I've cited in the references section), VE can be a major undertaking. A "job plan" is established, a team is formed and trained, and a project is initiated to reduce a product's cost. Now if it happens that you and your design team are responsible for developing automobiles, aircraft, major military systems, or other such incomprehensibly large and complex products, you might require this formal approach (again, see the references at the end of Part IV to begin your efforts). For the rest of us, a more tractable and much faster methodology can yield 90% of the benefit in 10% of the time.

4.1
Taking a "Quick Look" at Value Engineering

Before we proceed, I must justify the claim I made in the final sentence above: Is my "90 / 10" claim really viable? Can complex and sophisticated tools such as Value Engineering (or Six-Sigma Design methods, or Toyota's 3P process) be scaled down to something quick, straightforward, and applicable to almost any type of product? In my opinion, the answer is *absolutely, always, without exception*. Great ideas don't start out complex and sophisticated; they begin as some bright and shining insight, and evolve complexity as people try to connect that insight to the real world. The complexity and sophistication of a nuclear reactor has, at its core (pardon the pun), the equation $E=mc^2$. Six-Sigma Design began life as a fairly simple statistical analysis of defect rates, process capabilities, and product tolerances. Closer to home, the entire Lean Thinking universe revolves around five simple words: value, stream, flow, pull, perfection.

I have found that the reason why most new design tools and methods fail to "stick" within product development organizations is that they are just too darned complex and time-consuming. Often the tool itself is not at fault; it is human nature to take simple things and botch them up with unnecessary fluff (as is evidenced by virtually any word-processing program or TV remote control). What begins life as a flash of insight quickly becomes mired in mundane and trivial detail, until it dies of its own weight. One of my goals in this guidebook is to strip away as much of the unnecessary fluff as possible and expose the valuable core of each tool presented. To show you how the process works, I will illustrate this "filtering," using Value Engineering as a guinea pig.

The scaling of the VE methodology from a major corporate initiative down to a two-day, team-empowered affair is illustrated in Figure 4.3. In general, the scaling of any methodology is accomplished by: a) reducing the formality of the process, b) reducing the amount of rigor in information gathering, c) decreasing the involvement of upper management, d) making the tool more qualitative, and e) focusing on only the very cream of the opportunity crop. For the case of VE, we can reduce the formality of the process by moving from a staged-application approach to a quick-hit approach. Rigorous VE is typically applied in what is often called "nth-look" stages. Early in the concept / proposal phase of a development project, a "zero-look" application of VE is performed. This initial activity has as its goal the establishment of an optimal set of functions for the proposed product. As the development of the product progresses, VE events are held on a first-look, second-look,...nth-look basis. In this way, VE is deeply embedded in the formal product development process; not a bad thing if your product's complexity and price warrants such scrupulous attention. A more flexible application, however, can achieve much of the same benefit. If we craft a "Quick-Look" VE event that can be used at any time during development, from concept through launch, we can easily scale the effort to the needs of each specific product. A simple line extension might only require one Quick-Look event, whereas a major new platform initiative could utilize several events spread out in much the same way as the nth-look methodology described above.

Scaling the Value Engineering Methodology	
Full-Blown VE	*Quick-Look VE*
• Formal Structure – Zero look, first look, second look, etc….	• Informal Tool – Used on an as-needed basis when target cost cannot be achieved.
• VE "job plan" used to guide a major (often several month) project.	• "Job plan" becomes the agenda for a two-day event.
• Multidisciplinary information-gathering phase with detailed costing and a verification review.	• One week of preparation and information-gathering on a best-effort basis.
• Product functions are identified using "Argus Charts," "FAST Diagrams," or other formal tools.	• Functions are identified qualitatively using verb / noun structure and team intuition.
• Formal innovation phase taking several days or weeks to generate well-defined design options.	• Real-time brainstorming to generate possibilities, with only the most promising being pursued further.
• Evaluation and presentation phase to document recommendations and sell them to management.	• Creation of a published action list derived from results of Quick-Look VE Event.
• Total Duration – Several weeks to several months.	• Total Duration – Two to three days, but can be used iteratively if more opportunities exist.

Figure 4.3 – An example of how a complex, formal cost-reduction methodology (in this case, Value Engineering) can be effectively scaled down to suit even a relatively simple product development project.

4.1

So it goes for other aspects of VE. A major application of VE would demand a "job plan" that guides the design team through several weeks or months of detailed analysis, but that job plan can be scaled down to become the agenda for a two-day Quick-Look review. The amount of time spent on information gathering could be extensive for a rigorous application of the methodology, but can be "capped" at just one week for the Quick-Look VE event. Certainly some benefit will be lost, but if we believe Pareto, the leverage will be on our side; the really critical information will bubble to the surface after just a few days of intensive investigation. Even the use of analysis techniques within the VE process can be scaled down in a straightforward way. For relatively simple products, what is often referred to as the "verb / noun" approach to function identification will work quite well. If the product warrants more rigor, there are well-established techniques such as "Argus Charts" and "FAST (Function Analysis System Technique) Diagrams" that can enable the decomposition of even the most sophisticated, multilevel system products. It is important to realize that the use of a scaled-down, Quick-Look application of VE doesn't in any way preclude the use of selected tools from traditional VE. We gain *flexibility* without giving up the potential for rigor when it is appropriate.

Hopefully I've made my point. It would be a waste of your precious time for me to justify the scaling of the remaining tools in this guidebook. It is essential, however, that you trust the logic of scalability, because without it, cost reduction will forever remain the dominion of major-product firms. Whether you design commercial aircraft, or the hydraulic fittings embedded within that aircraft, your profits are your lifeblood. It's time that the tools of cost optimization be democratized to fit all products, great and small.

Section 4.2 — The Quick-Look Value Engineering Event

If you are the type who notices such things, this section is one of the longest in this guidebook. Actually, the number of pages I dedicate to a subject is almost always proportional to my sense of its importance. I realize that Value Engineering (VE) is not the most intuitive of cost-reduction tools; it requires time, collaboration, an open mind, and (god forbid) some creativity. Yet in a sense, Value Engineering is the beating heart of product design. You are doing VE every time you make a decision about what level of product performance to specify, or which features to include, or the level of customization to offer, or whether to paint your product passionate pink or cerulean blue. Each time one of your teammates comes up with a simpler and more elegant solution to a design problem, they get their ticket punched as a value engineer. What I propose is that you and your team become *experts* at this vital discipline after having gathered years of ad hoc experience. A week of preparation and two days of intensive brainstorming is all that is needed to begin acquiring this expertise, as summarized in Figure 4.4. The Quick-Look VE event is the quickest way to move your team from the bunny slopes of product design to shushing with the experts at Vail.

An Agenda for Value

A straightforward process flow for the Quick-Look VE event is shown in Figure 4.5. Notice that on the left-hand side of the figure, I have provided a strawman agenda for the event, based on my experience with products of low-to-moderate complexity. Remember that this tool is infinitely flexible, so if you feel more time is needed, by all means add some hours or even days. If you are a diehard skeptic, you might select just one element of your proposed new product and try this tool out as a one-day affair. In either case, the earlier you initiate the event the better; right after your preliminary specification is established is generally the ideal time.

Now that we've dispensed with the "when," we must decide on the "who." The short answer is, "all members of your core design team." Additional experts can be a plus, provided that they understand their role as advisors and idea catalysts (as opposed to bullies, prima donnas, or other annoying types). Should management be involved? My opinion is that as you look up through the organization from design team members, to team leader, to first-level manager, and so on, the appropriateness of their involvement decays expo-

4.2

"At a Glance" – Quick-Look Value Engineering Event

Overview –
Value Engineering (VE) is a powerful process for systematically identifying, clarifying, and prioritizing the required functions of a product, and subsequently generating lower-cost design alternatives that deliver the required functions at a lower total cost. The traditional VE methodology is quite time-consuming. This tool enables a development team to gain 90% of the benefits in a fraction of the time.

Primary Benefits –
Enables design teams to achieve major breakthroughs in cost reduction by encouraging innovative design alternatives that still deliver all of the required functionality and quality.

Best Suited Products –
This tool can be used for any product type, including service products.

Advantages –
There is no tool in this guidebook that can make a more significant difference in the total cost of a product. Consistent and successful application of VE can represent a sustainable competitive advantage.

Disadvantages –
Although the proposed Quick-Look VE tool is greatly simplified, VE is still a complex process requiring both discipline and the ability to innovate. It will take a few attempts to achieve excellence in the application of this method.

Impact on the Twenty Cost Levers –

I. Direct Labor				II. Direct Materials				III. Capital				IV. Design Cost				V. Overhead			
1a	1b	1c	1d	2a	2b	2c	2d	3a	3b	3c	3d	4a	4b	4c	4d	5a	5b	5c	5d
●	○	○	◉	◉	●	●	○	○	◉	●	◉	●	●	●	◉	○	○	○	○

Figure 4.4 – "At-a-glance" overview of the Quick-Look Value Engineering event.

nentially. Let this be an event that is both by, and for, the design team. Once the work is done and new cost-saving ideas are at hand, you can bring in the elephants and let them stomp around the room. Nothing important will happen without their blessing anyway, so why not give the design team some room to speak and create freely before bringing in the big guys.

One final note before we walk through the process. Way back in Figure 2.14, I showed that the product development process can be thought of as two interdependent loops: a design loop that is followed when the target cost of a product can be achieved, and a cost-reduction loop that is triggered when the target cost cannot be met. A portion of Figure 2.14 is reprised in Figure 4.6, to demonstrate that the Quick-Look Value Engineering tool fits quite nicely into that generic model. As the remainder of this guidebook unfolds, you will see that other important cost-reduction methods also follow this general process flow. Naturally, the choice of which tool to use depends on your type of product, the nature of the cost problem, and so on.

In the remainder of this section, I will describe in detail how to execute a successful Quick-Look VE (QLVE) event, following the circled numbers that appear in Figure 4.5. As

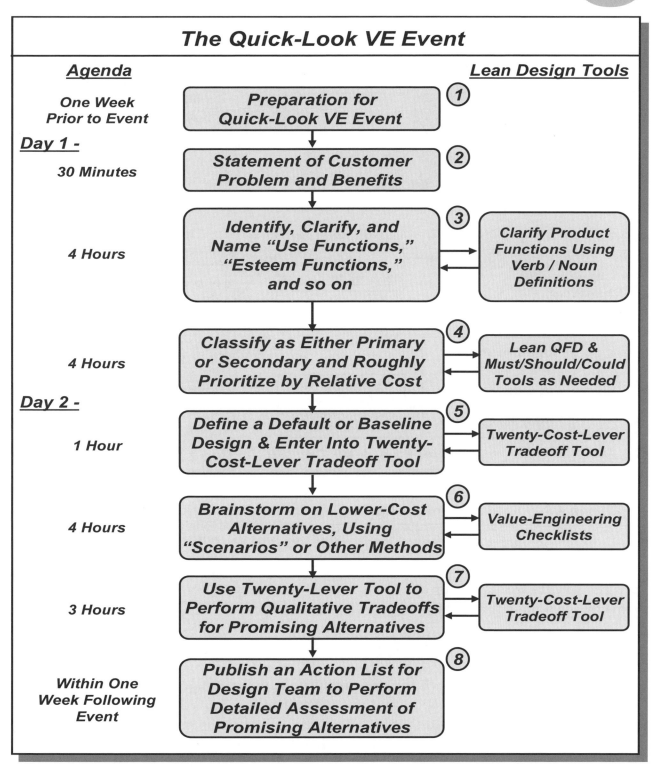

Figure 4.5 – A process-flow diagram for the Quick-Look VE event. Note that a strawman agenda is provided on the left-hand side of the figure, while recommended lean tools that can support this activity are offered on the right-hand side. The circled numbers next to each process step correspond to the numbered subsections in the text.

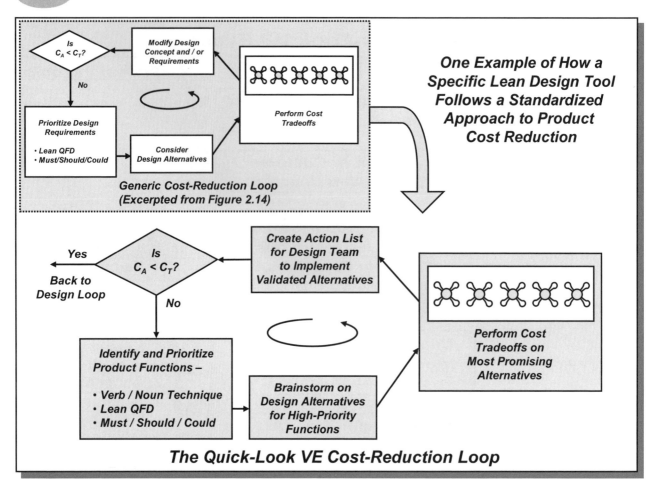

Figure 4.6 – An example of how the Quick-Look Value Engineering event fits into the generic cost-reduction process described previously in Figure 2.14. Other important tools within this guidebook will also follow this same general flow.

always, you are free to modify any of my suggestions based on your real-world circumstances. Just don't throw the baby out with the bathwater.

1) Preparation for the Quick-Look VE Event

I could walk you through the steps required to put on a QLVE event in a nice, dry, officious way, and then follow that dusty dissertation with a few well-worn case examples...but what fun would that be? Writing a guidebook is infinitely more tedious than reading one (if you can imagine that). Therefore, in the hope of making this important material more interesting for both of us, I'll resurrect our awesome designers-of-thingamajigs for another applied example. This time, however, we will set aside our already successful thingamajig line of business in favor of a new and exciting market opportunity; *whachamacallits*.

These days there is hardly a person out there who doesn't need a whachamacallit. Moreover, the core competencies and technologies involved in developing them are similar to those required to dominate the thingamajig market. Hence, our apocryphal design team decides to kick off a new product development project to create a line of market-killing whachamacallits. After extensive customer interviews and discussions, our team uses the Lean QFD and an initial application of the Must / Should / Could tool to arrive at a prioritized preliminary product (alliteration again) specification. Under normal circumstances, this would be the point at which a conceptual design effort would be initiated. The enlightened team leader, however, has learned of QLVE and decides that the team should give it a try. Naturally, when the team hears of this new tool, they sound off a rousing "Hurrah!" and enthusiastically select a date for the event (clearly, this is a *fictional* example).

The first step in preparing for a QLVE event is getting the team onboard. Hence, the team leader must first educate, then influence, then cajole, and if none of these tactics work, she must pull the stubborn ones aside and have a one-on-one. The "educate" part could be structured as an informal "class" taught by the team leader (or another willing facilitator). Since the whachamacallit team members are a bunch of quick studies, our leader simply asks each member to read this section of her guidebook.

Once the team understands the basic process, a two-hour "kickoff" meeting is scheduled, with the first hour dedicated to answering questions, and the second hour allocated for creating a list of the information that will be needed to support the QLVE event. The leader of our whachamacallit team calls this meeting roughly one week prior to the planned event. After initial questions have been answered, she asks the group to brainstorm on the types of information that might be useful for the event. Once a fairly comprehensive list fills her flip-chart, she asks each member of the team to vote for the five items of information that they feel are the most critical. She places a slash mark next to each winner and totals the slashes to determine the team's recommendations. After some discussion, a prioritized list of needed data items is finalized, as shown in Figure 4.7. Each member of the team then volunteers to gather a piece of that information over the next seven days. (Naturally, in the real world, you would have to substitute "reluctantly agrees" for "volunteers.")

Fortunately for our whachamacallit team, the team leader has some background in decision theory. Before adjourning the kickoff meeting, she admonishes the team to avoid getting hung up on the details. To illustrate her point, she draws the diagram shown in Figure 4.8. Here is her explanation:

"The way humans make decisions is a bit scary. People with aggressive, go-for-broke personalities will make their choices based on no *real* information at all. They might ask a few people for their opinions, hear an anecdotal story or two, and then just go for it. On the other side of the spectrum are individuals who typify the expression, "analysis paralysis." It is easy to get burned by making a bad decision (which is always remembered decades longer than a good one). Hence, a fairly large subset of decision-makers tend to be highly risk-averse. There is just never enough information, so a decision is never made.

- **Any conceptual design work that already exists**
  - *Drawings of similar existing products*
  - *Competitors products to reverse engineer*
  - *Existing mock-ups or prototypes*
  - *Rough sketches of current design ideas*
- **Cost information applicable to the proposed new product**
  - *Cost buildup of similar existing products*
  - *Critical-to-cost factors*
    - *Expensive or hard-to-find parts and raw materials*
    - *New suppliers*
    - *Low-yield processes*
    - *High-priced capital equipment*
    - *Complex subassemblies or process steps*
- **Contact data for experts that might be needed to support the QLVE event in real time**

Figure 4.7 – An example of a prioritized list of information items that the whachamacallit team agreed would be useful during their QLVE event. Although your situation might be different, the items shown are fairly typical.

To make matters worse, as the information-gathering process drags on, some of the data that was harvested early in the process will begin to grow obsolete. A market forecast that was valuable in July might have some value left in it by September, but around New Year's it's pretty much useless."

"The trick to making rational decisions is to realize that in the early stages of the information-gathering process, the value of information grows exponentially. After awhile, however, the process becomes less efficient, due to redundancy of information, the amount of detail involved, etc. So the Pareto Principle applies; roughly 80% of the valuable information available to a team can be harvested in the first 20% of the time. There is one big proviso, however. *The information-gathering team must work like a team, with clear and logical priorities and good communication.* Since I have complete confidence in your abilities to work as a team, we should have all the information we'll need to achieve some breakthroughs at our QLVE event in one week."

2) Statement of Customer Problem and Benefits

The next step for our whachamacallit team is to define, in very specific terms, the customer problem that their new product must solve and the benefits that it must deliver.

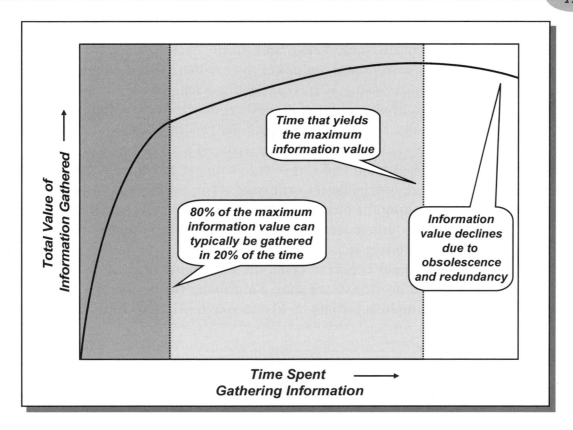

Figure 4.8 – Information gathering is subject to the Pareto Principle; 80% of the total available (and valuable) information can typically be harvested in the first 20% of the time. In fact, if the information-gathering activity goes on too long, obsolescence and redundancy will begin to erode the value of the data gathered early in the process.

Typically this analysis would have already been done during the development of the preliminary product specification, but a second look is always a good idea. At the QLVE kickoff meeting, the team leader (or selected facilitator) should propose a strawman problem and benefits statement for review and concurrence by the team. This way, only a few minutes at the beginning of the actual QLVE event will be needed to work the bugs out. Try to avoid making either overly general statements, or conversely, statements that are too specific for the product's intended market segment. For example, if your proposed product is a pasta-making machine, it would be too general to say that the device is intended to "make Italian food." Similarly, it would be unacceptably restrictive to say that the product is designed to "make spaghetti." A nice balance that clearly defines both the product's customer range and capabilities is ideal. A description such as the following would work well as a customer problem statement for a pasta maker:

> *"Customers for the Shlonco Pasta Maker are working parents and busy singles who wish to cook homemade spaghetti, linguini, and other specialty pastas, but don't have the time or skill to make excellent noodles in the traditional way."*

Almost always, the customer problem statement includes one or more of the following conditions: a) the customer wishes to save time, b) the customer needs to save money, c) the customer wants to improve quality of use of the product, d) the customer wants to be entertained, or e) the customer wishes to increase self-esteem. Often a combination of the above conditions may be required (recall the several types of value we discussed in the previous section). In any case, the "trick" is to carefully choose words that capture the true purpose of the product. For example, is the true purpose of a stylish pair of designer jeans to "comfortably cover the lower torso and legs of the customer to keep out cold and dirt?" Or would the value of the product be better expressed if the goal was to "attract attention from the opposite sex by making the customer appear more shapely, slender, and 'hot'?" The problem described in the former statement clearly should be solved as well, but it is table stakes compared with addressing the latter challenge.

Once a problem statement is agreed upon, the team must identify the specific benefits that the product should provide in the course of solving the problem. Continuing on with the designer-jeans example, a set of benefits, in rough priority order, might appear as follows:

- Build self-confidence and esteem
- Attract favorable attention from opposite sex
- Make customer look thinner
- Appear distinctive
- Be comfortable to wear

Note that "cover lower torso and legs" isn't even on the list. In fact, other than meeting local decency laws, *it is not mandatory that the product deliver this benefit*. Torn jeans don't cover the legs particularly well, and low-rise jeans don't cover much torso, but both styles attract attention and look distinctive. Preconceptions are like landmines; you and your team should have an almost paranoid attitude toward any assumption that appears to be etched in stone.

Returning to our whachamacallit example, the team agrees upon a strawman problem statement and benefits list during the kickoff meeting, as shown in the top half of Figure 4.9. On the first day of the actual QLVE event, the team leader begins the meeting by reiterating the strawman statement and reopening it for discussion and revision. After a half-hour of tweaking, the team arrives at the finalized statement shown in the lower half of the figure. Being the strong facilitator that she is, our team leader knows that firm time limits must be placed on each step in the QLVE agenda or the event will turn into a disaster. Say over and over in your mind (and perhaps out loud at the event); "A best effort is all that is needed, don't get stuck on trivial details."

3) Identify, Clarify, and Name Functions

Up to this point, the QLVE event looks pretty much like any other product design review. Here is where we get into the meat of Value Engineering; a unique approach to

Strawman Problem Statement and Benefits List –

"Customers for the whachamacallit product are former widget owners who require the same basic functions performed at a much higher speed and with greater ease of use."

Prioritized Benefits –
- Performs all widget functions
- Saves the customer time
- Enjoyable to use
- Has high status appeal among former widget owners

Finalized Problem Statement and Benefits List –

"Customers for the whachamacallit product are former owners of either widgets or dohickies who require the same basic functions performed at ten-times the speed and with higher entertainment value."

Re-prioritized Benefits –
- Saves the customer time
- Entertaining to use
- Has "sex appeal" to all techno-junkies
- Performs all functions of both widgets and dohickies.

Figure 4.9 – Two examples of a customer problem statement and benefits list for the whachamacallit product under development. The upper example is a strawman developed by the team one week prior to the QLVE event. The lower version resulted from a half-hour discussion with the team at the beginning of the event itself.

the identifying and naming of a product's functions. Recall that the functions of a product are the means by which benefits are delivered. For example, if cell-phone customers desire the benefit of nighttime use, the function which delivers that benefit might be: "Provide blue back-illumination of LCD screen and touch panel." This is where VE begins to work its magic. The latter statement, although typical of "function" statements made by many product designers, is really a *requirement* statement in functional clothing. There are several design assumptions and predispositions buried in that phrase. For example, why blue? Why back-illumination? And while we're at it, why an LCD screen, and is a touch panel the only design option? By adopting the function statement above, we have jumped from the customer-expressed desire for nighttime use *directly to the solution*. In so doing, we have precluded a host of possible lower-cost alternatives that might deliver the same benefit.

4.2

Value Engineering uses a semantic trick to strip away such premature design assumptions. *Each function must be described by only two words; a verb and a noun.* For the cell-phone example, a function that would provide the benefit of nighttime use would be described by, "illuminate controls." Now if an LCD screen was firmly specified for this product (and even this should be carefully scrutinized), we would modify our function description to read, "illuminate LCD." We would not, however, lump the touch panel into that same function description. Why? Because illuminating the touch panel is a *separate function*. It might turn out that providing different lighting sources for the LCD and the touch panel is actually less expensive. In any case, start with zero assumptions, but quickly move toward a sensible balance.

Before I provide you with the details of how to use this formidable technique, let's look at a few examples of how powerful this simple approach can be. Back in the early 1960's, the U.S. government was relentlessly driving its defense contractors to deliver a manned lunar landing system before 1970 (the famous "Kennedy Challenge"). The obstacles were mind-boggling; not only did the system have to get astronauts to the surface of the Moon safely, it had to bring them back! Weight was problem number one, with the actual lunar landing craft having by far the tightest weight restrictions. Every pound of landing craft (referred to as the Lunar Excursion Module, or LEM) that touched the surface of the Moon required thousands of pounds of fuel (and millions of taxpayers' dollars) to get it there.

In fact, the constraint was so severe that the contractor for the LEM didn't believe it could be achieved. Grumman Corporation struggled mightily to squeeze every ounce out of the LEM, but the target still seemed unachievable. The surprising solution that Grumman engineers came up with is described in Figure 4.10. A huge amount of effort had been expended trying to make the two seats in the LEM less massive. Finally, at an ad hoc design meeting, an engineer proposed something totally off-the-wall; why not get rid of the seats altogether? With a gravitational load of near zero g's and a short flight time, *couldn't the astronauts just stand*, restrained in comfortable impact harnesses? Of course this solution worked and the rest is history, but if that engineer hadn't stripped away a supposedly "fundamental" assumption (that important passengers *always sit*), the U.S. might have suffered another embarrassing technological defeat at the hands of the Soviet Union.

A more recent example also comes from the exploration of space. It seems that NASA has been throwing hardware at Mars for most of our lifetimes, but the results have been mixed, to put it politely. Awe-inspiring victories such as the original Viking lander, the famous little Pathfinder robot, and more recently, the sophisticated Spirit / Rover surface explorers, have been tainted by crash landings and lost satellites. In their desperation to reduce mission risk (while maintaining an incredibly tight budget), NASA engineers were forced to strip away their assumptions about how to land an object safely on Mars.

Figure 4.10 – An example of how using verb / noun functional descriptions can eliminate design preconceptions and assumptions, and potentially lead to breakthroughs in both cost and performance.

It had always been assumed, for example, that to place the delicate instruments carried in a Mars lander on the surface demanded a *soft landing*, as shown in Figure 4.11. A soft landing requires retrorockets, a sturdy landing-gear assembly, lots of complex software, an unbelievable amount of additional fuel (both for the landing and to carry the extra weight of lander hardware), and frankly, a lot of luck upon arrival on Mars. All it takes is one unexpected boulder or crevice and that billion-dollar baby becomes another source of rust for the red planet.

Here's where Value Engineering, and in particular the verb / noun functional description tool, came into play. What is the basic function that must be performed by a Mars landing system? Why, to *land on Mars*, of course. There is no explicit need for a *soft landing*, nor is it necessary that the lander arrive at a precise location (i.e., within feet of a specific target). All that must occur is that the secondary function of "*protect instruments*" be achieved, meaning that the exploration vehicle and instruments must be fully functional upon landing. So why not just wrap the Rover in huge and durable airbags and let it bounce its way to a stop in Mars' low gravity? I just love solutions like this, because at first your reaction is, "You've got to be kidding," but after a few moments, you see the elegance and simplicity of the idea. Again, history has validated this non-sequitur design

Example #2 – Spirit / Rover Mars Landing System

- Primary Function – Land on Mars
- Secondary Function – Protect Rover

Cost Problem –
Traditional soft-landing systems (top image) require retrorockets, landing pads, and complex guidance-control software. The mass of such systems is very large, and the success rate for planetary landings has not been stellar.

Incorrect Preconception –
That a soft landing on a planet demands slowing the craft to a stop on the planet's surface.

Breakthrough Solution –
Believe it or not, airbags! Since a precise landing location was not critical, a system of parachutes and airbags protected the Rover payload at a tiny fraction of the weight and cost of traditional landing systems (see bottom image).

Images courtesy of NASA

Figure 4.11 – Another example of the power of verb / noun functional descriptions. The highly successful Mars Spirit / Rover exploration mission owes its success, in great part, to an airbag landing system that would never have been considered without first stripping away design preconceptions.

approach, and the cost savings have been monumental. Without stripping away preconceptions, however, and focusing on the basic function to be performed, this breakthrough would never have occured.

Hopefully, your interest is piqued regarding the innovative power of using verb / noun functional names, so let's see how this tool can work on more mundane, Earth-based products. The first step in creating a function list for any product, from pencil to power plant, is to have the design team brainstorm on all possible functions that the product might be expected to perform *as a system*. These are referred to as *primary functions*, whereas supporting or optional functions are referred to as *secondary functions*. Consider, for example, the lowly pencil. (Note that I will put a finer point on the definition of primary and secondary functions in the next subsection, and yes, that was yet another pun.) If your team were to brainstorm on the possible primary functions of a pencil, hopefully they would come up with the logical answer; enable writing on paper. Possible secondary functions might include, for example: erasing marks, serving as a chew toy for nervous people, etc. Once you have a relatively comprehensive list of functions, force yourselves to strip away all but the most basic verb / noun description of each function, as shown in Figure 4.12. The statement "enable writing on paper" would become "makes marks," and so on.

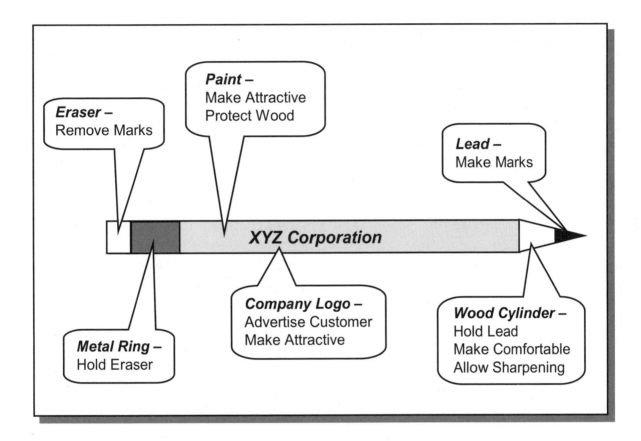

Figure 4.12 – Example of how the primary and secondary functions of a pencil would be identified, clarified, and named using the verb / noun description technique.

Once all of the system-level functions have been clarified in this way, consider each major component, subsystem, or subassembly, and perform the same brainstorming analysis. How deeply you dig should be driven by cost considerations. If a component or subassembly is a minor cost item, just skip it. On the other hand, if there is an expensive component or process that is buried deep within a product, it would be worthwhile to include it in your analysis. Usually, the functions of components or subassemblies are secondary to the primary function(s) of the product, but this is not always the case. Hence, it is best to list all functions, from system-level to component-level, and subsequently prioritize them, as will be described in the next subsection. Note that the decomposition of functions within a product almost always follows a system hierarchy, so if you've become knowledgeable in systems thinking, you'll have another opportunity to apply it during your QLVE event.

4.2

Now let's return to our whachamacallit team to see how they perform this brainstorming and clarification activity. By the way, if you haven't figured it out by now, *there is no such thing as a whachamacallit.* It is, in fact, a "universal example" that allows me to demonstrate the catagorization of primary and secondary functions, hardware and software design elements, electronic and mechanical components, and so on. I hope I haven't disappointed you.

Our illustrious team leader has now flipped to a blank sheet of paper on her easel, and addresses the team:

"Now that we have a reasonably good definition of the customer problem and expected benefits for our product, we're going to perform a functional analysis of the whachamacallit. We'll start at the level of the entire product system, and work our way downward to subsystems, major components, etc. Remember that we have a time limit for this effort, so let's focus on just the design elements and functions that have high cost-saving potential. We have some cost numbers and guesstimates that have been prepared by various team members, so we can refer to that information whenever there is any doubt about relative costs."

"For each element in the system, we are going to define its function or functions with just a verb and a noun. Don't worry too much about choosing the optimal words right now; we can refine our wording after we have prioritized the functions. No sense in wasting time debating semantics on functions that will later be eliminated. Okay, so who wants to start suggesting the functions of the product as a whole?"

The results of the whachamacallit team's brainstorming on product functions is shown in Figure 4.13. As you can see, the system (meaning the entire product) has several functions, addressing use value (e.g., "Perform Function A"), esteem value (e.g., "Look Attractive"), and exchange value (e.g., "Operate Reliably"). In addition, several components and subsystems were also selected for functional decomposition. Note that software was included on their list. You might wonder how software can have an impact on product cost; after all, the production cost of duplicating software is essentially zero. Actually, that's exactly the point. It may be possible to alter the functionality of a product's software to either reduce the cost of hardware elements, or entirely eliminate costly materials by converting a hardware function into a software function. Also keep in mind that for some products, software represents a very large non-recurring design investment. Since you still have to pay back that investment throughout the life of the product, reducing unnecessary design complexity in software can have a powerful effect on overall product profitability.

4) *Classify as Either Primary or Secondary, and Prioritize*

With a host of system and component functions listed on a flipchart, the whachamacallit team is ready to select a prioritized subset that will serve as cost-reduction candidates. The template shown in Figure 4.14 enables a quick and useful prioritization of functions, and also provides space to classify those functions into several catagories. Why

Design Element	Verb / Noun Function Name
System –	Perform Function A
	Perform Function B
	Operate Easily
	Look Attractive
	Appear Customized
	Operate Reliably
Components –	
• *Enclosure*	Protect Product
	Look Attractive
	Hold Attachments
	Contain Power Cord
• *Software*	Control System
	Interface with User
	Monitor Performance
	Entertain User
	Enable Upgrades
• *Handle*	Move System
	Protect Hand
	Feel Comfortable
• *Circuit Card*	Power System
	Respond to Software
	Provide Signals
	Process Signals
• *Gear Box*	Transfer Power
	Multiply Torque
	Reduce Vibration
	Drive Wheels
• *Wheels*	Move System
	Steer System
	Support System

Figure 4.13 – An excerpt from the whachamacallit design team's brainstorming on both the system- (i.e., product-) level functions and major component-level functions. Note that each design element can have several functions, including those that provide use, esteem, scarcity, and exchange value.

do we need to classify the functions? Well, if you are short on time, you could probably eliminate the classifications and include just the scoring system shown in the three right-hand columns. It is often useful, however, to categorize each function by whether it contributes to use value, esteem value, and so on. This information may be helpful when discussing design alternatives to ensure that each type of value is either retained or enhanced by a proposed change in design.

Another useful, but optional, categorization involves whether a function is primary or secondary to solving the customer's problem. Interestingly enough, *it is typically the secondary functions that have the greatest cost-saving potential.* Primary functions are virtually etched in stone for many product types; they are fundamental to the marketability of the product. Secondary functions, on the other hand, support the execution of primary functions, so they may have more flexibility in interpretation. In Figure 4.14, for example, the primary function of the whachamacallit enclosure is defined as "Protect Product." It's rather hard to eliminate that function entirely, and great care will be required to extract cost from it without compromising either the robustness or the perceived quality of the product.

The secondary functions of the enclosure are potentially better candidates. In particular, the esteem function defined as "Look Attractive" is subject to a great deal of interpretation. The enclosure could be made of an expensive-looking material, or given an interesting shape and texture, or coated with an attractive paint, and so on. Hence, it is likely that there are more cost-saving opportunities in the "Look Attractive" secondary function than there would be in the "Protect Product" primary function.

The "mandatory" part of the template involves using a two-metric scoring approach to prioritize your product's functions. The first metric, which is scored on a 1-5 scale (sound familiar?), assesses the *relative cost* of each function. Relative cost is semi-quantitative; we just need to know if a given function is high, medium, or low cost, relative to other functions under consideration, as shown in Figure 4.15. Use actual cost numbers if they are available (and provided that costs can be allocated to individual functions with some credibility). Otherwise, use your collective heads and make some educated guesses. The same logic applies to the second metric: *improvement potential*. If there is really only one possible design approach for a given function, or if that function has received a lot of cost-reduction attention in the past, give it a low score for improvement potential. If there are several substitute approaches possible, or if that aspect of the design is relatively new or immature, give it a high score.

When both scores have been agreed upon by the team, multiply them together to arrive at a priority ranking for each function. Please note: *it is hypercritical that you and your team prioritize cost-reduction opportunities before you begin discussing design alternatives.* You have a fixed amount of time to brainstorm on alternatives. If you squander that time on some low-priority design element, the value of the entire QLVE event will be undermined. In the next subsection, our whachamacallit team will begin with the highest priority opportunity (i.e., the "Appear Customized" secondary function of the overall prod-

Design Element	Function Name	Use Value	Esteem Value	Scarcity Value	Exch. Value	Relative Cost (C)	Improvement Potential (P)	Ranking (C x P) ↓
System –								
Primary –	Perform Function A	x		x		5	3	*15* ↓
	Perform Function B	x		x		3	2	6
Secondary –	Operate Easily	x	x			1	1	*1*
	Look Attractive		x			3	4	*12* ↓
	Appear Customized		x	x		5	4	*20* ↓
	Operate Reliably	x				2	3	6
Enclosure –								
Primary –	Protect Product	x			x	3	3	*9* ↓
Secondary –	Look Attractive		x			3	4	*12* ↓
	Hold Attachments	x				1	3	3
	Contain Power Cord	x				1	3	3
Software –								
Primary –	Control System	x				5	3	*15* ↓
	Interface with User	x	x			2	2	4
Secondary –	Monitor Performance	x				3	5	*15* ↓
	Entertain User		x		x	3	2	6
	Enable Upgrades	x				2	2	4
Etc…	Etc…							

Figure 4.14 – The first few lines of the whachamacallit team's ranking of functions for cost-reduction potential. The functions are classified as either primary or secondary, and assigned to one or more of the four categories of value. A ranking system is then used to assign a priority to each function. The arrows at the far right indicate which functions were selected by the team for inclusion in the next phase of their QlVE event.

> **Relative Cost (1 – 5 scale) –**
>
> 1 - Very minor cost item: < 1% of total product cost
> 2 - Minor cost item: ~ 1% of total product cost
> 3 - Medium cost item: 1% – 3% of total product cost
> 4 - High cost item: 3% – 5% of total product cost
> 5 - Very high cost item: > 5% of total product cost
>
> **Improvement Potential (1 – 5 scale) –**
>
> 1 - Very low potential, mature or fixed-cost item
> 2 - Low potential, commodity part or relatively mature
> 3 - Medium potential, some flexibility in design or materials
> 4 - High potential, new or immature design with known alternatives to be considered
> 5 - Very high potential, known to be a costly item with alternatives already under consideration

Figure 4.15 – Guidelines for a two-metric priority-ranking approach that were provided to the whachamacallit team prior to completing the template shown in Figure 4.14.

uct), and work their way down the list in rank-order. In principle at least, this approach will assure that their (and your) event will yield the highest benefit for the time spent.

One final note. For products that warrant a more detailed examination, you may wish to add some time to your QLVE event at this point in the agenda and pull out your Lean QFD and Must / Should / Could lean design tools (see Part II). If you've already used one or both of these tools to optimize product functions and performance requirements, then sanity-check those results against your ranking of cost-improvement opportunities. If you haven't used these tools yet, now would be a good time to interrogate your list of functions to see if any can be eliminated, downscaled, or made into an optional "could have." It would be a shame to go through the effort of reducing cost on a function that is really superfluous to the product from the customer's perspective.

5) *Define a Default or Baseline Design*

It's time once again for a quick climb to 40,000 feet to see where we are in this QLVE process. We have defined the customer's problem and the benefits that they expect from our product. Although this work should have been done earlier in the development process (during preliminary specification development), it is important that it be restated for the QLVE team so that all thinking in the room is properly aligned. We then brainstormed on the functions that we believe the product must perform, and listed them starting with the system as a whole and moving to those subassemblies and components that we believe have high relative costs. Then in the previous step we classified those functions as either primary or secondary, and prioritized them based on their potential to yield significant cost savings.

We now must put on our innovation hats, cast aside all prior assumptions about the design of the product, and come up with a host of alternatives. Big alternatives, small alternatives, heavy ones, light ones, ones that go bump in the night. No ideas are dumb, and there should be no negative feedback (that includes eye-rolling, snickering, and rude noises). Seriously, it is important to cast the very largest of nets, since often the idea that will save you a fortune is so unexpected or perverse that it will be filtered out by all but the most open-minded brainstorming environments.

Before you let your creative juices fly, your QLVE team must select a baseline or default design concept for each high-priority function that will be analyzed. We are going to make use of our Twenty-Cost-Lever tradeoff tool (discussed in Section 1.6 and shown in Figure 1.29). To do so, it is best to identify a baseline that receives a "zero" ranking for all cost levers. A baseline design concept is usually one of the following:

1) The design approach currently in use on similar products within your firm.
2) The design approach used by a competitor in markets for which you have no similar products.
3) What your designers are most comfortable with for this new product.
4) A low-risk, moderate-cost alternative that you're reasonably sure will work.

It's not really important which design option is used as the baseline and which are the cost-saving alternatives; it all comes out in the wash once scoring is done. Our goal in selecting a baseline is to make it clear when a new or innovative concept is "better" than our traditional, stogy thinking. If we set the baseline to zero, a positive total score from the Twenty-Cost-Lever tool means that we may increase our potential profitability by pursuing that option. If the baseline turns out to be the lowest cost alternative, then we can pat ourselves on the back for making a good choice of baselines, and proceed to the next cost-saving opportunity on our prioritized list.

6) *Brainstorm on Lower-Cost Alternatives*

Once a baseline design concept has been defined for each high-priority function, it is time to start churning out alternatives. Start with the top-ranked opportunity on your list (the one with the highest score from the template shown in Figure 4.14), but note that it is important to set a time limit for brainstorming on this first cost-saving opportunity. You have just a few hours to make it through your entire list, so I suggest carving up the time allotted for this step into slots with durations that are proportional to the cost-saving potential of the item. For example, the whachamacallit team identified seven high-priority opportunities (see Figure 4.14), with scores ranging from twenty to nine. If they follow the agenda I propose in Figure 4.5, only four hours are allowed for brainstorming on alternatives. Hence, it would be reasonable for the team to agree on the following allocation of their time:

System – Secondary Function – Appear Customized:	50 minutes
System – Primary Function – Perform Function A:	40 minutes
Software – Primary Function – Control System:	40 minutes
Software – Secondary Function – Monitor System:	40 minutes
System – Secondary Function – Look Attractive:	30 minutes
Enclosure – Secondary Function – Look Attractive:	20 minutes
Enclosure – Primary Function – Protect Product:	20 minutes

It is important that the QLVE facilitator keeps the flow of ideas moving forward. It is just too easy for meetings like this to stall on a single idea. Get a bell or some other obnoxious noisemaker and use it to break up log jams and get people onto the next concept. Jot down each proposed design alternative on a flipchart, with only enough detail to remind the team of what was meant by the suggestion. You will have time to discuss the promising alternatives in more detail during the last step in your QLVE event.

Let's take a look at some of the design alternatives that the whachamacallit team came up with, as shown in Figure 4.16. I've intentionally kept the alternative list for each opportunity short (and eliminated some rather uninteresting opportunities as well), so you can see how a variety of different situations might be handled. Clearly, the specific nature of your firm's products will determine what type of cost-saving opportunities you will address in this step. If you have a team of innovative animals, it should be easy for them to generate a wealth of alternatives in a short period of time. If your team's innovation wheels are a little rusty, I've provided a suite of idea-inspiring checklists in Figure 4.17 that cover several categories of design element. The references provided at the end of Part IV contain even more hints and suggestions for creative idea generation if your team is particularly ossified.

Before I leave you to peruse the checklists, I have one final (but reluctant) suggestion. Although it is important to place time limits on this step of the process, *it is the most important step in the QLVE event.* If you overrun your allocated time, it really isn't all that deadly, since in principle, the rest of the QLVE event could be completed either at a later time or by a smaller group of people. So if you believe that there is a huge benefit in continuing to harvest ideas, or if you just can't keep the ball rolling at the desired pace, don't panic. Just keep the pressure on and use the last steps in the event as a "shock absorber" to take up any slip in schedule.

Sheet 1 of 2

System – Secondary Function – Appear Customized: 50 minutes

> ***Baseline*** – Allow choice of designer colors and three different enclosure configurations: freestanding, tabletop, and portable.
> - Offer one basic color for chassis and include several replaceable cover plates with different color options.
> - Offer only a single designer color, and a color-match option at a higher price.
> - Design product to have a modular enclosure that can be reoriented to serve as either tabletop or portable version.
> - Eliminate freestanding option since the tabletop version can be placed on any convenient surface that's at a comfortable height.

Software – Primary Function – Control System: 40 minutes

> ***Baseline*** – Software controls basic product functions and manages power consumption and routing. Most active user functions are handled with hardware knobs and buttons.
> - Eliminate all hardware controls and add a touch-sensitive screen for user interface with software controls.
> - Eliminate costly motion-control hardware and replace with a software motion encoder.
> - Use automatic software routines for the most common operating modes and provide only the minimum necessary manual controls for exceptional situations.

Software – Secondary Function – Monitor System: 40 minutes

> ***Baseline*** – Software monitors all system functions, including power consumption, speed, status, position, etc.
> - Eliminate software monitoring function entirely.
> - Eliminate all but power monitoring.
> - Use alarms for dangerous situations, but otherwise eliminate active monitoring function.
> - Make active monitoring an optional feature, but only for non-hardware-based parameters. No additional hardware for monitoring system.

Figure 4.16 – A look at the results of a brainstorming activity performed by the whachamacallit team to identify lower-cost design alternatives. This is not a complete listing; for the reader's benefit some of the team's opportunities have been skipped and the number of design alternatives under each heading has been truncated.

Sheet 2 of 2

Enclosure – Secondary Function – Look Attractive: 20 minutes

> **Baseline** – Use stainless steel and chrome trim for basic components, with a choice of designer colors for front panel.

- Use replaceable color plates for front panel.
- Eliminate chrome trim and use anodized aluminum instead.
- Eliminate stainless steel in favor of powder-coated steel.
- Use injection-mold plastic instead of metal enclosure.
- Use commercial-off-the-shelf enclosure and modify in factory.
- Use enclosure from XYZ product and add chrome accents.
- Use a clear plastic front panel that would allow user to "see the action."
- Use a rough-surface sheet-metal product that reduces fingerprints.
- Allow user to insert a plaque with their name on it.
- Hire industrial design firm to create a sculptural enclosure design.
- Go for "heavy-metal" look using simple bends and inexpensive rugged-looking exposed fasteners.
- Die cast the enclosure and polish to a high shine.

Enclosure – Primary Function – Protect Product: 20 minutes

> **Baseline** – Use 16 gauge stainless steel for enclosure panels, with reinforced corners for drop / shock protection. Use a fan and filter combination to provide cooling and eliminate dust.

- Use 22 gauge stainless steel with stamped ribbing to increase strength.
- Use injection-mold plastic enclosure with interior foam to protect product against drop / shock exposure.
- Use a hermetically-sealed enclosure.
- Eliminate fan and use passive cooling (e.g., a heat exchanger and natural chimney effects for airflow).
- Fill interior of product with epoxy.
- Fill interior of product with polyurethane expanding foam.
- Eliminate filter and specify that product cannot be used in a high-dust environment.

Figure 4.16 – (Continued)

Some Questions to Inspire Creativity in Your QLVE Team (Page 1 of 3)

Any Design Element (General) –

- Can the design element be eliminated?
- Does it overshoot performance requirements?
- Is there a lower-cost material that can be used?
- Is there a lower-cost manufacturing process that can be used?
- Can parts be eliminated?
- Can assembly be simplified?
- Can tooling cost be reduced?
- Have we considered commercial-off-the-shelf alternatives?
- Should we outsource this element instead of making it here?
- Does the element need all of its features?
- Is there a better, simpler way to perform the required function(s)?
- Would it be less costly to modify a standard part?
- Can the cosmetics of the part be reduced or simplified?
- Can the number of different materials required be reduced?
- Is the design compatible with automated production?
- Can it be made smaller, lighter, thinner, with less bends, with less welds, etc.?
- Can the tolerances be relaxed?
- Can the function be combined with another function?
- Can the shape be changed / simplified?
- Is the position of the element optimal?
- Should the type of motion be changed (e.g., from rotational to translational)?
- Is one requirement driving the overall cost of the design element?
- Can standard tooling be used?
- If we cannot do it the way we described in the baseline, what would be our next choice? The choice after that?

Figure 4.17 – Some questions that the QLVE event facilitator can use to trigger creative thinking among the design team.

Some Questions to Inspire Creativity in Your QLVE Team (Page 2 of 3)

Mechanical Design Elements –

- Can a coarser surface finish be used?
- Can a casting be replaced by a modified extrusion?
- Can two parts be combined?
- Are all threads standard?
- Can standard cutting tools be used?
- Are material dimensions compatible with standard raw stock?
- Can welds be replaced by bends?
- Can nearly identical parts be made identical?
- Can furnace welding be substituted for manual welding?
- Can masking be eliminated for plating or painting steps?
- Can the assembly be designed for single-orientation machining?
- Can tolerances be relaxed by using slots, spacers, shims, etc.?
- Can adjustments be made automatic or eliminated entirely?
- Can fasteners be eliminated, or replaced by fewer or simpler?

Electrical Design Elements –

- Can a non-standard part be replaced by a standard part?
- Can the number of printed circuit board (PCB) layers be reduced?
- Can the size of circuit boards be made standard?
- Can circuits be made self-adjusting?
- Can a hardware function be transferred to software?
- Would an application-specific integrated circuit (ASIC) be less costly than a printed circuit board?
- Can power dissipation be reduced?
- Can noise shielding be reduced or minimized?
- Can connectors be eliminated?
- Can two wiring harnesses be combined?
- Are PCB parts compatible with automated pick-and-place machines?

Figure 4.17 – (Continued)

Some Questions to Inspire Creativity in Your QLVE Team (Page 3 of 3)

Electrical Design Elements – (continued)

- Has testability been considered?
- Is there adequate access for in-circuit test probes?
- Are nodes isolated to allow ease of testability?
- Are holes in PCBs of a standard size?
- Can dual-in-line-pin (DIP) sockets be eliminated?
- Can passive cooling (e.g., a heat exchanger) replace active cooling?
- Will the design withstand required vibration and thermal-cycle testing?
- Can a hand assembly operation (e.g., installing jumper wires) reduce the cost of a PCB?
- Does the PCB or electronic assembly require a specified coating or epoxy potting?
- Can conductive plastics be used in place of metal shielding or ground planes?

Software Design Elements –

- Can software code from other products be reused?
- Is there commercial code that could serve in place of custom code?
- Are industry standards being met?
- Can hardware functions be moved to software?
- Can adjustments, testing, maintenance, etc., be handled by software?
- Can simple alarms be substituted for quantitative system monitoring?
- Can the user interface software be simplified?
- Can the user interface hardware be simplified?
- Can an interface-builder software application save development cost?
- Can the code be fully tested prior to integration with hardware?
- Can the code be easily modified to correct unforeseen problems?
- Is the code modular so that upgrades or fixes will be less costly?

Figure 4.17 – (Continued)

7) Use Twenty-Cost-Lever Tool to Perform Tradeoffs

The most efficient way to accomplish this tradeoff step is to load the Twenty-Cost-Lever tool onto a spreadsheet (easy to do) so that the calculations are automated and a record of each tradeoff can easily be saved. First load in the baseline design, with all parameters set to zero. Then begin with the highest priority cost-saving opportunity from Step 6 ("System – Secondary Function – Appear Customized" for the whachamacallit team). As a group, go through each proposed design alternative and discuss its potential for cost savings, as well as its producibility, and its ability to deliver the function in question. At this point you could use yet another 1-5 ranking scale, but even I am getting tired of that scoring method, so let's do something a little different. After a brief discussion period, have each member of your QLVE team go up to the flipchart and place a slash mark next to the three alternatives that they feel are the most viable. Once everyone has had a chance to vote for their top three, add up the slash marks and select the two alternatives that have the highest total scores. These design options will be taken further in this event; the remainder should be retained for possible future consideration by the core design team.

After just such a voting session, the whachamacallit team has selected two design alternatives for further analysis. They are (from Figure 4.16):

Option 1) Baseline design.
Option 2) Design product to have a modular enclosure that can be reoriented to serve as either tabletop or portable version.
Option 3) Eliminate freestanding option since the tabletop version can be placed on any convenient surface at a comfortable height.

These options correspond to the column entries in the Twenty-Cost-Lever tradeoff tool shown in Figure 4.18. Weighting factors should have been selected by the core team during specification development, but should be given a sanity-check before proceeding. Rather than having the entire group discuss each design option listed in the tradeoff tool, I suggest selecting one or two people to work on each alternative and come up with a set of scores. These scores can then be reviewed by the larger group and validated or changed if necessary. Remember that we are not making any final decisions here; our goal is to sort out nonviable alternatives and focus the attention of the core design team on alternatives with high cost-saving potential. Qualitative guesstimates are fine for this rough sorting activity.

As can be seen in Figure 4.18, both of the selected alternatives receive a relatively high positive score when compared to the baseline design approach. Clearly no rigorous cost analysis was performed, but from a qualitative standpoint, a recommendation to move forward with these two possibilities is certainly warranted. Just to make the process of using the Twenty-Cost-Lever tool as clear as possible, let's walk through the logic for Option 2 in the figure. The first "knob" listed in the template is *direct labor*. Under this

Cost Levers	Weighting	Option 1	Option 2	Option 3
I. Direct Labor				
A. Simplify Processes	1	0	3	3
B. Reduce Skill Level	2	0	0	0
C. Automate Processes	1	0	0	0
D. Reduce Test Costs	1	0	3	2
Subtotal =		0	6	5
II. Direct Material				
A. Reduce Scrap	1	0	2	2
B. Eliminate Parts	1	0	5	4
C. Low-Cost Materials	1	0	0	0
D. High-Volume Parts	1	0	2	0
Subtotal =		0	9	6
III. Assignable Capital				
A. Eliminate Batches	1	0	0	0
B. Outsource Processes	1	0	0	0
C. Optimize Tooling	3	0	4	2
D. No Dedicated Equipment	2	0	0	0
Subtotal =		0	12	6
IV. Design Costs				
A. Design Reuse	2	0	3	0
B. Eliminate Complexity	1	0	-2	2
C. Avoid Gold Plating	1	0	0	0
D. Optimize Make vs. Buy	1	0	0	0
Subtotal =		0	4	2
V. Factory Overhead				
A. No Factory Changes	2	0	2	2
B. Reduce WIP	1	0	-1	1
C. Reduce Handling	1	0	2	0
D. Reduce Consumables	1	0	0	0
Subtotal =		0	5	5
Total Scores =		0	36	24

Figure 4.18 – Results of the whachamacallit team's assessment of design options for their highest priority cost-saving opportunity. As can be seen, both alternatives (Options 2 and 3) have significant positive scores relative to the baseline. These options should be recommended to the core design team for detailed investigation and possible implementation.

category, the QLVE whachamacallit team agrees that a modular enclosure design that could be used for two of the three proposed product versions would significantly simplify the manufacturing process (one less dedicated production line required). Testing costs would also be reduced, since a single set of tests could cover both product versions. Moving to the next category, *direct material*, the cost of scrap might decline due to commonizing on a single modular architecture. The number of version-specific parts would certainly be reduced, and the volume of the parts used for the modular design should increase proportionally.

Under *assignable capital*, the big benefit results from the elimination of some version-specific tooling; the modular architecture would employ the same set of molds, jigs, etc., for both market segments that it addresses. *Design costs* would improve as well, although the complexity of the modular design might be slightly greater. Finally, with one less production line to implement, the impact on *factory overhead* is significantly reduced, due to fewer factory changes and less overall material handling. We do, however, take a minor hit with respect to work-in-process inventory: The combined modular-version assembly line might carry higher WIP than with separate lines for each version. (Keep in mind that this is just an example – the motivation and logic behind these scores is, by definition, correct.)

Once the top-priority cost-saving opportunity has been evaluated through the tradeoff tool, it's on to the next candidate opportunity, and so on. If you run out of time, you can assign action items to complete the analysis work "off-line" and request that the results be reported to the core design team at a later date. At this point, you have basically completed the two-day QLVE event. A few minutes should be spent at the end of the meeting to review the design alternatives that received high positive scores from the Twenty-Cost-Lever tool. Before the meeting adjourns, however, there is one last step to complete, as described below.

8) Publish an Action List for More Detailed Assessment

Assign actions! Never walk out of a review such as the QLVE event without having assigned action items, including names and due dates, for any follow-up work that is needed. If the tradeoff process ran short of time, assign people to complete this activity as soon as possible after the event date. For each of the design alternatives that received high scores, assign an individual to be responsible for filling out a Cost Improvement Recommendation template, such as the one shown in Figure 4.19. The person who suggested a "winning" design alternative is a good choice to complete the recommendation sheet (that's the price they pay for being clever). Allow no more than a week for this task, with the completed recommendations being delivered directly to the core design team leader for disposition. A copy of each recommendation template should also be provided to the director of engineering (or other staff-level executive) for incorporation into a product development database or other such central idea repository.

4.2

Cost Improvement Recommendation
QLVE Event Dates: Analysis Performed by: Product: Part Number: *Author Signature*
Design Element Under Consideration –
Baseline Design Approach –
Recommended Alternative Approach –
Conceptual Sketches and Details –
Estimated Source(s) and Magnitude of Cost Savings –

Figure 4.19 – A suggested format for documenting a recommended design alternative derived from the QLVE event. An individual should be assigned to complete this template for each "winning" idea before adjourning the event.

4.2

Just a quick note about "follow-through" and we will (finally) move on to an entirely new topic. The QLVE event can yield dramatic cost savings, *but only if the core design team takes the recommendations from the event seriously.* Therefore, some process for ensuring that the team considers each recommendation is needed. My suggestion is to have an independent, staff-level manager verify that each alternative has been considered by the team before the conceptual design of the product is approved for further development. Many of the "great ideas" that bubble out of a QLVE event will turn out to be turkeys once they are looked at in detail. Each idea, however, deserves at least a brief consideration by the team, and the *really* great ideas should be embraced. Don't let the time and effort expended on a QLVE event go to waste because the core design team didn't have the discipline to follow through.

Section 4.3 — Sponsoring a Design Challenge

Although the Quick-Look Value Engineering (QLVE) event only requires a week of prep time and a couple of intensive days of team activity, even this commitment may be excessive for your specific situation. Suppose, for example, that your target cost appears to be achievable...except for just one or two high-cost design elements. In this situation, it may be hard to justify disrupting a lot of peoples' schedules and burning over a week of your team's time. Is there a more modest tool that can help solve specific cost problems without demanding a major organizational fire drill? If there wasn't one, why would I bring it up?

In this final section of Part IV, you will learn a very effective way to attack cost problems that can also inject some fun into your organization. Before we consider this neat little lean design tool, however, let's take a brief look at the general topic of *concept selection*. Assuming your team consists of open-minded folks, you will probably consider several design concepts for your new product before down-selecting to a preferred choice. On smaller projects, this process may take place entirely in the head of a single designer, but if a cost problem arises (or any other roadblock, for that matter), this tradeoff process becomes everyone's business. There are two general ways of performing conceptual design tradeoffs, other than the QLVE approach described in Section 4.2. One of them has become something of a classic; the so-called "Pugh Method" for concept selection. The other is notable for its roots in Toyota Motor Company's product development process. Both of these approaches are effective, but can require at least as much time as a QLVE event (the Toyota approach, in particular, may only be suited to high-ticket, high-volume products). Hence, at the end of this section I will stew these two methods together in a pot, and see if we can't cook up a truly noninvasive approach to solving specific cost problems during new product development.

Concept Selection According to Pugh

In 1981, Stuart Pugh, a professor of engineering at the University of Strathclyde in Glasgow, Scotland, suggested a simple and relatively effective way of sorting out multiple design concepts. Admittedly, the description that I provide herein is simplistic; Dr. Pugh's book (see the References section at the end of Part IV) provides a very readable and detailed discussion, should you decide that this approach is right for you. Fundamentally, the Pugh Method is quite similar to the QLVE event, except that it is more focused on optimizing engineering design rather than on cost reduction. An overview of this alternative methodology is provided in Figure 4.20. In a sense, the Pugh Method for Concept Selection is the logical next step in the design process, once the QLVE event has been completed. For smaller projects (or ones without major cost issues), it might make sense to skip the QLVE tool in favor of moving directly to the Pugh Method.

"At a Glance" – Pugh Method for Concept Selection

Overview –
A somewhat simpler alternative to using a full-blown QLVE event for performing concept tradeoffs. A two-dimensional matrix is used to qualitatively evaluate various alternative design concepts in relation to a baseline approach. Scoring is done using pluses, minuses, and neutral symbols, and covers a broader range of design attributes than QLVE.

Primary Benefits –
Quick but effective way to sort out design alternatives. Can be used by a large team or a single individual. Covers a comprehensive set of design criteria.

Best Suited Products –
This tool can be used for any product type, including service products.

Advantages –
Simplicity and speed. Easy to understand for first-time users. Eliminates poor design alternatives clearly and quickly.

Disadvantages –
Not explicitly a cost-reduction tool. May be too qualitative to perform accurate tradeoffs among nearly equivalent design options. Lack of weighting factors limits effectiveness of tool.

Impact on the Twenty Cost Levers –

I. Direct Labor				II. Direct Materials				III. Capital				IV. Design Cost				V. Overhead			
1a	1b	1c	1d	2a	2b	2c	2d	3a	3b	3c	3d	4a	4b	4c	4d	5a	5b	5c	5d
●	○	○	◉	◉	●	●	○	○	◉	●	◉	●	●	●	◉	○	○	○	○

Figure 4.20 – "At-a-glance" overview of the Pugh Method for Concept Selection.

The methodology begins, predictably, with the harvesting of a large suite of possible design alternatives. In this case, however, the design alternatives are developed to a greater level of detail, including some rough estimates of performance and a visual depiction of each proposed approach. Generating design alternatives could be accomplished in the manner described in Section 4.2, but the Lean Design Challenge tool discussed later in this section is a fast and fun way to harvest a host of options. One of the distinctive aspects of the Pugh Method is its emphasis on the sharing of elements among design alternatives; often a "Frankenstein" concept will turn out to be the optimal solution. Hence the need for more detail, such as schematic sketches, before the tradeoff process begins. As an example, some design alternatives for a canister vacuum's "allow movement" function are shown in Figure 4.21.

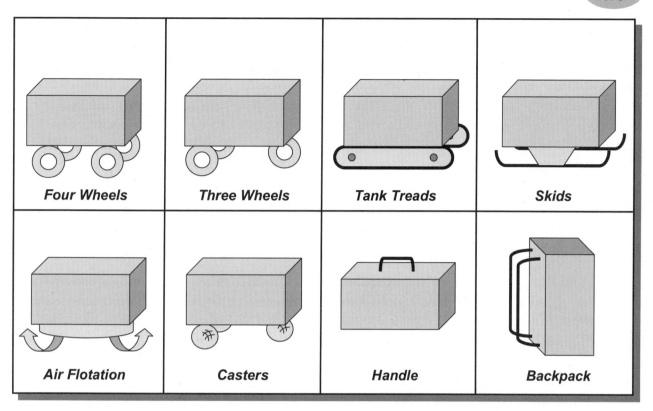

Figure 4.21 – Some alternative conceptual designs for a canister vacuum product's "allow movement" function. Sketches such as these are typically used to help communicate concepts during Pugh Method evaluation.

As can be seen in the example, not all alternatives will make a lot of sense, but there may be some aspect of one option that can be combined with another to form an unexpected breakthrough. As a side note; believe it or not, my mother owned a vacuum in the mid-sixties that used the exhaust from the motor to lift the canister on a cushion of air (see figure). It didn't work worth a darn, but in those thoroughly modern sixties, it was just one more step toward the Jetson's lifestyle. In any case, once options have been gathered and briefly described, a matrix such as the one shown in Figure 4.22 is used to select promising candidates. Along the left-hand column, all major design criteria for the given function are listed. Pugh recommends a fairly comprehensive list, with no weighting factors. The design alternatives are listed along the top of the matrix, often accompanied by simple sketches that are provided for clarity. At the junction between each criterion and design alternative, a "score" is determined, based on how well the alternative supports that criterion. As with the QLVE event, a default design approach is chosen, and all other options are compared to that baseline. Rather than a numerical score, Pugh suggests a "+" for "better than the default," a "-" for "worse than the default," and an "S" representing "same as the default."

Once the scoring is complete, we simply add up the "+'s" and "-'s" (ignoring the S-for-same scores). Design alternatives with more pluses than minuses deserve further consideration. If there is a dramatic winner, it may be sufficient to just select that choice and move forward. As with all methods for concept selection, more detailed analysis by the core design team is essential to validate the qualitative results of a selection tool. Your choice of concept selection method is really a matter of taste and experience; the primary difference between my QLVE event and the Pugh Method is that my approach places significantly more emphasis on cost as a driver for selection. Using the two approaches in concert may be an effective compromise. Certainly money isn't everything... unless, of course, your firm isn't making enough of it.

Concept Selection the Toyota Way

Before providing you with a snapshot look at the "Toyota Way," I must reiterate my concern over using the automobile industry as a role model (if your firm happens to make cars, I withdraw my concern). The auto industry is so atypical of modern business that translating methods used therein to your own situation may prove to be hazardous. Their products sell at both very high prices and very high volumes, and all of their products are *essentially the same*. This combination allows them to justify inordinate expenditure on upfront design, factory capitalization, marketing, and so on. What works for the eight-hundred-pound gorilla may well be anathema for the smaller creatures of the jungle.

Okay, now that I've vented, let's see what the inimitable Toyota is up to. A few years back, Dr. Durward Sobek, a professor of mechanical engineering at Montana State University, taught himself Japanese and paid an extended visit to the Land of the Rising Sun. His observations are well put forth in several papers referenced at the end of Part IV, but I'll summarize them here for the literature-averse reader. Toyota has proven to be more productive at product design than their competitors (meaning that they require less labor hours to complete a typical vehicle design), and obviously their products have proven to be market winners. Yet they don't use any strange and mysterious CAD tools, are not obsessed with Total Quality Management methods, and generally are organized in much the same way as other automakers. It seems that their edge in product design is more a matter of philosophy than of clever tricks.

Two specific aspects of their development process are distinguishing: 1) they consider multiple design solutions at virtually every step, and aggressively compete those alternatives to refine their designs, and 2) they delay design decisions for as long as possible, consistent with an acceptable development schedule. Toyota's approach has been dubbed "Set-Based Concurrent Engineering" by the scholars who have studied their process, in reference to the "sets" of possible design solutions considered at each level of development. For example, a set of perhaps ten to twenty candidate exterior designs might be generated at the onset of a new vehicle project. As the development process proceeds, the set will gradually be trimmed until a final design eventually solidifies. In many cases,

Design Alternatives / Design Criteria	4 Wheels	3 Wheels	Treads	Skids	Air Float	Casters	Handle	Backpack
Support 10 lbs.		S	S	S	-	S	-	-
Minimal Friction		S	-	-	+	S	-	-
Turning Radius		S	-	S	+	S	+	+
Smooth Movement	Default Design	S	-	-	+	S	-	-
Lightweight		+	-	S	+	S	-	-
Nice Appearance		S	-	S	S	+	S	-
Handle Stairs Easily		S	-	-	-	S	+	+
Easy Assembly		+	-	S	+	S	+	+
Low Cost		+	-	+	+	-	+	S
High Reliability		S	-	+	+	S	+	+
Number of Parts		+	-	+	+	S	+	+
Totals +	0	4	0	3	8	1	6	5
Totals −	0	0	10	3	2	1	4	5

Figure 4.22 - At the heart of the Pugh Method for Concept Selection is a simple evaluation matrix that lists all of the major design criteria for a given product function. Each design alternative is given a "score" based on its potential performance relative to a default design choice. A "plus" indicates that a concept performs better than the default, a "minus" implies worse performance than the default, and an "S" (for "same-as") means that the concept would perform equally well.

Toyota will actually establish several completely independent teams to "compete" with each other for the best design. Often these competitions result in a merging of approaches, causing Dr. Sobek to coin a phrase that has become something of a mantra in the auto industry: "Conflict makes better cars."

Furthermore, this idea of considering trade-spaces rather than point designs extends to every important aspect of their product. Once the general platform and body style have been refined, subsystems and components are given the same set-based attention, as shown in Figure 4.23. Often the final refinements are left to suppliers, with only a basic design envelop provided by Toyota. The benefits of casting such a large design net should be intuitively obvious. What is not obvious is how Toyota maintains the discipline to keep its options open without sacrificing time-to-market.

In the late 1980's, Ford Motor Company used a similar approach to develop their highly successful redesign of the Mustang sportscar. Three separate teams were formed

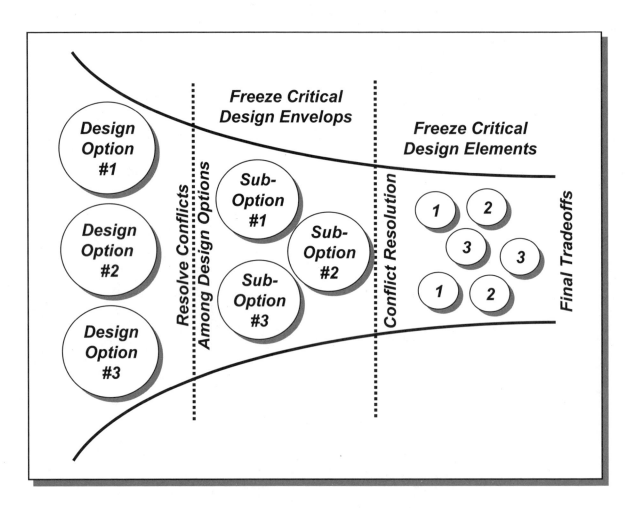

Figure 4.23 – An illustration of how Toyota's product development process utilizes "sets" of possible design solutions rather than a point-design approach. By competing multiple options at every stage of design, they achieve a higher level of design refinement without sacrificing time-to-market.

to develop, in parallel, three distinct design concepts. To ensure that the teams would consider a broad range of possible solutions, each group was given the name of a famous (at the time) personality for inspiration. The first group was called the "Rambo Team," and as you might imagine, their charter was to design a raw muscle car. The second group, dubbed the "Schwarzenegger Team," was tasked with designing a more "politically correct" muscle car (if you get my drift). Finally, the third team was titled the "Bruce Jenner Team." (Incidentally, Bruce Jenner was an Olympic decathlon gold medalist back when dinosaurs roamed.) Presumably, this team's goal was to design a version of the Mustang that resembled the athlete; sprightly to be sure, but not built for heavy lifting. The ultimate product turned out to be an amalgamation of the three concepts, and proved to be a market winner.

Attack Cost Problems with a Lean Design Challenge

All of you readers out there whose firms have enough time, money, and resources to form several redundant design teams, raise your hands. Come on now, don't be shy. Well, I'm sorry to say that I don't see many hands. The logic of competing several design options is inescapable, but then so are the practical constraints of typical businesses. Hence the need for another lean design tool, which I somewhat obviously call the Lean Design Challenge. Using this tool, much of the benefit gained from a set-based design approach can be captured by virtually any firm, as described in Figure 4.24. In principle, you could even use this tool if your firm has only one designer, although the competition aspects of it might not be quite as riveting.

Suppose your firm has identified an exciting new product opportunity, but upon reviewing possible design concepts, you find that the costs are just too high. It seems that a breakthrough is needed to allow further development of the product. Unfortunately, your designers are quite busy with lower-risk projects, so forming a study team just doesn't make sense. Should you sideline this golden opportunity? Perhaps the cost problem involves just a single part or process step that's preventing the product from meeting its target cost. In any case, some innovation is needed to overcome a cost barrier and enable a profitable product to be launched.

Whoever is burdened with the cost problem (I'll refer to that person as the "sponsor") can harness the design smarts of their entire firm by issuing a Lean Design Challenge. A Design Challenge Announcement form, such as the one shown in Figure 4.25, is posted on a corkboard near to where designers congregate (or alternatively, distributed by e-mail, or posted on a company intranet site). The start date and product are identified, and a "challenge number" is assigned (assuming that your firm holds multiple design challenges). More important, an *end date* is identified, based on the importance and complexity of the design challenge. For minor cost troubles, the allotted time should be kept short; a week might be appropriate for relatively simple challenges. For those challenges that seek a product-level cost breakthrough, the allowed time could be months or even years.

4.3

"At a Glance" – The Lean Design Challenge

***Overview** –*
A quick and easy way to foster innovation within your organization. The Lean Design Challenge involves notifying all designers within your firm of a specific design problem; often a cost or performance barrier that must be overcome for a new product to become viable in the marketplace. Designers submit concepts; the best ideas are rewarded with recognition and a non-monetary prize. This is only used for very high-leverage opportunities, and only after the design team has reached an impasse.

***Primary Benefits** –*
Breakthrough ideas generated at a very low cost. In particular, solutions to cost problems that might have been missed by the new product design team.

***Best Suited Products** –*
This tool can be used for any product type, including service products.

***Advantages** –*
Can be fun for the designers involved if the tone is kept supportive and positive. Intended to spur healthy competition, with acknowledgement for all who participate. Not disruptive to other projects, provided that some simple "rules" are followed.

***Disadvantages** –*
If your organization has an entrenched "not invented here" syndrome, there may be some designers who will feel threatened by open competition. Could become a distraction if not managed properly.

***Impact on the Twenty Cost Levers** –*

I. Direct Labor				II. Direct Materials				III. Capital				IV. Design Cost				V. Overhead			
1a	1b	1c	1d	2a	2b	2c	2d	3a	3b	3c	3d	4a	4b	4c	4d	5a	5b	5c	5d
●	○			○	●	●	○			●	◉	●	●	●	◉	○			

Figure 4.24 – "At-a-glance" overview of the Lean Design Challenge product improvement tool.

The announcement form should also include space for a brief description of the specific design element under consideration and the current best design concept (assuming one exists). Finally, enough space should be provided for a detailed description of the design challenge. The challenge may involve reducing cost at the same performance level, or it might require a combination of both cost *and* performance improvement. At the bottom of the form, the sponsor should provide contact information to allow participants to ask questions, and for the submittal of design ideas. The goal of this challenge is to get as many minds as possible working on the problem for just a very brief look. We certainly don't want to have designers obsessing over design challenges, so some discipline in the implementation of this tool is needed.

Designers who decide to participate are given a Challenge Response form to complete, as shown in Figure 4.26. Along with the necessary administrative stuff is a space for participants to describe their ideas, primarily in visual form (*not a CAD drawing*...just a hand-drawn sketch). The participant is also asked to provide a qualitative estimate of what impact their idea would have on product cost and performance.

Design Challenge Announcement
Start Date: End Date: Product: Challenge Number:
Design Element Under Consideration –   Reference(s) –
Current Best Design Concept –   Reference(s) –
The Design Challenge –   ☐ Performance Improvement   ☐ Cost Reduction
For questions, or to submit Challenge Response forms, contact - _____ Sponsor Signature Sponsor Contact Information

Figure 4.25 – The Design Challenge Announcement template. This form can be posted in a designated area, or circulated by e-mail or intranet to all designers within a firm. A specified period of time is allotted for submittals of concept alternatives. All participants are recognized for their submittals, and the "winner" (if there is one) receives a symbolic reward.

4.3

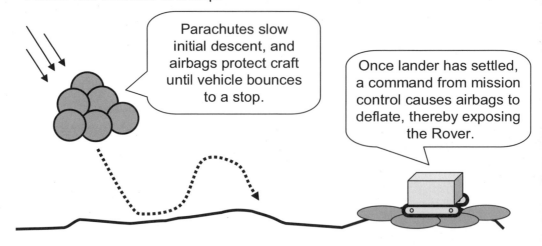

Figure 4.26 – The Challenge Response template that designers can use to submit their "innovative" concepts. The above form has been filled out by a (fictional) member of the Mars Spirit / Rover design team.

Once the end-date has been reached, the challenge sponsor gathers up all of the submittals and reviews them. If a concept appears to be worth pursuing, it is given to the appropriate design team or to the director of engineering for further analysis. All that remains is to recognize the participants and reward the "winners." There are many ways to accomplish this, but I like to include all participants in the recognition process, which could consist of a certificate, a free lunch, an e-mail thank-you, etc. The winners might be presented with an "innovation award" in the form of a plaque, and perhaps some minor cash prize or equivalent. Note that the innovations that are generated by the Lean Design Challenge might prove to be patentable, so be careful to maintain appropriate records if such potential exists.

There are a number of situations that can benefit from issuing a Lean Design Challenge. They include:

- A design team is stuck on a cost problem and can't seem to push past it.
- A new product opportunity has great market potential, but the target cost seems impossibly low.
- One of your existing products is being undercut in the marketplace and a cost breakthrough is needed to save it from the bone yard.
- A competitor has come up with a scary new product, and your firm needs to innovate past it to retain market share.
- You are being held hostage by an unsatisfactory supplier and would like to design their components out of the next generation of the product.

As a final note, friendly competitions such as this one have proven extremely effective, both within a firm and as an open challenge to science and industry. The first man-powered aircraft, the first man-powered flight across the English Channel, and many other breakthroughs in aviation have resulted from a challenge being issued (and a substantial prize being offered). If "conflict makes better cars," then it stands to reason that a little friendly competition among creative and highly motivated people can make a better product for your firm.

Notes

Part IV

Recommendations for Further Learning

Unlike previous "References" sections, I've included essentially *all* of the worthwhile books on the subject of Value Engineering. Each of the books listed below has its advantages, and although there is a great deal of overlap, I feel that this important subject deserves some extra attention. The literature papers on Toyota's product development process are all quite readable, so don't be intimidated.

Value Engineering and Analysis

***** ***Techniques of Value Analysis and Engineering, 2nd Edition,*** Miles, L. D., 1972

This is really the source for much of the conceptual material covered in the books that follow. Excellent, readable, and prescient, Miles provides the kind of detailed engineering examples that should appeal to any design practitioner. This book was out of print the last I looked, but there are used copies available from Amazon.com and others.

***** ***Value Analysis to Improve Productivity,*** Fallon, C., 1971

A contemporary of Miles, Fallon served as President of the Society of American Value Engineers during the 1970's. A perspective similar to the book mentioned above, but with a slightly more philosophical tone. It includes fine descriptions of the history of Value Engineering, and a great discussion on the categories of value.

***** ***Value Engineering: A Systematic Approach,*** Mudge, A. E., 1989

This is my personal favorite, in part because it is somewhat more current. This is also the best book available, in my opinion, for the implementer of Value Engineering. Tons of detail, including job plans, templates, case examples, forms, and other practical necessities.

**** ***Value Engineering: A Blueprint,*** Brown, J., 1992

For those of you looking for an "easy-read" entry into the world of Value Engineering, this book is a good choice. Nowhere near the content of the above works, but clean and clear explanations make the barriers to entry minimal.

*** *Value Engineering: A Plan for Invention,* Park, R., 1999

A nice, clean book, much like the "easy-read" one mentioned directly above. Perhaps slightly more emphasis on innovation as the source of value breakthroughs. It is a fine book that only pales when compared to the other works in this field.

Design Competition and Selection

***** ***Total Design: Integrated Methods for Successful Product Engineering,***
Pugh, S., 1991

A great book in all respects. Perhaps the most insightful book available on overall product design, with an excellent discussion of the "Pugh Method" that comes directly from the source.

***** *"Toyota's principles of set-based concurrent engineering,"* Sobek II, D. K., Ward, A. C., and J. K. Liker, 1999, *Sloan Management Review*, Vol. 40, No. 2, Winter Issue

Personally, I don't find the "Toyota Way" of product development all that unique or astounding. In the auto industry it may be unusual to perform multiple design competitions or to delay decisions on critical design elements, but in electronics or aerospace, these practices are fairly common (albeit on a smaller scale). Still an excellent article, and if you're a student of Toyota, a very nice piece of hands-on research.

**** *"The second Toyota paradox: How delaying decisions can make better cars faster,"* Ward, A. C., Liker, J. K, Cristiano, J. J., and D. K. Sobek, II, 1995, *Sloan Management Review*, Vol. 36, No. 3, Spring Issue

The above article is more comprehensive and insightful, but this one focuses on the "decision-delaying" aspect of Toyota's design philosophy.

**** *"Another look at how Toyota integrates product development,"* Sobek II, D. K., Liker, J. K, and A. C. Ward, 1998, *Harvard Business Review*, July-August Issue

Readable and practical, but a bit watered down from the first article listed above on this topic. Typical HBR tone; just enough to sate your immediate appetite, but you're hungry again in a few hours.

Preparing for Production: The "3P" Process

5.1 - What's a Lean Factory Look Like?

5.2 - Overview of Toyota's 3P Process

5.3 - The "How's it Built?" Review

5.4 - The "Seven-Alternatives" Process

Part V

> *"Coming together is a beginning: keeping together is progress: working together is success."*
>
> Henry Ford

> *"If we don't discipline ourselves the world will do it for us."*
>
> William Feather

Section 5.1 — What's a Lean Factory Look Like?

In Part V we will consider the substantial benefits of developing a product design in parallel with its associated production processes. In fact, our goal will be to integrate these two activities so tightly that your new product fits into your factory like hand in glove. The key to achieving this intimate compatibility is *product and process co-development*. As the product design evolves, so should the processes that will be required to manufacture it, literally in lockstep. Materials specified for the product should be reconciled with the factory's current inventory, supplier base, and handling capability. The flow of assembly should match as closely as possible to existing process flows. Design tolerances must be matched to process capabilities to ensure minimal scrap and quality defects, etc.

How can this be accomplished without slowing down development or unnecessarily encumbering your already overburdened designers? Not surprisingly, we will use Toyota Motor Company's well-proven Production Preparation Process (3P) as a pathfinder. Also not surprisingly, I will recommend a somewhat minimalist implementation of their extraordinarily thorough approach.

Before we get into the details, however, it is worthwhile reviewing just what we mean by a lean factory, and how a lean product design can make your production peoples' lives a great deal easier. First of all, a lean factory is not a monolithic concept. In reality, lean manufacturing is characterized by an evolving set of tools and techniques which may or may not make sense for a specific situation. An implementation that makes sense for the automotive industry may be inefficient for a shampoo manufacturer or a producer of highly customized electronics. With that in mind, let's take a look at the typical attributes of a lean factory.

Just-in-Time (JIT) Inventory Management – Perhaps the most universal characteristic of a lean factory is its miserly management of raw and work-in-process (WIP) inventories. In the bad old days, factories would order railcar-loads of material at a time, and process that material in huge, supposedly economical batches. The result was an enormous drain on available capital, floor space, material-handling equipment, and labor. Moreover, materials that were stored for extended periods often suffered damage, defects, or other degradation. Lean manufacturing mandates a significant reduction in inventory levels, as measured by "inventory turns per period." Hence, suppliers are asked to make frequent small shipments rather than a few monstrous ones. Internal to the factory, batch processes are minimized or entirely eliminated. The goal is for needed materials to arrive

5.1

Design for Lean Manufacturing	
Lean Manufacturing Attribute	Lean Design Opportunity
JIT Inventory Management	• Selection of suppliers that support JIT delivery schedules • Consolidation of suppliers • Selection of suppliers that will manage an on-site inventory
Pull Systems	• Reduction in the number of subassemblies • Compatibility of product with one- or few-piece flow • Standardizing on fewer parts • Design products to be assembled on demand rather than built to finished goods inventory (reduced cycle-time)
Flow-Lines / Workcells	• Reduction in the number of subassemblies • Design for compatibility with existing flow-lines or workcells • Design for top-down or single-orientation assembly • Grouping of parts by process flow (group technology)
Batch Elimination	• Selection of processes that allow for small batches or one-piece flow (avoid large and costly capital equipment)
Other Opportunities	• Design for testability and easy inspection • Design products to be self-aligning, self-adjusting, etc. • Reduction in small-parts content (fewer fasteners, etc.) • Compatibility of raw material requirements with standard available dimensions, thicknesses, etc.

Figure 5.1 – Ways in which lean product design can improve the compatibility of a new product with a lean manufacturing environment.

"just-in-time" to produce only those products which can be immediately sold. Factories should not serve as warehouses; they should be pipelines that take in materials and ship out products in the shortest possible cycle-time.

Pull Systems - A pull system is an approach to managing manufacturing flow that avoids such dinosaurs as master scheduling (and other MRP-based workflow-management tools) in favor of an event-driven system. When a factory receives an order (or a firm production forecast is submitted to the factory, for the case of long cycle-time products), a series of events is triggered that results in the required products being produced. This sequence begins, in a sense, at the shipping dock, and flows upstream through finished goods, subassemblies, component processing, and finally to raw-material inventory. Some form of signal is used to indicate how much should be produced at each step in the process to exactly match what is needed to meet current orders. Often the pull signal comes in the form of a *kanban* card (Japanese for "signal card"), a specially designed parts holder, or some other simple visual method.

Flow-Lines and Workcells - Once inventory levels are under control through implementation of JIT and pull systems, the next big opportunity for cost improvement is reduction of material handling and movement. In the past, materials might be moved (literally) *miles* from their arrival at the factory until their exit as finished goods. A lean factory utilizes tightly integrated flow-lines or U-shaped workcells to virtually eliminate wasted movement.

One-Piece Flow - If all of the above is in place, the next step in a factory's lean journey might be to drive their flow-lines toward one-piece flow. Elimination of batch processes is one of the hardest economies to grasp, since our intuition tells us that big batches must be less costly to process. The tradeoffs are subtle, but critically important. A batch process requires a significantly longer production cycle-time, and forces the product mix into batch-size increments (which likely will not match orders or forecasts). Hence, inventory cost increases, while responsiveness to customers decreases. Moreover, large-batch equipment tends to be hard to move, costly to maintain, and of limited flexibility. Certainly there are some processes that just can't reasonably be done in a one- or few-piece flow arrangement, but innovations in equipment design have made these situations the minor exception rather than the rule.

There are a number of other, lower-level tools that are synonymous with a lean factory (e.g., andon lights, *takt* time, etc.), but the above attributes are the most fundamental and ubiquitous. So how does this manufacturing milieu impact product designers? A summary of possible design factors that can enable compatibility with lean manufacturing is provided in Figure 5.1. The remainder of Part V will delve into how product and process co-development can easily be integrated into an efficient product development process.

Notes

Section 5.2 — Overview of Toyota's 3P Process

Previously in Section 4.3, I suggested that Toyota's product development process was "unique" in two primary ways: they use a set-based approach for defining product specifications, and they delay finalizing their design decisions until as late as possible in the process. Some would argue that Toyota is unique in a third way; they have implemented a formal Production Preparation Process (3P). Personally, I am reluctant to single out Toyota for embedding a detailed manufacturing preparation process within their product development methodology. Many firms have been successful in this regard, in particular those who follow the Advanced Product Quality Planning (APQP) standard for product development. Toyota does deserve credit, however, for elevating the concept of product and process co-development to a very high level of sophistication. Fortunately for us non-carmakers, there are two techniques within the Toyota 3P process that can, with a bit of adaptation, be extremely valuable to any firm.

Parallel and Interwoven Processes

The Toyota 3P process is summarized in Figure 5.2. Manufacturing process developers are guided through a "narrowing funnel," from rough concepts, through concept tradeoffs, and finally to a process that is qualified and ready for product launch. In a real sense, Toyota operates two parallel and interwoven processes, as illustrated in Figure 5.3. Each process feeds and informs the other in a relatively seamless manner. As design concepts are being proposed, the processes needed to produce those concepts are being considered. More definition on the design side allows for more definition on the process side, and so on.

As with most product development processes, 3P is divided into "phases," based on the maturity of design information. The "information phase," which is executed in parallel with the conceptual design of the product, involves gathering of product documentation, identification of parts and raw materials, and a rough estimation of how the product will be built. In the next phase, referred to as the "creative phase," process design alternatives are considered as the product design begins to mature. Finally, as detailed drawings and bills-of-material are being generated on the product-design side, the "redefine phase" is conducted. In this phase, the final production process is solidified, capital equipment is purchased and qualified, and the factory layout is completed. If everything goes according to plan, product design documentation arrives on the factory floor from the product-design funnel "just in time" to perform a pilot production run using the production process developed in the 3P "funnel."

5.2

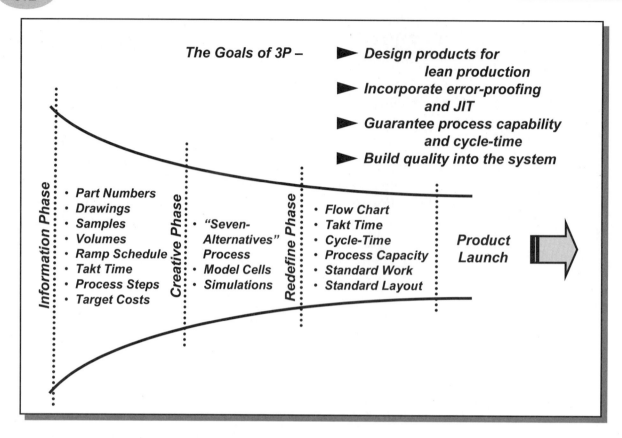

Figure 5.2 – Overview of the Toyota Production Preparation Process (3P). Note the similarity between this "narrowing-funnel" process and the Set-Based Concurrent Engineering process illustrated in Figure 4.23.

Inside of the 3P funnel, there are lots of clever tricks that Toyota has come up with. In the next two sections, we will take a closer look at how they perform initial assessments of manufacturing capability and how they go about generating process-design alternatives. Just to complete the high-level picture, however, I'll outline some of the most important activities that take place during the Toyota 3P process.

Making Sure that Value Flows

One of the hallmarks of a lean factory is a smooth and efficient flow from raw materials, through *flow-lines* or *workcells*, and into finished-goods inventory, ready for shipment. The 3P process mandates early consideration of flow in the development of manufacturing methods and factory layout, as shown in Figure 5.4. In general, the distance from receiving to stock is minimized, and if possible, raw materials and parts are delivered directly to the factory floor at the point of use. The production process is arranged into flow-lines wherever possible, or U-shaped workcells if more flexibility is needed to handle a specific mix of products. Remember that an ideal factory is a "pipeline" that converts raw

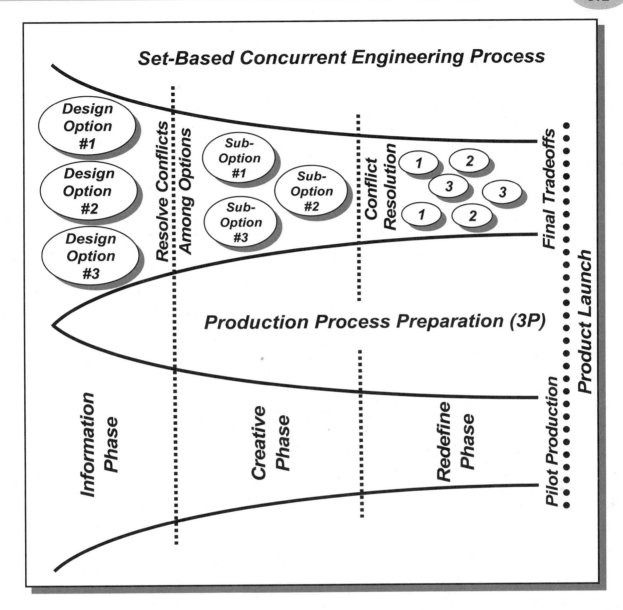

Figure 5.3 – The 3P process is tightly interwoven with the design and development of the product itself. In a sense, they are two parallel and synchronized processes with a high degree of information flow and feedback between them.

materials into high-value finished goods in the least possible time and with a minimum of material movement and inventory carrying cost. (Just as a side note to liven things up, when the Iron Curtain fell in 1990, Western economists and consultants were asked to assess the production capabilities of Soviet factories. After some careful study, the initial team of experts concluded that most factories in the good old USSR *actually subtracted value*: Quality and efficiency were so poor that the finished goods these factories produced were worth less than the raw materials from which they were made.)

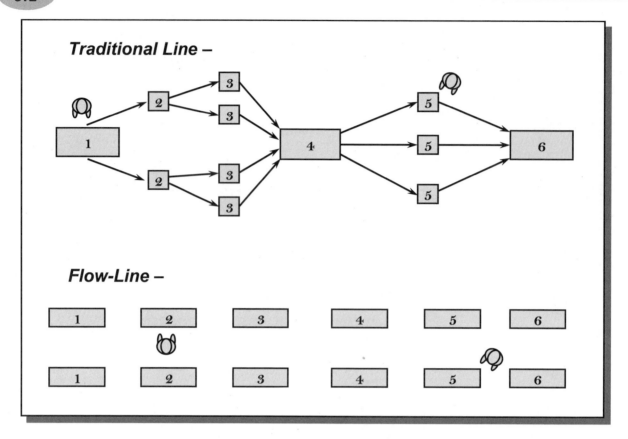

Figure 5.4 – The 3P process emphasizes early consideration of factory layout and flow of materials to enable high-efficiency flow-lines or U-shaped workcells wherever possible.

Modeling the Factory of the Future

One of the things that I believe Japanese firms get right is their extensive use of mock-ups and other physical models to represent both future product designs and future factory implementations. We in the West are just a little too infatuated with our solid-model CAD systems and factory simulation software. At several points during the 3P process, physical models are constructed that allow the process design team to experiment with various layouts, machine configurations, material storage schemes, and so on. At a minimum, a two-dimensional model is created that includes a factory floor plan sketched to scale and movable bits of cardboard to represent various machines, people, storage, etc. More often, a three-dimensional model is created that allows clear visualization of proposed changes to the factory. Toyota and other sophisticated companies create high-quality 3D scale models and maintain them from project to project as an ongoing resource. The models are used several times during 3P to analyze *takt* time (the number of products per unit time that can be produced), capacity, flow, material movement, and WIP inventory.

Checklists and Catch Phrases Abound

Those of you who have spent time with a lean manufacturing *sensei* have probably been barraged with checklists and so-called "catch phrases." I think this must be a cultural thing, since the emphasis on such lists appears to be far greater than in a typical Western firm. Given that I'm a huge fan of checklists, however, this aspect of the 3P process is near and dear to my heart. The purpose of a checklist or catch-phrase list is to jog your brain into considering multiple aspects of a problem. For example, the Fifteen Catch Phrases for Factory Optimization, shown in Figure 5.5, are designed to help you remember such diverse considerations as ensuring that equipment is easy to move, making operator stations narrow, and reducing equipment cycle-time. Personally, I don't find that the phrases and lists coming out of Japan translate all that well into Western manufacturing lingo. It would probably make more sense for your designers, process developers, and operations people to get together and create your own list of memory joggers, based on known and learned best practices.

Fifteen "Catch Phrases" for Factory Optimization

1. Production preparation should be lightning fast
2. Equipment layout should permit easy material flows
3. Use additive equipment
4. Use equipment that allows easy changeovers
5. Make equipment easy to move
6. Use versatile equipment
7. Make operator stations narrow
8. Equipment and layout should allow people to move easily
9. Eliminate wasted equipment cycle-time
10. Use equipment for small, swift flow-lines
11. Use short, vertical flow-lines
12. Production can be pulled along
13. Quick changeovers
14. Link machines for smooth loading and unloading
15. Use multiple lines and rectified flows

Figure 5.5 – An example of a "catch-phrase" list that is typical of those used in the Toyota 3P process. These catch phrases are intended to jog the brains of process designers into considering all critical aspects of lean manufacturing.

5.2

The 3P Kaizen Event

There are two activities within the 3P process that I believe deserve special attention. The first is the 3P *Kaizen* Event. The concept of the *kaizen* event has evolved over the past two decades into a mainstay of modern manufacturing. Although the format is extremely flexible, a typical *kaizen* event requires a week-long commitment from those involved. Since the objective of the event is to achieve immediate process improvement, the *kaizen* team is given both the authority and materials to implement changes on the spot. The first day is usually spent mapping out the existing process (presumably one that has high potential for cost, quality, or cycle-time improvement). As the week progresses, a future-state process flow is developed that would potentially eliminate non-value-added activities, excessive inventory, etc. The final step, usually an all-nighter between the fourth and fifth day, involves actual implementation and testing of the changes. Equipment is moved, tools are reorganized, flow is redirected, until the desired improvement has been achieved. If you haven't participated in one of these energizing events, put it on your "things-to-experience" list. For those of you that have been in a sensory-deprivation chamber since the lean movement began, there are several excellent references on how to hold *kaizen* events listed at the end of Part V.

The goal of the 3P *Kaizen* Event is to interrogate the proposed manufacturing approach at the early stages of product development, and subsequently refine it as the launch date approaches. Unfortunately, blocking off five consecutive days of a team's time might represent a big obstacle for many organizations. To remove this roadblock (along with your last excuse for not doing true product and process co-development), I'll describe in Section 5.3 one of my "Reader's Digest" tools that captures the essence of the 3P *Kaizen* Event in a single day.

Consideration of Alternative Processes

The second notable activity within Toyota's 3P process is often called the "Seven Alternatives." Those of you who have been paying attention throughout this guidebook will note a pattern here. Excellence in product design and development depends fundamentally on the consideration of multiple options at virtually every stage of product creation. This is true in spades for the weighing of manufacturing process alternatives. Since a version of this tradeoff activity will be described in detail in Section 5.4, I won't go deeper here. Suffice to say that the identification of processes that optimize quality, tooling cost, labor cost, and cycle-time, can mean the difference between profit and loss. So the next time you sign off on a capital requisition for six or seven figures, ask yourself whether your process designers looked beyond the obvious. In my experience, considering non-obvious options for process design can literally *knock a zero off* of that hefty capital request.

Section 5.3

The "How's it Built?" Review

As you've likely gathered, I am a big fan of one-day events. In my experience, it is relatively easy to get almost any group of people into a room for a day or less to focus on a truly important topic. When it comes to product cost reduction, there are few "truly important topics" that can rival the *manufacturability* of your new product. Of course the Toyotas of the world have an army of people whose sole job in life is to ensure manufacturability. If you are the commander of (or a grunt within) such an army, you may find the lean design tool described in this section to be a bit too quick and easy for your taste. For the vast majority of you who more closely resemble platoon sergeants, however, the "How's it Built?" Review described in Figure 5.6 should be an excellent fit.

Who, What, and When

The purpose of a "How's it Built?" Review is to bring together product and process designers for a highly productive meeting of the minds on manufacturability. (Incidentally, I would normally use a three-letter acronym at this point to reference this new tool, but for some reason "HBR" just left me cold; hence, from now on I'll call it the HB Review.) Although cross-functional teams and concurrent engineering practices are intended to foster collaboration and feedback between product designers and process designers, in practice this partnership often needs a catalyst. The HB Review is a forum in which the manufacturing folks get to shine, for once tipping the development scales in the direction of cost and yield rather than performance and features.

The outputs from this review include feedback on the current state of production process planning and a host of action items for both sides of the design aisle that will improve cost, reduce scrap, slash overhead and capital, etc. Ultimately, the responsibility for executing an HB Review rests with the development team leader. From a practical standpoint, however, the manufacturing engineer or process development engineer on your team should take the lead. Attendees should include the core design team and an appropriate assortment of operations people, perhaps including toolmakers, shop forepersons, process engineers, the facility manager, and the director of operations.

Now that the "who" is out of the way, we can consider the "what" of an HB Review. Prior to the review, the facilitator (again, either the development team leader or process development engineer) must gather the following categories of information:

5.3

> ### "At a Glance" – The "How's it Built?" Review
>
> **Overview –**
> An excellent tool to improve communication and interaction between design engineering and process engineering during new product development. A one-day (or shorter) meeting is held at several points within the development process to focus on manufacturability issues, such as cost, cycle-time, scrap rate, quality assurance, and so on. The highlight of the meeting is a walk-through of the proposed production process by the facilitator or other process-design specialist.
>
> **Primary Benefits –**
> Puts manufacturability issues on the front burner (at least briefly). A great way to break down barriers between product and process designers. Can generate lots of valuable ideas for cost, cycle-time, and yield improvements.
>
> **Best Suited Products –**
> This tool can be used for any product type, but is best suited to discrete manufacturing.
>
> **Advantages –**
> Can be a fun and energizing experience for both sides of the design aisle. Minimal time commitment in return for high-value improvement suggestions.
>
> **Disadvantages –**
> No real disadvantages, provided that your organization can muster the discipline to get both process and product designers in a room for a day.
>
> **Impact on the Twenty Cost Levers –**
>
> | I. Direct Labor | | | | II. Direct Materials | | | | III. Capital | | | | IV. Design Cost | | | | V. Overhead | | | |
> |---|---|---|---|---|---|---|---|---|---|---|---|---|---|---|---|---|---|---|---|
> | 1a | 1b | 1c | 1d | 2a | 2b | 2c | 2d | 3a | 3b | 3c | 3d | 4a | 4b | 4c | 4d | 5a | 5b | 5c | 5d |
> | ● | ● | ● | ● | ● | ◉ | ◉ | ◉ | ● | ○ | ◉ | ● | | ○ | | | ○ | ◉ | ● | ◉ |

Figure 5.6 – "At-a-glance" overview of the "How's it Built?" Review lean design tool.

- What are the critical processes required to manufacture the new product?
- What are the design tolerances that will be difficult to meet?
- What capital equipment will be required?
- What will the layout of flow-lines and workcells look like?
- What is the plan for JIT material management?
- What will be the capacity and *takt* time of the new value stream?
- What is the plan for quality assurance?

Although it would be great if the entire core design team pitched in to help gather this information, it is more likely that your manufacturing engineering representative will have to do essentially all of the preparation. This is not an undue burden, however, since the process of answering all of the "whats" listed above must be done regardless of whether an HB Review is held or not.

Since the true purpose of the HB Review is to break down barriers between process and product designers, the timing of the event is crucial. If product design decisions have already been made by the time your team begins considering manufacturability, you're out of luck. There are actually two logical windows of opportunity for an HB Review. The highest priority timeframe is early in the development process, roughly in sync with consideration of conceptual design alternatives. Since one of the most critical tradeoff factors in conceptual design should be manufacturing cost and producibility, it makes sense to hold an HB Review just before the final down-select of a conceptual design. A second opportunity occurs during prototype validation. With prototypes available, it may be possible to conduct Design-of-Experiments (DOEs, see Section 6.2) or other statistical tests to optimize process capability or to investigate critical-to-quality issues. These tests can help validate your proposed manufacturing strategy, and should provide lots of fuel for an HB Review. Holding reviews at both points in your development process is advisable, but if that would be a hard sell, opt for the early review where your leverage is the greatest.

The How of a "How's it Built?" Review

A sample agenda for a one-day HB Review is shown in Figure 5.7. Note that a full day would typically be required for a moderately complex system product. If your product is monumentally complex, you should consider dividing the design along system partitions and holding an HB Review for each major subsystem. For simpler products, a couple of hours will likely suffice. Use common sense to scale the duration of the review to the volume of information that must be covered. An initial meeting notice should be sent out several weeks in advance, *after the availability of critical decision-makers has been confirmed*. Don't waste your time holding an HB Review that doesn't have a quorum of appropriately large elephants to put some teeth (or tusks?) into your decisions and actions.

On the day of the review, begin with an overview of current "best thinking" on the product's design. Be sure to define the maturity level of the design; it can be frustrating for HB Review attendees if designers are continually saying, "Sorry, that can't be changed." After this initial overview, I suggest a short discussion on the important issues associated with manufacturing the new product. This is a good way to help open the minds of both product and process designers, particularly if some truly challenging issues are raised. Keep a list of the important points, and go back through it near the end of the review to ensure that all critical topics have been covered.

After these preliminary activities, the process design engineer (or other appropriate expert) presents a "How's it Built?" proposal. Keep the formality to a minimum; try to use existing forms of documentation rather than creating a bunch of one-time-use slides. Although the contents of such a manufacturing-plan proposal are highly product-dependent, the topics I've listed in Figure 5.7 are a good starting point. One element of the proposal deserves special attention, however. The most important step in the presentation of a "How's it Built?" proposal is a *walk-through of the proposed manufacturing process*. In this walk-through, the facilitator explains the production flow, how material will move, where capital equipment will be located, and so on. It is vital that a visual model be used for this walk-through, as shown in Figure 5.8. A scaled, plan-view drawing of the factory

5.3

Product XYZ "How's it Built?" Review
August 32, 2036

Proposed Agenda –

8:00 – 8:30	Overview of Current Product Design
8:30 – 9:00	Brainstorming on Critical Cost / Yield Factors
9:00 – 11:00	Walk-Through of Proposed Manufacturing Plan -
	• Factory Layout Model
	• Capital Equipment List
	• Capacity and *Takt*-Time Calculations
	• Critical-to-Cost / Critical-to-Quality Issues
	• Other Selected Topics
11:00 – 12:00	Factory Tour (Optional)
12:00 – 1:00	Working Lunch – Discussion of "How's it Built?" Proposal
1:00 – 3:00	Structured Brainstorming on Improvements
3:00 – 4:00	Ranking of Improvement Opportunities
4:00 – 4:30	Assignment of Action Items

Figure 5.7 – A sample agenda for a one-day "How's it Built?" Review. Note that a full day will not be needed for relatively simple products. This agenda should be scaled to suit the complexity of the manufacturing challenge.

will work quite well, particularly if the facilitator uses a transparent overlay to indicate changes in layout and equipment. If time and funds permit, the manufacturing engineering function within your firm might consider creating a semi-permanent 3D model of the factory. This model could then be used to play "what if" games during *kaizen* events, HB Reviews, and other factory-related activities. One way or another, a visual model is critical to the communication of your manufacturing strategy.

If the HB Review is being held at the same location as your factory, it is a great idea to take the attendees for a physical walk-through, so that they can better relate your model to reality. If everyone at the meeting is familiar with the factory floor, this step may not be necessary. It's important to make things real, but don't waste people's time. At about the midpoint of the HB Review (lunchtime for the one-day agenda), hold an informal critique of the "How's it Built?" proposal. Take copious notes on a flipchart to capture any valuable observations, but try not to stop the flow of conversation. This open forum is just a precursor to the more structured discussion that follows, but it is a great way to get people thinking.

Creating a Two-Dimensional Factory Model

Step 1 –
Create a scale drawing of your factory layout in "plan view." Use artist's foam board or heavy cardboard as a backing.

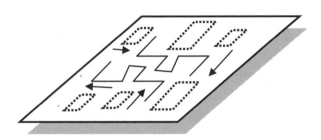

Step 2 –
On a piece of clear acetate, sketch your proposed "future state" for the factory (do your sketch in red ink).

Step 3 –
Join the acetate to your "current-state" layout using clear packing tape. Orient the "hinged" side so that the model can be either hung or laid flat on a table.

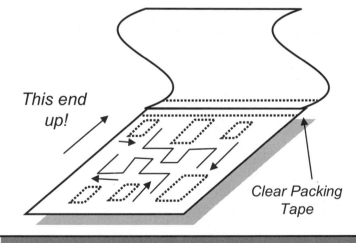

Step 4 –
Make up some scale cardboard cutouts of all new equipment, racks, tables, workspaces, etc. Use these cutouts to brainstorm alternatives during your "How's it Built?" Review.

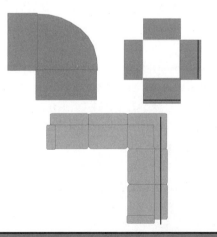

Figure 5.8 – A suggested way to create a useful two-dimensional factory layout model. If you have the time and money, a more advanced, three-dimensional model can dramatically improve your team's ability to visualize flow, scale of machines, routing of material conveyers, etc.

5.3

Now for the payoff. After a bit of open debate, hand out a checklist such as the one shown in Figure 5.9 to all attendees. Note that the example I've provided is just a starting point. Your list need not be significantly longer, but you should certainly go through my suggestions and word them more precisely, and perhaps substitute more relevant topics. The more closely you align the checklist topics with your real-world situation, the more high-value inputs you will gather from the HB Review.

Before you start soliciting improvement suggestions, ask the group to quickly go through the checklist and rank-order the topics for discussion. A 1-10 scale works fine (don't worry, we'll come back to my old favorite 1-5 scale in a few moments). The purpose of this cursory ranking is to (as always) get the most from your collective time together. A "10" score would imply a topic that has huge cost, quality, or cycle-time impact on the proposed new product. Lower scores indicate less relative impact, while a "1" score translates to "skip it."

Start with the "10's" and work your way down the list. Ask the participants for suggestions that might help reduce cost, time, scrap, and so on. Don't spend more than a few minutes on each topic, unless the group is laying some golden eggs. Keep an eye on the clock, and as you approach your allocated time, quickly scan the remaining topics on the list to see if anything important has been missed. You might also challenge the attendees to suggest topics that should have been listed, and be sure to record these new topics for inclusion on future lists.

Only one step remains. Now what would that final step be...? Hopefully, you have identified a pattern among the lean design tools you've already learned. What do we always do at the end of almost every lean design activity? Give yourself an "A": We must always *prioritize the outputs* of any brainstorming activity to maximize the value of the *action items* that will be assigned. Great ideas should bubble to the top for immediate attention, while lesser ones can be subordinated or even completely ignored. A template for harvesting and ranking manufacturability improvement ideas is provided in Figure 5.10. The scoring should be performed as a group, using a "show of fingers" to indicate each attendee's vote. On a 1-5 scale, what is the probability that an improvement suggestion could realistically be implemented? A high score indicates a certainty, whereas a low score implies it's time to move on to the next idea. Similarly, on a 1-5 scale, what would be the impact on cost, quality, and cycle-time if the suggestion proved to be successful? Here, a high score connotes major impact, while a lower score indicates minor impact. Take the product of these two scores and you have a quick prioritization of improvement ideas. For suggestions that have received a high relative ranking (I like to use a combined score of > 8 as my cutoff criterion), ask for volunteers to pursue that idea further. Always, always, always assign a responsible person and completion date for any action item that you actually wish to see completed.

"How's it Built?" Review Manufacturability Checklist (Page 1 of 3)	Importance (1–10 Scale)
I. Inventory and Supply-Chain Optimization	
i. Have commercial-off-the-shelf (COTS) parts been considered for all non-critical components?	
ii. Has a make vs. buy analysis been performed on critical components? Has obsolescence of components been considered?	
iii. Have suppliers provided design guidelines or rules?	
iv. Have suppliers identified cost-saving opportunities?	
v. Has the design taken maximum advantage of commonly used parts within our existing inventory?	
vi. Has the number of suppliers been minimized?	
vii. Have suppliers agreed to support our JIT strategy?	
viii. Can the number of new or unique parts in this product be reduced?	
ix. How can raw-material requirements be optimized to reduce process waste?	
x. How can incoming inspection be minimized or eliminated?	
II. Process Capability	
i. Has manufacturing defined the critical processes that will drive production cost and yield?	
ii. Have the capabilities of critical processes been quantitatively defined?	
iii. Have design margins been matched to process capabilities for all critical processes?	
iv. Have statistical process control limits been estimated and verified?	
v. Have Design-of-Experiments (DOEs) been run to minimize the process sensitivity of critical steps?	

Figure 5.9 – The checklist shown above can serve as a guide for the "structured brainstorming on improvements" activity shown in Figure 5.7. This is just a generic starting point; your firm should develop an expanded version based on the specific nature of your products and manufacturing capabilities. Note that a ranking system is used to help focus discussion on the most fruitful topics.

"How's it Built?" Review Manufacturability Checklist (Page 2 of 3)	Importance (1–10 Scale)
III. Design for Testability	
i. Have all essential production tests been identified?	
ii. Has the potential for suppliers to perform testing been considered?	
iii. Has easy access been provided for all tests?	
iv. Has a clear "pass / fail" criterion been defined for all production tests and inspections?	
v. Have all tests been simplified as much as possible?	
vi. Have self-test and self-adjust features been utilized?	
vii. Have the ranges and accuracies of test equipment been considered?	
viii. Has a product cost model been created that includes yield loss and scrap cost at each critical process step?	
ix. Have all modes of operation of the product been specified and verified?	
IV. Capital Equipment and Tooling	
i. Has capital equipment been selected for one- or few-piece flow?	
ii. Have several alternative processes been considered for each process step that requires new capital equipment?	
iii. Can capital equipment be used for multiple products, or will the new equipment be dedicated to the new product?	
iv. Has soft tooling been considered as an option?	
v. Can the new equipment be easily moved, retooled, adjusted, maintained, expanded, etc.?	
vi. Is the throughput of new equipment and tooling adequate to meet both current and future demands?	

Figure 5.9 – (Continued)

"How's it Built?" Review Manufacturability Checklist (Page 3 of 3)	Importance (1–10 Scale)
V. Design for Lean Manufacture	
i. Has the product been designed to reduce or eliminate batch processes?	
ii. Are the selected suppliers on a "pull" production system?	
iii. Is the product designed for one-piece or few-piece flow?	
iv. Has the *takt* time for production been considered in the partitioning of the product into subassemblies?	
v. Has the existing capability of manufacturing cells been considered in the product's design?	
vi. Do any manufacturing processes require new training?	
vii. Have fasteners and other minor parts been minimized?	
viii. Has the product been designed for top-down or single-orientation processing and assembly?	
ix. Are common components and tools used wherever possible?	
x. Is there adequate hand / tool access for each assembly operation?	
xi. Have all critical-to-quality steps in the manufacturing process been identified and optimized?	
xii. Have parts using similar processes been "grouped" to be manufactured in a single workcell?	
xiii. Has the ambiguity been taken out of assembly steps (e.g., avoiding parts that can be oriented in several ways)?	
xiv. Has the physical movement of material been minimized for the fabrication of this product?	
xv. Has the use of hazardous materials been minimized?	
xvi. Have Failure Modes and Effects Analysis (FMEA) sessions been performed on the design, process, etc.?	

Figure 5.9 – (Continued)

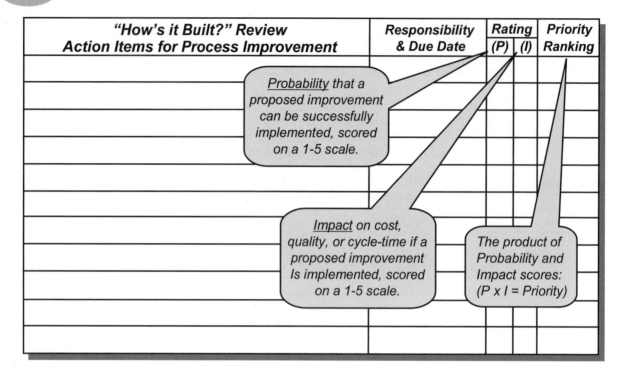

Figure 5.10 – Your HB Review is not complete until a detailed set of action items has been assigned. Opportunities for process improvements should be gathered in a brainstorming session, and then ranked in importance using the two-variable scoring system shown above.

See how easy that was? A "surgical-strike" approach to achieving product and process co-development, and ultimately, product cost optimization. Undeniably, it would be better if product and process designers held hands throughout the product development process, anticipating each other's needs and rubbing each other's shoulders. Assuming that this little slice of heaven isn't happening in your firm, the "How's it Built?" Review can begin the process of breaking down barriers and getting people on both sides of the design fence to understand each other a little better.

Section 5.4 — The "Seven-Alternatives" Process

One of the best techniques to come out of the Toyota 3P methodology is something called the "Seven-Alternatives" Process, as summarized in Figure 5.11. Yes, I know, we have been generating alternatives for better than half of this guidebook. This is certainly not the time to turn off our innovation engines, however. One of the most significant factors in the success or failure of a new product is the cost of capital equipment. Recall that this non-recurring investment must be paid back during the market life of the product. Hence, it is easy for your initial capital investment (e.g., tooling, fixtures, material-handling equipment, machines, etc.) to eat up all of your profits. The wrong choices here could render the rest of your cost-reduction efforts fruitless.

To avoid just such a catastrophe, Toyota introduced a technique that forces the tradeoff of several (actually seven to be exact) possible manufacturing processes for each high-cost / high-capital design element. Why seven? You'll have to ask your local Toyota dealership, but seven seems to work quite well. When should you use this technique? It could be incorporated into the "How's it Built?" Review described in Section 5.3, but it *should* be employed shortly before the approval of major product-specific capital expenditures.

Before we move on, I have a little brainteaser for you. Please take a moment to consider one of the following simple design elements (whichever is the most familiar to you): a) a hollow metal cylinder with one closed end, b) a box-like plastic enclosure, c) an electronic circuit element, or d) a mechanical fastener used for final assembly. For the element you've chosen, make a list of as many possible fabrication processes as you can think of. Don't let prejudices get in your way; any method that will yield the desired design element should be listed. Can you come up with seven alternatives?

The Multivariable World of Capital Optimization

Life is full of tradeoffs. Do we invest in robotic automation or set up a manual assembly line? Would product-specific fixturing pay for itself over the life of our new product? Is there some way to avoid six-figure investments in molds or dies? For a given product, there are a number of variables that must be considered to optimize product-specific capital investment. They include:

5.4

"At a Glance" – The "Seven-Alternatives" Process

Overview –
Quick and powerful approach to reducing the cost of dedicated capital equipment and tooling, or for resolving yield, cycle-time, or other manufacturability issues. A small team is assembled to generate at least six alternatives to the baseline manufacturing process for any costly or troublesome design element. These alternatives are then qualitatively evaluated, and promising options are selected for a more detailed cost tradeoff analysis.

Primary Benefits –
Great way to foster "out-of-the-box" thinking among product and process designers.
Can lead to dramatic reduction in expenditures for dedicated capital, tooling, fixtures, etc.

Best Suited Products –
This tool can be used for any product type, but is best suited to discrete manufacturing.

Advantages –
Value-added will almost certainly be worth the time spent. Can make the difference between a profitable product and a non-starter.

Disadvantages –
No real disadvantages, provided that enough time is taken with promising alternatives to perform some fairly accurate cost tradeoffs before a choice of manufacturing process is made.

Impact on the Twenty Cost Levers –

I. Direct Labor				II. Direct Materials				III. Capital				IV. Design Cost				V. Overhead			
1a	1b	1c	1d	2a	2b	2c	2d	3a	3b	3c	3d	4a	4b	4c	4d	5a	5b	5c	5d
●	●	●	◉	◉	○	○	○	●	●	●	●		○		●	◉		●	◉

Figure 5.11 – "At-a-glance" overview of the "Seven-Alternatives" Process tool for reduction of product-specific capital investment.

- The total estimated volume that will be produced over the product's market life.
- The critical tolerances that will determine yield.
- The physical properties that will determine performance.
- The labor hours required for the selected processes.
- The cost of equipment repair and maintenance, and replacement of consumables.
- The wear-out life of each machine, tool, or fixture being considered (in number of units produced before replacement or refurbishment).
- The approximate non-recurring cost of capital equipment for each process under consideration.
- The impact on the factory (e.g., layout, power availability, environmental controls, etc.) for each process option being considered.

I know this is a daunting list. As usual, we will avoid the "complexity trap" by using rough estimates for the data listed above. Before we perform our cost tradeoffs, however, we need to scrounge up those pesky alternatives.

A smaller team can be used for the "Seven-Alternatives" Process meeting than was necessary for the HB Review; just the core design team and perhaps a few process experts (such as those folks on the shop floor who actually know *just about everything*). How much time you allocate depends on the number of cost-saving opportunities, the magnitude of capital investment, and the complexity of the production process. Typically, a half-day is about right for a product of average complexity and a capital requisition of moderate scale. The general process to be followed is shown in Figure 5.12, but I'm reluctant to make this another "agenda-with-firm-time-limits" tool. There is so much money to be saved using this technique that as long as the discussion is moving forward, I would give the group all the time it needs.

Start with your capital equipment list for the new product being developed. Establish a baseline approach for each process under consideration that seems the most plausible at the time of the meeting, and estimate the investment required for each baseline option. Now for each process step that requires significant capital investment, brainstorm with the group to identify at least seven alternatives (six new options plus the baseline). Note that reduction of capital investment is not necessarily the only focus of the "Seven-Alternatives" Process. Other possibilities include reduction of scrap, improvement of

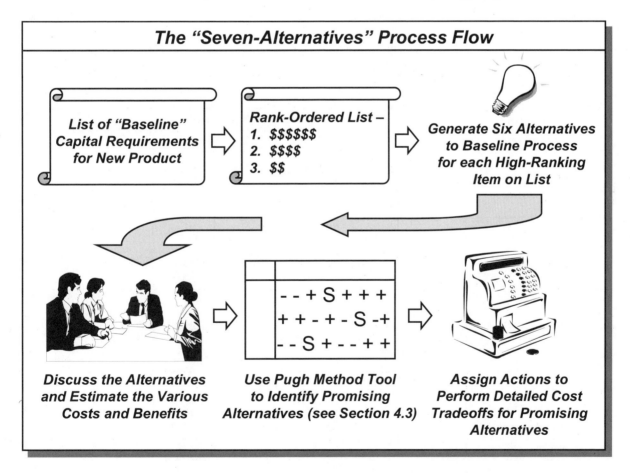

Figure 5.12 – The steps necessary to execute a "Seven-Alternatives" Process meeting. Note that the agenda should be kept loose; with good facilitation, the group will tend to naturally gravitate toward the most important capital-reduction opportunities.

5.4

quality, reduction of touch labor, reduction of floor-space requirements, elimination of hazardous materials, and so on. Naturally, your choice of focus should be driven by the nature of your product and the relative costs involved.

I must pause here to make a critical point. The success of the above brainstorming on process alternatives vitally depends on the process knowledge of your team. If team members are not aware of an alternative, it can't be considered. There are some relatively obscure manufacturing techniques that can prove to be godsends when the conditions are appropriate. Moreover, process technology is changing at an ever-increasing rate, so even if your internal expertise was world-class a few years ago, it may be ready for a booster shot. Although there are a number of books that can help in this regard (see my recommendations at the end of Parts V and VI), the most current information will come from trade publications. If you read about a promising new process in one of the trade freebees, contact the supplier and request their design rules and process-capability data. You might even consider creating a process-tradeoff database to capture the benefits and costs of each applicable process alternative. However you accomplish it, your process vocabulary should continuously improve over time.

Once you have chosen seven alternatives from your brainstorming session, you are ready to do some evaluation. At the beginning of this section, I asked you to come up with seven process options for producing some relatively simple design elements. Compare your

Design Element	Process Alternatives						
	1	2	3	4	5	6	7
Metal Cylinder with Bottom	Deep-Drawn	Cut From Tube Stock & Welded	Milled from Solid Bar Stock	Rolled from Sheet Stock & Welded	Liquid Metal Injection Molded	Sand Cast	Die Cast
Plastic Enclosure	Injection Molded	Compression Molded	Vacuum Formed	Structural Foam Molded	Welded from Sheet Stock	Milled from Solid Stock	Extruded and Machined
Electronic Circuit	Single-Layer Printed Circuit Board (PCB)	Multilayer PCB	Flexible PCB	Wirewrap Circuit Board	Multi-chip Module	Surface Mount vs. Through-Hole	Application Specific Integrated Circuit (ASIC)
Mechanical Fastener for Final Assembly	Screws	Pins	Clips	Barbs	Captive-Nut Fasteners	Rivets	Velcro

Figure 5.13 – Seven alternative processes for the manufacture of a metal cylinder, a plastic enclosure, an electronic circuit, and a mechanical fastener used for final assembly.

answers with those provided in Figure 5.13. If you scan across the process alternatives for each design element, you will likely recognize considerable differences among them. Tooling costs can be dramatically different, quality levels can vary, in some cases secondary processing might be needed to complete the desired part. These and other factors must be considered in your tradeoff analysis.

Before we continue, I must say a few words about subjective ranking tools. At this point, you have been exposed to a number of variations on the same theme: "Come up with alternatives and rank them using some hair-brained scoring method that the author suggests." Moreover, you've probably noticed that the schemes I recommend change from tool to tool. In some cases I've used a ten-point scale, in some cases a "+ / -" scale, sometimes a weighting factor is included, other times not. It's enough to make you think that I'm being highly subjective about subjective scoring.

Actually, there is method to my madness; scoring schemes should be tailored to the level of granularity needed for a specific ranking chore, as shown in Figure 5.14. If all you are interested in is a quick relative ranking of options, the scales shown near the top of the figure will work just fine. As the degree of desired "accuracy" increases, so does the time and difficulty required to gain a consensus from a group. Which scoring strategy you choose is really up to you and your team. For example, I don't see why you couldn't substitute the scheme of your dreams in any of the tools described in this guidebook. Just follow two general rules: 1) always choose a scoring system that reflects the amount of detailed information available (i.e., less accurate scoring when less information is on hand), and 2) don't waste time trying to turn a subjective tool into a quantitative one.

Now back to our regularly scheduled example. The tool I've selected to evaluate our process options is a modification of the Pugh Method that was discussed in Section 4.3, as shown in Figure 5.15. I've entered the seven alternative processes from the "plastic enclosure" row of Figure 5.13 to illustrate how the ranking proceeds. Along the left-hand column, a number of critical tradeoff factors are listed. Although the ones I've suggested are a good starting point, the list your team uses should be based on your specific manufacturing circumstances. The goal of this step in the "Seven-Alternatives" Process is to quickly identify whether any of the six new process alternatives have a chance of besting the baseline. Hence, using the very qualitative Pugh Method makes sense in this context. To provide just a bit more resolution to our ranking, however, I've allowed for "++" and "- -" scores that communicate extreme agreement or disagreement with each tradeoff factor. It might also make sense for you to add a weighting-factors column to the matrix; as always, don't be afraid to modify the tool to suit your personal preferences.

Once the pluses and minuses are totaled, we look for alternatives that received the highest net positive scores. Since this is a very rough ranking tool, choices such as Alternative #2 in the figure are essentially a wash with the baseline (these might deserve further consideration if there is some compelling reason to move away from the baseline process). One choice, Alternative #7, stands out as having significant cost-saving potential. At this point in your "Seven-Alternatives" Process meeting, you can adjourn; you have identified a promising option to pursue further.

A Hierarchy of Subjective Scoring Techniques

Decreasing "Accuracy" ↑

- Yes / No Guesstimate
- Relative scoring using "+", "-", and "S" (Pugh Method)
- Relative scoring using "++", "+", "S", "-", "--"
- Relative scoring using "+", "-", "S", plus weighting factors
- Relative scoring using a numerical scale from –5 to +5
- Relative scoring using a –5 to +5 scale, plus weighting factors
- Absolute scoring using semi-quantitative metrics on a 1–10 scale
- Absolute scoring using quantitative metrics on normalized scale

Increasing Time and Difficulty ↓

Figure 5.14 – Subjective scoring techniques span a broad range; from simple guesstimates to much more detailed and semi-quantitative schemes. The approach you select should be based on the amount of information available and the degree of "accuracy" you wish to achieve. Don't waste people's time, however, trying to make a subjective ranking into a quantitative one.

The final step in the "Seven-Alternatives" Process is the most intimidating, yet it need not be a roadblock, provided that you follow the example shown in Figure 5.16. You must now (drum-roll please) calculate the estimated cost of the promising process alternative and compare it to the baseline. The potentially scary part is that capital investment decisions will be based upon your results. Fortunately, however, extreme accuracy is not required, since the whole point of the "Seven-Alternatives" Process is to identify process alternatives that offer *significant* savings. If two processes are even close to each other in cost, you should go with the low-risk, well-understood choice (typically the baseline). If the potential savings are dramatic, then the calculation I've provided in the figure should give you all the accuracy you'll need. Nonetheless, it is worthwhile to have your financial and operations people validate your calculations.

Let's walk through the example in Figure 5.16. The cost factors that I believe are the most critical are listed at the top of the figure. Your specific situation may warrant inclusion of additional parameters, but don't neglect the ones I've identified. Starting from the top, non-recurring engineering may be required to design a tool or fixture, or at a minimum, to interface with an outside toolmaker or equipment supplier. Naturally, we must consider the cost of tooling and equipment in our tradeoff calculation, but it is also

Design Element – Plastic Enclosure	Process Alternatives						
	1	2	3	4	5	6	7
Critical Tradeoff Factors	Injection Molded (Baseline)	Com-pression Molded	Vacuum Formed	Structural Foam Molded	Welded from Sheet Stock	Milled from Solid Stock	Extruded and Machined
1. Helps to meet takt time goals	Baseline Process	-	-	-	-	-	S
2. Supports one-piece flow		S	S	S	S	S	S
3. Minimal touch-labor		S	-	S	- -	- -	-
4. Poke-Yoke (error-proofing)		-	- -	S	-	S	S
5. Requires minimal new equipment		+	-	S	+	+	S
6. Quality / accuracy of output		- -	- -	-	-	+	S
7. Minimal tooling lead-time		+	+	S	+	+ +	+
8. Rapid setup and changeover		+	S	S	+	S	+
9. Minimal tool-room maintenance		S	S	S	+	-	S
10. Minimal tooling cost		+ +	+ +	+	+ +	+ +	+ +
11. Not dangerous, dirty, or difficult		S	S	S	- -	-	S
12. As simple as possible		+	+	S	- -	-	S
13. Equipment is readily available		S	S	S	S	S	S
14. Process is low-risk or known		-	-	S	S	S	S
15. Minimal maintenance is needed		S	S	S	-	-	S
16. Requires minimal time to develop		S	S	S	S	S	S
POSITIVE SCORES	N/A	6	4	1	6	6	(4)
NEGATIVE SCORES	N/A	5	8	2	10	7	1

Figure 5.15 – A continuation of the example provided in Figure 5.13. The "plastic enclosure" set of seven alternative processes has been expanded into a Pugh Method tradeoff matrix. Note that only Alternative #7 stands out as being worthy of further consideration.

5.4

important to compare the number of units that can be produced before the capital investment must be replaced. Is it possible that some "secondary" capital equipment will be required to support the primary investment (e.g., racks, benches, conveyers, etc.)? What about the labor cost of installation and initial setup? All of these costs must be considered in your calculation.

The factors I've described so far represent the non-recurring cost elements of a manufacturing process choice. On the recurring side, we must consider the relative impact each process alternative will have on direct labor and materials. The most important cost tradeoff will usually involve direct labor versus tooling / equipment costs (as would be the case for an investment in process automation). Material costs should not be overlooked, however, particularly if one of the process choices creates significantly higher waste or scrap. Finally, the cost of maintenance should be considered. This represents an overhead charge for most firms, but since it has to be paid for somehow, it should be included in your tradeoff calculation. Often the maintenance cost is so low that it can be ignored. This is not always true, however, particularly with touchy new processes, so keep the term in your calculation and neglect it if it's small.

Now we sum the costs for each alternative (see the middle portion of Figure 5.16). Note that I've included a term for "recurring capital cost." This reflects the limited life of most tooling and equipment. If the total production volume for your product exceeds a tool's use-life, another big chunk of capital must be expended to replace it. This is illustrated in the example I've provided: the tooling cost for the baseline process dwarfs that of Alternative #7, but the baseline tooling can yield ten times as many acceptable products before replacement. Ultimately, this proves to be the deciding factor between the two alternative processes, as can be seen in the lower right-hand corner of the figure. At low-to-moderate volumes, Alternative #7 would be an excellent choice, primarily due to the low tooling cost. This savings outweighs the significantly higher direct labor cost until production quantities approach 50,000 units. At these volumes, the baseline finally comes into its own, after the monstrous capital investment has been sufficiently diluted. Hence, your choice of process in this case is straightforward...all you need is an accurate market forecast. As I've mentioned previously, beware of optimistic forecasts when it comes to making capital decisions. If you underestimate total production volume and choose a process based on that conservative number, you really can't go too far wrong. If you overestimate total production volume, however, and justify your capital investments accordingly, *your firm could lose a fortune.*

Cost Tradeoff Calculation for Process Alternatives

Alternative #1 – (Baseline) Plastic Injection Molding

Non-recurring Engineering – $10,000
Tooling Cost (per mold) – $250,000
Estimated Tool Life – 50,000 units
New Equipment Cost – $30,000
Installation Cost – $10,000
Recurring Labor Cost – $5.00 per unit
Recurring Material Cost – $2.00 per unit
Maintenance Cost – $ 0.10 per unit

Alternative #7 – Extruded & Machined

Non-recurring Engineering – $7000
Tooling Cost (per die) – $5000
Estimated Tool Life – 10,000 units
New Equipment Cost – $30,000
Installation Cost – $10,000
Recurring Labor Cost – $11.00 per unit
Recurring Material Cost – $2.00 per unit
Maintenance Cost – $ 0.20 per unit

Non-recurring (NR) Labor –
  $10,000 + $10,000 = $20,000
Non-recurring Capital –
  $250,000 + $30,000 = $280,000
Recurring Labor Cost –
  $5.00 + $ 0.10 = $5.10
Recurring Materials Cost –
  $2.00
Recurring Capital Cost –
  Occurs at volumes greater than 50,000 units*

Non-recurring (NR) Labor –
  $7,000 + $10,000 = $17,000
Non-recurring Capital –
  $5000 + $30,000 = $35,000
Recurring Labor Cost –
  $11.00 + $ 0.20 = $11.20
Recurring Materials Cost –
  $2.00
Recurring Capital Cost –
  Occurs at volumes greater than 10,000 units*

Alternative #1 –
  Recurring Cost per Unit =
  $5.10 + $2.00 = $7.10
  Allocation of NR Cost per Unit* =
  ($280,000 + $20,000) / No. of Units

Alternative #7 –
  Recurring Cost per Unit =
  $11.20 + $2.00 = $13.20
  Allocation of NR Cost per Unit* =
  ($35,000 + $17,000) / No. of Units

	Cost per Unit at the Following Production Volumes		
	5000	20,000	50,000
Alt. #1	$67.10	$22.10	$13.10
Alt. #7	$23.60	$16.05	$14.64

Figure 5.16 – A sample calculation of the relative cost of two process alternatives: a baseline process and a promising option derived from the "Seven-Alternatives" Process. Note that this is a continuation of the example shown in Figure 5.15.

5.4

Make vs. Buy – A "Mandatory" Alternative

Once while I was teaching a workshop at a large aerospace firm, the subject of make vs. buy came up. The cross-functional audience had lots of questions about when it is best to outsource, and held many misconceptions about the benefits and disbenefits thereof. During the discussion that followed, the critical importance of considering outsourcing (at all levels of the product, from basic parts to entire assemblies) as a process alternative was highlighted. What was most striking to me, however, was the audience's response to a simple question. I asked, innocently enough, "Who within your firm is responsible for make vs. buy decisions?" The first response came from the procurement folks: "We don't make those decisions. It's dictated to us on the bill-of-materials before we begin getting quotes and selecting suppliers."

Next, the operations people spoke up: "Usually, we get involved if there is a capacity or capability issue, but we don't have the final say." A familiar pattern was beginning to emerge.

After probing further, it became clear that this firm did not have a viable make vs. buy decision process. These critical choices were made in some ad hoc way, often driven by personal bias, history, habit, and of course, incorrect assumptions. Unfortunately, it is beyond the scope of this guidebook to help you develop such a process if your firm is similarly lacking. You can easily fill this void, however, at least on a temporary basis, by insisting that outsourcing be considered every time you employ the "Seven-Alternatives" Process. In fact, outsourcing might prove to be a good choice to use as the baseline process, since it is the easiest to quantify from a cost standpoint.

Let me be very clear that outsourcing is not always a good idea. There has been much hype in the literature about "virtual manufacturing" and "horizontal integration." As with most things related to business, there is no right or wrong answer; the only correct answer is "it depends." A good rule-of-thumb is that any part which is not well-aligned with the current manufacturing capabilities of your factory should be outsourced. Yet even this "rule" is not valid much of the time; you really need to do the tradeoff on a case-by-case basis.

To assist you in this analysis, I've provided in Figure 5.17 some legitimate reasons why firms should make a part versus procuring it from an outside supplier. The most common justification for keeping a part in-house is that it is "strategic." Again, this word is often misused. Some legitimate situations that indicate a design element *might* be "strategic" include:

- The item provides a clear competitive advantage for your product.
- The item contains proprietary or competition-sensitive information.
- Making the item helps justify a major capital investment.
- Making the item significantly contributes to your firm's profit goals.
- The item represents a critical factor in forming an alliance or joint venture.
- Making the item is necessary to protect the company's reputation.

The Make vs. Buy Tradeoff

Reasons to "Make"

- It is cheaper to make the part than to buy it.
- There is capacity available to make the part.
- The part requires unique expertise to fabricate.
- The part's design is changing rapidly.
- The part contains proprietary knowledge.
- The possible suppliers for the part are not acceptable.
- Transporting the part would be too costly.
- The process technology involved supports your factory's core process competencies.

Reasons to "Buy"

- It is cheaper to buy the part, when all costs are considered.
- There is no capacity currently available.
- Significant capital investment is required.
- Demand fluctuates dramatically.
- Internal expertise does not exist.
- Process involves hazardous materials.
- Process technology is improving rapidly, requiring continuous reinvestment.

Figure 5.17 – Advantages and disadvantages of making a design element versus purchasing it from a supplier. Note that any high-cost / high-capital item should be reviewed for make vs. buy, unless the item is clearly "strategic."

You don't have to throw around the "S" word to justify in-house production, however. There are other perfectly valid reasons to make, the most compelling of which is that it will enhance your new product's net profitability. If, after going through the pros and cons, your team agrees that outsourcing is at least a possibility, include it in your "Seven-Alternatives" Process. You might be surprised how attractive this option may appear once all the costs are considered. In one recent case, a firm was facing into a $2.5 million capital requisition for product-specific equipment and tooling. After performing the "Seven-Alternatives" Process, the outsource option appeared the most promising. When the cost calculations were done, it turned out that by choosing buy over make, the firm could reduce its capital expenditure by *two million dollars.* Not bad pay for a day's work.

Notes

References

Part V

Recommendations for Further Learning

Unfortunately, there are not many published accounts of the Toyota 3P process. At the time of this writing, it is still primarily the domain of scholars and consultants. However, the books I've recommended below should provide the reader with enough details to support the tools described in Part V. If you wish to learn more about lean manufacturing in general, just search on Amazon.com and you'll find a host of useful resources. I've highlighted some lesser-known works that I think deserve your time and attention.

Lean Manufacturing

(Note: See also the reference under "Toyota 3P Process.")

★★★★★ *The New Manufacturing Challenge,* Suzaki, K., 1987

I know it may seem slightly dated, but I just love this book. It was the first book I read when I began researching lean manufacturing, and it is still the only one I use on a regular basis. Clear, concise, humble, and readable; just an all-around great reference without all of the buzzword hype.

★★★★★ *Quick Response Manufacturing,* Suri, R., 1998

This is really a landmark book on high-velocity, low-waste production, and the author didn't even put the word "lean" in the title! Particularly useful if you are struggling with a high-mix production environment.

APQP Process

★★★★ *Advanced Quality Planning: A Commonsense Guide to AQP and APQP,* Stamatis, D. H., 1998

The APQP is as close to a "standard" product development process as you're likely to find. I don't necessarily endorse the process as a whole, but if the reader were to do a little intelligent tailoring, you should find yourself with an excellent methodology for product and process co-development.

Toyota 3P Process

***** ***The Toyota Way,*** Liker, J. K., 2003

This book is hot off the presses as of this writing, and its one of the best available on how Toyota works its magic. Not only a fine account of lean manufacturing "best practices" but also some excellent tips on the product development front.

Manufacturability Reviews (The "How's it Built?" Review)

***** ***Product Design Review,*** Ichida, T., 1996

This is a practical guidebook, and I mean that in the sense that the book you are holding is a practical guidebook. The author provides templates, step-by-step instructions, checklists, and agendas for a wide range of design reviews, including manufacturability reviews.

**** ***The Kaizen Blitz,*** Laraia, C., Moody, P. E., and R. W. Hall, 1999

This is a nice how-to book on the execution of a successful *kaizen* event (a format which can easily be co-opted for use in manufacturability improvement). I like the positive "can-do" tone, and the practical advice from experienced practitioners.

Developing Process Alternatives

(Note: See also references suggested under "Design for Manufacture and Assembly" in Figure 6.24 of Section 6.3.)

***** ***Tool and Manufacturing Engineers Handbook (series),*** Society of Manufacturing Engineers (SME)

This series, with a volume on each major category of manufacturing process, is the most doggone valuable set of texts you could hope to find. A tremendous resource for developing process alternatives, and a mandatory read for anyone serious about optimizing manufacturing cost.

Performing Cost Tradeoff Calculations

***** ***Target Costing and Kaizen Costing,*** Monden, Y., 1995

Just in case I didn't scare you away from performing those daunting tradeoff calculations, here is a reference that can shed some light on the topic. As with all of his books, Monden has made a complex topic approachable.

Part VI

Attack Direct Costs During Detailed Design

6.1 - What's a Process Capability?

6.2 - Six-Sigma / Robust Design

6.3 - Design for Manufacture and Assembly (DFMA)

6.4 - Achieving Continuous Cost Improvement

Part VI

> "We succeed in enterprises which demand the positive qualities we possess, but we excel in those which can also make use of our defects."
>
> Alexis de Tocqueville

> "People never improve unless they look to some standard or example higher and better than themselves."
>
> Tryon Edwards

> "Small opportunities are often the beginning of great enterprises."
>
> Demosthenes

Section 6.1 — What's a Process Capability?

It's been a long journey. We began our lean-design sojourn by proving our product's worth during initial project selection and prioritization, and were rewarded with a core development team and a target cost. Throughout our wanderings, customers have spoken to us, warning us away from pitfalls and showing us the pathway to enlightenment (or at least to market success). The very form of our product has been transformed along the way, from a stubbornly unique individual into a symbiotic contributor to our firm's profit-generating system, sharing parts, processes, raw materials, and capital equipment with its peers. We've feasted at banquets of design and process alternatives, thereby nourishing customer value while keeping much of our gold in our pockets. What more could be expected of a weary adventurer?

Rest not, my itinerate designer; there are still miles (or at least a few dozen more pages) to go before you sleep. Finally, finally, finally, we have arrived at the detailed-design stage of your new product. Certainly, many of the tools and ideas that will be described in Part VI could and should be employed earlier in the development process. They are, however, the most product-specific, detailed tools in this guidebook, so although the chronology may not be precise, this set of topics represents a logical place to bring our journey to a close. Of course, the end of a journey through lean product design means the beginning of a very different adventure; one that will yield bounty for years to come if we've been faithful to our quest for cost reduction.

Waging Battle Against Our Sworn Enemy – Variability

Here's a quick test of your manufacturing I.Q. What is the one type of design element that suffers absolutely zero variability when produced in quantity? No, it's certainly not hardware; there is no type of hardware in the world that can be manufactured without at least some variability. It isn't electronics either. Everything about an electronic circuit has the potential for variability, from the tolerances of passive components to differences in delay times and noise levels from one integrated circuit to another. What about chemicals, pharmaceuticals, household detergents, and so on? Despite their best efforts, continuous-process manufacturers must fight a daily battle against variability in raw materials and process parameters. Give up? The only design element that can be reproduced indefinitely with zero variability is *digital media*: software, digital video, graphics, etc. Everything else is subject to change without notice.

6.1

Now it is certainly true that the variability in some products is so low as to be virtually undetectable. It would be rather hard to observe the variability among batches of a prescription drug, but it's there, just a few decimal places to the right of the zero. Moreover, the variability in a product might not make the slightest difference to customers. I'm sure that there is noticeable variability in the solder joints within your DVD player, but as long as the product works properly, who cares? Hence, we can begin to put words to our struggle with variability:

Manufacturing variability must be controlled to a level that ensures both customer satisfaction and cost-optimized production.

Hopefully, if we've done a good job thus far in our lean design process, the customer satisfaction portion of the above mandate is neatly embedded in our product specifications, test and inspection guidelines, and quality assurance procedures. But do we have the same assurance that our product can be produced to those standards at optimal cost? Any product can be produced to essentially any standards, provided that money is no object. How can quality be guaranteed while still aggressively pursuing profits? In other words, can we control variability on a budget?

First, let's take a look at how variability drives product cost. Since every manufacturing process has variability, the development team for a new product must specify a design tolerance for each critical-to-quality attribute. For now, let's assume that they have done their best to make the product design "robust," meaning that tolerances are as accommodating as possible of manufacturing variations (we'll come back to this topic later). How do the manufacturing folks respond to these specified design tolerances? They consider various process alternatives from a standpoint of "precision" and "accuracy"(or whatever passes for these metrics in your industry), and select the best option. Here's the tricky part, however. How do they make that selection? They can't just go with the most accurate process out there; it will likely cost a fortune. It is also unreasonable for them to go with a cheap-and-dirty process that can't come close to holding the required tolerances. There must be a happy medium in which the yield of acceptable product is balanced with the cost of equipment, training, and so on: A tradeoff of defect cost versus process cost.

This struggle with variability is illustrated in Figure 6.1. For simplicity, let's consider a manufacturing process whose statistical variability displays a "bell-shaped" (i.e., standard normal) distribution. If we've set up our process correctly, the center of the distribution should coincide with the nominal value specified for our product. As we move outward from the nominal value, a steadily decreasing number of units will display variability of a steadily increasing magnitude. This behavior becomes decidedly antisocial when parts begin showing variations that go beyond the upper or lower specification limits for the product. Anything produced beyond these limits must be rejected, and either relegated to the scrap bin or sent back through the process line for rework.

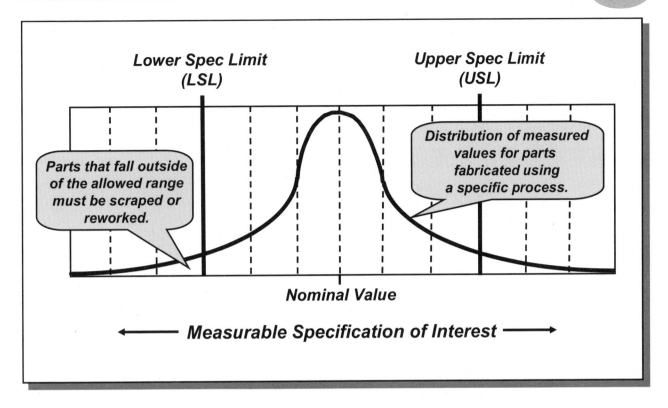

Figure 6.1 – A typical variability distribution for a manufacturing process step. Note that parts whose actual measurements fall outside of the "upper-spec-limit / lower-spec-limit" range represent quality defects (i.e., scrap).

What is most interesting about the diagram in Figure 6.1 is that it clearly illustrates the tradeoff that we must address. If our goal is to reduce or eliminate scrap (and all of the wasted time and money it represents), then there are actually *two ways we can go about it*. We could tighten the variability distribution of the process (i.e., the ability of the process to hold tolerances), or we could loosen the tolerances of the design. Either action would tend to reduce the number of units that fall into the scrap regions of the distribution.

Before describing how to perform this tradeoff, I'll introduce some formal metrics of process variability. Manufacturing engineers recognize that extreme precision is not what's critical to cost-effective, high-quality production. What is essential is that each process be *capable*, meaning that the ability of the process to hold tolerances has been properly matched to the specified tolerance ranges of the design. This process capability can be represented by a statistical metric called the *Process Capability Ratio* (C_p), as described in Figure 6.2. Somewhat arbitrarily, the manufacturing engineering folks have defined C_p as the ratio of the total tolerance band of a given specification (i.e., the upper spec limit minus the lower spec limit), to six times the standard deviation of the process' variability distribution. For those of you who took probability and statistics as a summer

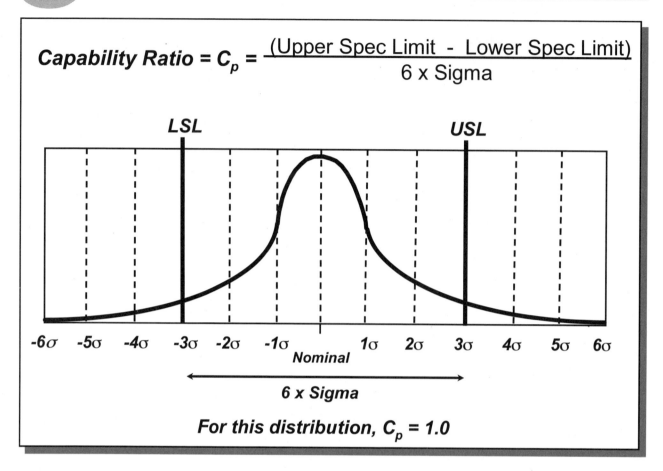

Figure 6.2 – The definition of the Process Capability Ratio (C_p), shown in both equation and graphical form. Note that, somewhat arbitrarily, $C_p = 1.0$ defines a "capable" process. Despite this rather self-assured definition, a "capable" process will still generate a significant number of quality defects.

course, the standard deviation is a measure of the "width" of a statistical distribution. Larger standard deviations (usually symbolized by the Greek letter "sigma" or σ) indicate a broader variability distribution; smaller ones signify a tighter distribution. So C_p is really just a measure of the width of the variability distribution as compared to the acceptance band of the product.

You might be wondering why the denominator of the C_p ratio includes a "six-times" multiplier. Somewhere in the lost knowledge of the ages there must have been a reason. It certainly can't be justified by the statement that "a process with $C_p = 1$ is 'capable'." Perhaps in the past, a process with $C_p = 1$ would have been considered awesome, since a C_p of unity means that only 0.3% of units produced will be out of tolerance. But is this level of scrap acceptable today? Consider the following scenario. Assume that your entire factory can achieve $C_p = 1$ at every process step. This means that one in three hundred parts would be defective in each of, say, fifty process steps for a moderately complex product. Since the yield-loss of a product is multiplicative, the percentage of finished products that would pass through your factory without a defect would be roughly 86%. Back when the definition of C_p was established, this might have been considered an acceptable yield. Today, however, many industry sectors (most notably the automobile industry) are demanding essentially *zero defects*. Hence, to survive in our quality-obsessed age, firms have two choices: either significantly improve the process capabilities of their factories or do a whole lot of expensive testing and inspection.

This mandate led one famous firm to develop an equally famous cost-reduction / quality-enhancement program, known as Six-Sigma Design. This powerful design methodology will be surveyed in Section 6.2. For now, let's see what might be required to get those yields up. As C_p increases, the yield of quality parts increases, as shown in Figure 6.3. Since the number of defects falls off asymptotically (i.e., very fast, for the non-mathematicians), we don't need to improve C_p much beyond unity to achieve significantly lower scrap percentages. In fact, if we could match our process capabilities to our product tolerances in such a way that we achieve $C_p = 2$, our defect rate would be vanishingly small. So small, in fact, that we could virtually eliminate testing and inspection – every product produced would be a winner!

To illustrate this concept, let's consider the silly example shown in Figure 6.4. Suppose you are a do-it-yourselfer with more ambition than ability. Your spouse, who has an unrealistically high opinion of your capabilities, asks you to make a nice piece of furniture for your home. Full of enthusiasm, you rush to your workshop, only to discover that your precision table saw is covered with junk (a common condition in my garage). Rather than taking the time to clean it off and tune it up, you pull out your chainsaw and start cutting pieces for your spouse's dream cabinet. Needless to say, the yield of acceptable parts for your project will be humiliatingly low. Embarrassed but not defeated, you decide

Process Capability Ratio (C_p)	Percentage of Parts Outside of Specification Limits
0.50	13.36%
0.67	4.55%
1.00	0.30%
1.33	64 parts-per-million
1.66	~ 1 part-per-million
2.00	~ 4 parts-per-billion

Figure 6.3 – The percentage of parts produced by a process step that would be considered defective, as a function of the C_p of the process. Note that the defect rate drops exponentially as C_p increases. At $C_p = 2.0$, the scrap rate is essentially zero.

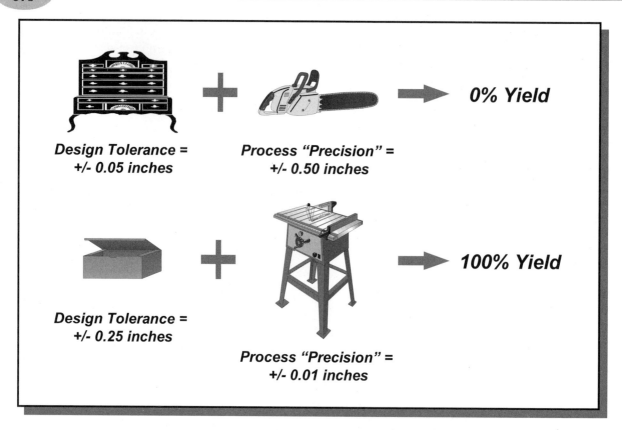

Figure 6.4 – An exaggerated example of how the matching of design tolerances to process capabilities (the ability of a manufacturing process to hold tolerances) can affect the yield of high-quality products.

that perhaps a more modest project would better suit your abilities. You decide to try building a simple wooden box with a loose-fitting lid, and to increase your probability of success, you clean off your table saw and start cutting lumber. Now things go much better; whereas the chainsaw had a very low process capability when applied to a Queen Anne cabinet, your table saw has an extremely high process capability when applied to a loose-tolerance box.

All of this capability stuff will come home to roost in the next section. For now, just a few important observations about the matching of process capabilities to product tolerances. First, note that the definition of C_p incorporates both product information and process information. In other words, it is meaningless for a manufacturing engineer to state that a process is "capable" without linking it to a specific product. Although a chainsaw is wholly inadequate to produce fine furniture, it is more than capable of cutting down a tree. Second, remember that C_p can be improved by either relaxing product tolerances *or* by narrowing the variability distribution of the process, as shown in Figure 6.5. Which of these is easier to do? Naturally, it depends on the product and the process, but in general, it is much easier and cheaper to find innovative ways to relax product tolerances than to buy higher-precision equipment. Finally, it is important to recognize that although every manufacturing process has variability, not all processes will have nice, smooth, bell-shaped distributions. Processes that experience the wear of cutting tools over time, for example, will display a skewed variability distribution. Low-rate production processes with relatively low statistics might have variability distributions that are all over the map: if you only produce a few units per month, the statistical error will be very high. Moreover, many manufacturing processes involve manual labor (with all the human error that entails). What does variability mean in that context? What kind of distribution might manual assembly display, and how would we calculate its C_p? These questions and more will be addressed by the legendary Six-Sigma Design methodology described in the next section.

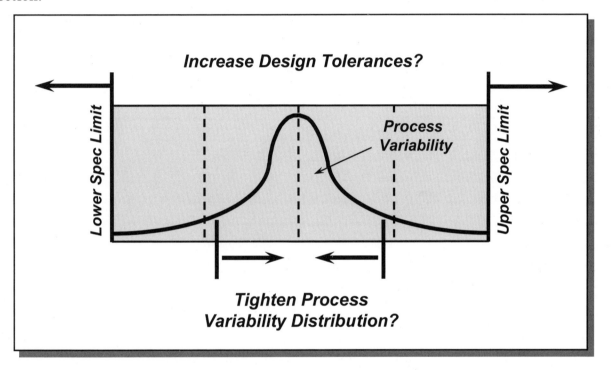

Figure 6.5 – A reminder that the number of manufacturing defects caused by process variability can be reduced by either relaxing a product's design tolerances or by tightening the process' ability to hold tolerances.

Notes

Section 6.2 — Six-Sigma / Robust Design

In the world of product cost reduction, the methods of Six-Sigma Design (also known as Design for Six-Sigma, or DFSS) are by far the deepest, richest, and most broadly deployed. This presents a daunting challenge for yours truly; condensing this huge body of work into a meaningful few pages makes me feel like the ant that climbed up the tail of an elephant with sex on its mind. Nonetheless, I will accept the challenge...with a bit of explanation.

It is important to recognize that, unlike many of the other topics covered in this guidebook, there are *vast* resources out there supporting Six-Sigma Design. Books have been written at all levels, from basic to advanced. Consultants and trainers are available by the railcar-load, and unlike the typical clueless-MBA management consultants, most of these folks can deliver on what they promise. In fact, your firm may already have an infrastructure of so-called "blackbelts" and "greenbelts" who have been formally trained in these tools (there is even a pretty good chance you're a blackbelt yourself). Clearly, there are limited opportunities for me to add value to such a well-developed subject area.

One opportunity that does avail itself is the placing of Six-Sigma methods in their proper context relative to the pantheon of available tools for cost reduction. This is important, because as the Six-Sigma Design philosophy has evolved from its roots as a very specific approach to variability control and defect reduction, it has "absorbed" a number of unrelated but synergistic tools. This acquisitive behavior has been driven largely by consultancies that desired a more comprehensive toolset for their clients. Hence, the Six-Sigma approach of Motorola fame has expanded through mergers and acquisitions into a loosely connected behemoth. As additional tools and techniques have been added, the breadth of problem that can be solved has expanded at the expense of clarity and focus. Today, it is not unusual for a Six-Sigma Design training program to include Taguchi Methods (also known as Robust Design tools, a sophisticated offshoot of Six-Sigma), Failure Modes and Effects Analysis (FMEA), Design of Experiment (DOE), Statistical Process Control (SPC), and of late, an assortment of "lean" tools that allow Six-Sigma consultancies to hitch their wagon to the Lean Enterprise train. I will endeavor to organize and position the various tools within the Six-Sigma catchall, and provide the reader with a concise description of how each important tool works (both its benefits and limitations). A lean design tool, called the Six-Sigma Cost-Reduction Guide, will help you sort through the maze and get to the cheese.

6.2

Another opportunity for me to add to this party is in connecting Six-Sigma to the broader subject of product cost reduction. Six-Sigma has its roots in quality assurance, and although all quality issues ultimately impact cost, that relationship is not always clear. The ability to calculate the benefits of a Six-Sigma project is important, since in my experience only a fraction of blackbelt projects are deemed to be worth the investment by the firms that sponsor them. A second lean design tool, called the Cost-of-Poor-Quality Calculator, will help the reader to determine the potential cost benefits of applying Six-Sigma methods and to justify the investment such an activity would require.

Finally, I must mention that if you really are a Six-Sigma blackbelt, or at least a well-read practitioner, this section will provide you with limited new information. I hope you will scan it for context, but I won't be offended if you skip to the next topic. For the rest of you who are either vaguely familiar with (or intimidated by) Six-Sigma, the material that follows should break down barriers and give you a solid foundation for continued learning.

What is the Cost of Poor Quality?

The expression "quality is free," although catchy as heck, is something of a misnomer. Actually, it should be reworded to say "an investment in assuring appropriate levels of quality will pay itself back over the life of a product." Not a very good title for a book, but a more accurate statement to be sure. There is nothing free about validating and maintaining the capabilities of production processes, nor are tests and inspections performed by unpaid volunteers. Achieving market-satisfying quality may require using more expensive materials, more precise machines, and most important, a "robust" product design that can shake off manufacturing variability without working up a sweat. How does this investment pay dividends? The payback for excellent quality comes from a variety of sources, ranging from the tangible (e.g., reduction in wasted materials and labor caused by high scrap rates), to the more esoteric (e.g., improved market reputation and customer satisfaction).

In these enlightened times, the cost of poor quality (COPQ) has become a critical factor for most products. Market share is won and lost based on quality issues, and some industries will shun any firm with a less-than-stellar quality record. Designers are therefore faced with yet another challenge: How can quality be assured at the absolute minimum cost? The first step is to define as precisely as possible what quality levels are required for your product. Remember that it is possible to overshoot even on something as vital as quality. A personal computer that will function flawlessly for five years, for example, will satisfy most consumers. On the other hand, designing a PC that will keep crunching ones and zeros for a hundred years is clearly an overshoot; most customers wouldn't pay more for such extreme reliability. Quality (along with its time-based manifestation, reliability) represents yet another critical "function" of your new product. How this function is performed is up to the design team to determine, and there are, as always, several alternatives. The following is a quick survey of ways in which COPQ can be managed:

Option 1 – The product is produced with marginal quality. The negative effects of poor quality are then offset by an extended warranty and an appropriately low price.

Option 2 – The product receives 100% testing and inspection to all specifications that are of interest (or noticeable) to the customer.

Option 3 – The product receives partial testing and inspection, enabled by the application of Statistical Process Control (SPC) and lot-sampling techniques.

Option 4 – The product receives virtually no testing or inspection, made possible through the application of Six-Sigma Design principles.

Each of these options has its benefits and drawbacks; *there is no right or wrong answer.* Although it may seem almost barbaric these days to produce a product with marginal quality, there are circumstances under which this option makes the most economic sense. The quality of many low-priced consumer electronics products, for example, is far from ideal, but a good warranty makes these items palatable to customers on a budget. Some second-tier automobile manufacturers offer stupendous warranties (in some cases longer than you would care to own the car) to allay consumer fears over endless costly repairs. Those disposable cameras that folks take to Disneyworld are not much competition for a Nikon, but that's the whole point; they're *disposable.* I don't necessarily endorse this option, but I can appreciate the logic of it.

A more common solution is for firms to implement draconian testing and inspection to overcome intractable quality problems. Although this option gains points for purity of spirit, it is ham-handed to be sure. Manufacturing test and inspection are *non-value-added activities.* Using such wasteful means to compensate for poor quality just compounds the cost problem; you pay for both the scrap *and* the testing that identifies it. Much of this waste can be avoided by moving toward Option 3; deploying Statistical Process Control along with lot-sampling techniques on all "critical-to-quality" processes. The non-recurring cost involved may be significant, but the investment is often justified by immediate savings in both scrap and testing costs.

The final option on my list didn't exist before Motorola "invented" it in the 1980's. Imagine the *chutzpah*; a production line for pocket pagers (the pathfinder product for early Six-Sigma breakthroughs) that has *no test or inspection.* Just build the darned things, pack them up, and ship them out! Through aggressive product and process co-development, Motorola was able to implement a production line with such over-the-top capability that the defect rates were vanishingly small. An enticing option to be sure, but be careful. All that process capability comes at a high price, and may only make sense if you are

6.2

planning to produce *millions of units*. Achieving an optimal balance between process capabilities and defect rates, however, *always* makes sense. We will, therefore, begin our exploration of Six-Sigma methods by introducing a lean design tool that will help you calculate how process capability impacts total product cost: the Cost-of-Poor-Quality (COPQ) Calculator, described in Figure 6.6.

Understanding the subtle relationship between process capability and defect rates is where Dr. Genichi Taguchi has focused much of his groundbreaking work. (Note to the reader: The tools collectively known as Taguchi Methods are arcane, even by Six-Sigma standards. Hence, other than this quick mention, they will be left to the intrepid reader to investigate. I've provided an excellent reference at the end of Part VI, however, for the ambitious student.) In the past, firms have taken an overly simplistic view of product tolerances; a production part was either "in tolerance" or in the scrap bin. This black-and-white perspective underestimated the true impact of process variability, and therefore gave an unrealistically optimistic picture of how much poor quality actually costs a firm.

"At a Glance" – The Cost-of-Poor-Quality Calculator

Overview –
The cost of poor quality (COPQ) reflects the costs incurred as a result of defects, scrap, testing, inspection, returns, warranty charges, and the negative impact on product price and reputation. This tool demonstrates, in a simplified way, how COPQ can be estimated and compared to the cost of enhancing process capability (and thereby reducing defects).

Primary Benefits –
Can help designers select optimal product tolerances, as well as inform decisions on when to invest in enhanced process capabilities.

Best Suited Products –
This tool is best suited to discrete manufactured products, and particularly high-volume products, but can be adapted to almost any product type.

Advantages –
The cost of capital can be a major factor in the profitability of a new product. By trading off the cost of poor yield with the cost of purchasing new and better equipment, your investment in dedicated equipment can be significantly reduced.

Disadvantages –
This calculation depends on several "fuzzy" factors, including the market forecast for the new product, and the estimated defect rates of both a baseline and enhanced process. This limits the accuracy of the calculation.

Impact on the Twenty Cost Levers –

I. Direct Labor				II. Direct Materials				III. Capital				IV. Design Cost				V. Overhead			
1a	1b	1c	1d	2a	2b	2c	2d	3a	3b	3c	3d	4a	4b	4c	4d	5a	5b	5c	5d
⊙	○	⊙	●	●						○	○		⊙			○			

Figure 6.6 – "At-a-glance" overview of the Cost-of-Poor-Quality (COPQ) Calculator.

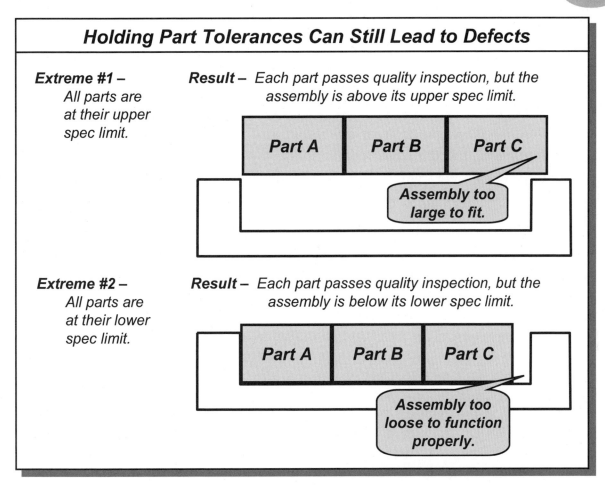

Figure 6.7 – A simple four-part product that displays the effects of tolerance stackup. When variability cancels, the cubes will fit properly. But if all cubes vary in the same direction (just by random bad luck), the overall assembly will fail, even though each cube is within its specified tolerance band.

To understand this concept more clearly, consider the example shown in Figure 6.7. You're responsible for designing a simple four-part product; three cubes that must fit into a rack. For your customers to be satisfied with this product, the cubes must fit snugly into the rack without rattling around. After some prototyping, you design the three cubes so that a nominal .003 inch gap remains when they are placed into the rack (note that for simplicity, I'm assuming in this example that the rack itself can be produced to perfect tolerances). This gap is achieved by defining the appropriate nominal specifications for each cube. Since you know that there will be some variability in the manufacturing process, you must assign each cube a tolerance range. What should it be? Quite logically, you might say to yourself, "On average, the random variability among the cubes will tend to cancel itself out. Hence, a relatively loose tolerance of +/- .003 inch will work just fine." Well, it will work...some of the time. What if the three cubes tend to vary in the same direction (on the large side, for example)? All it would take is > .001 inch variation in each of the three cubes to cause them not to fit into the rack. Likewise, if all three cubes display variability on the small side, the cubes would rattle around like dice. So it appears that the cubes must be very close to their nominal value to attain the overall quality desired by the customer.

What tolerances *should* you select for your cube-and-rack product? It depends on economics. Your original +/- .003 inch tolerance band could be achieved with cheap, low-capability equipment, but the defect rate of the final assembly would be significant. As you tighten up the tolerance band, the defect rate goes down as the cost of equipment, testing, inspection, etc., goes up. Based on this tradeoff, you might decide to go with a much tighter +/- .001 inch tolerance band for each of your cubes, thinking that this would assure essentially a 100% yield of acceptable final assemblies. Well, think again.

It is true that this tighter tolerance will assure that the final assembly can actually *be assembled*; at the worst, the cubes will be a very tight fit. Yet how would the customer react to a product at the extremes of your "acceptable" variability? Would they appreciate having twice the desired gap, for example, when the variability of all three cubes happens to be at the lower extreme? At the other end of the spectrum, would they enjoy having to cram the cubes into their rack and pry them out with a screwdriver? Assuming you decided to test for this unacceptable performance at the final assembly step in your process, you would be forced to rework a number of units, thereby wasting time and resources.

It seems that the black-and-white concept of quality has failed us. Even though each cube is within its tolerance, the quality of the final assembly may still be questionable. This is exactly the point that Dr. Taguchi made when he defined his now-famous Taguchi Loss Function, as shown in Figure 6.8. Rather than thinking of conformance to specifications as being a yes / no affair, Taguchi recognized that as parts deviate from their nominal specification, the cost of poor quality increases continuously, even within the "allowed" tolerance range. More precisely, he defined a quadratic function that typifies the behavior of COPQ versus variability in most products. With this more sophisticated perspective on process capability, it is obvious that a tolerance band significantly tighter than +/- .001 inch would be required to truly optimize the process-cost-vs.-product-quality tradeoff for the cube-and-rack assembly. That being said, the actual calculation of the Taguchi Loss Function is probably not warranted for the average product development project. Hence, we will keep Taguchi's point in the back of our minds while we pursue a more practical calculation of the cost of poor quality.

We are now prepared to develop an estimating tool for COPQ. Before your quality-assurance experts burn me in effigy, however, let me emphasize that the following discussion is greatly simplified. Clearly, a precise calculation of this type is virtually impossible, but we can get close enough to inform our decisions about product tolerances and investment in enhanced process capabilities. The first step in generating a practical estimate is to recognize that not every element in a product design plays a role in COPQ. Only those elements that are "critical-to-quality" will contribute significantly to the cost-of-poor-

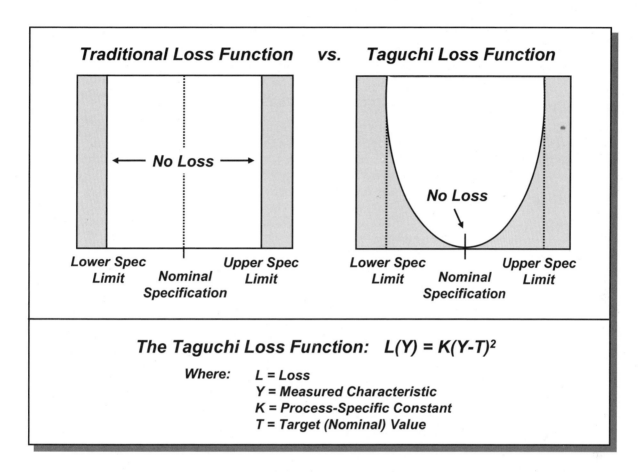

Figure 6.8 – Graphical illustration of the Taguchi Loss Function. Unlike the black-and-white vision of traditional quality control, Taguchi recognized that the cost of poor quality typically increases quadratically with deviation from the nominal value, even inside of the "allowed" tolerance band.

quality equation. Typically, these items include parts with tight tolerances, difficult assembly steps, or other challenging yield factors. (Note the term "yield" in this context means "percentage of parts that meet specifications on the first pass through the process.") Furthermore, among these critical-to-quality elements, there will usually be a single, dominant yield-killer; a process whose defect rate is the highest of all processes within your production line. Ideally, this "limiting" process step would be the focus of your first application of the COPQ Calculator, since this is most likely your highest cost-reduction leverage point.

6.2

To make the calculation of COPQ as clear as possible, I've made a number of simplifying assumptions. They include:

- For the product of interest, there is a yield-limiting process within your factory that will be the focus of your calculations.
- For the yield-limiting process, there is a well-understood "baseline," and the percent yield of that baseline can be estimated (see the next subsection for a "how-to" discussion).
- There is an "enhanced" process available whose estimated percent yield (i.e., its capability) is significantly better than that of the baseline process.
- Rework is assumed to be impractical. If rework makes economic and technical sense in your industry (and be careful here – the cost of rework is usually greater than you think), it will tend to improve the cost picture for the baseline process.
- Overhead impact and other second-order effects are neglected. Note that depending on your choice of baseline and enhanced processes, these effects can go either for or against the baseline.

You should feel free to include additional factors that are significant in your industry; I'm certain your quality experts will have suggestions on how to enhance the calculations that follow. Rework, in particular, can be a major cost factor for some processes. Note, however, that rework usually creates far more "damage" to a flow-line than just the time and materials required to disposition a defect, reroute the part, reprocess the part, and retest the part. Consider the disruption to flow, the capacity that is squandered, and so on. These costs will be buried in overhead, but as we know, someone has to pay for them. As a general rule, a lower defect rate (i.e., a higher first-pass yield) has a favorable impact on overhead costs, production cycle-time, and production capacity.

With all of the necessary caveats in place, we can now walk through the COPQ Calculator shown in Figure 6.9. The fundamental COPQ tradeoff calculation is presented at the top of the figure. In words, this equation states that the differential cost of enhancing the capability of a process step must be balanced against the differential savings gained by an improvement in yield. If the cost of upgrading process capability is significantly lower than the savings that will be accrued due to reduced defect rates (i.e., C_Δ in the figure is significantly less than zero), you should make the investment. As with all the semi-quantitative tools in this guidebook, however, if the calculated value of C_Δ is close to zero, you should either study the problem further, or just go with the lower-risk baseline approach.

The remainder of the figure provides a template for calculating each term in the C_Δ equation. The implementation costs for both the baseline and enhanced process capabilities are predominantly non-recurring, so the simple sums that are indicated should suffice. It is important to note that if you already have a baseline capability in place, the only costs that should be included in the calculation of C_B are *new investments* required to adapt the process to your product. As with all of the terms in the Calculator, there can be many second-order effects that result from implementing an enhanced production process, but the ones I've included are usually the heavy-hitters.

The Cost-of-Poor-Quality Calculator

The Equation -

$$C_\Delta = \left\{ \begin{pmatrix} \text{Cost of Enhanced} \\ \text{Process Capability} \end{pmatrix} + \begin{pmatrix} \text{Cost of Poor Quality} \\ \text{@ Enhanced-Process Defect Rate} \end{pmatrix} \right\} -$$

$$\left\{ \begin{pmatrix} \text{Cost of Baseline} \\ \text{Process Capability} \end{pmatrix} + \begin{pmatrix} \text{Cost of Poor Quality} \\ \text{@ Baseline Defect Rate} \end{pmatrix} \right\}$$

$$= (C_E + C_{EPQ}) - (C_B + C_{BPQ})$$

An investment in enhanced process capability may be justified if C_Δ is <u>significantly</u> less than zero.

The Calculator -

$$C_B = \sum \left\{ \begin{array}{l} \text{Cost of Baseline Capital Equipment = } \square \\ \text{Cost of Installation and Setup = } \square \\ \text{Cost of training = } \square \end{array} \right\}$$

$$C_E = \sum \left\{ \begin{array}{l} \text{Cost of Enhanced Capital Equipment = } \square \\ \text{Cost of Installation and Setup = } \square \\ \text{Cost of Enhanced Training = } \square \end{array} \right\}$$

V_T = Total Forecast Production Volume for Product = ☐

Y_B = Estimated Percent Yield of Baseline Process = ☐

Y_E = Estimated Percent Yield of Enhanced Process = ☐

Y_N = Net Yield Difference between Baseline and Enhanced Process (in Percent)
   = $(Y_E - Y_B)$ = ☐

$$C_{PQ} = V_T \times Y_N \times \sum \left\{ \begin{array}{l} \text{Per-Unit Cost of Materials* = } \square \\ \text{Per-Unit Cost of Labor* = } \square \end{array} \right\}$$

$$+ V_T \times \left\{ \begin{array}{l} \text{Negative Price Delta Due to} \\ \text{Unsatisfactory Quality = } \square \end{array} \right\}$$

$(C_E + C_{EPQ})$ ⚖ $(C_B + C_{BPQ})$

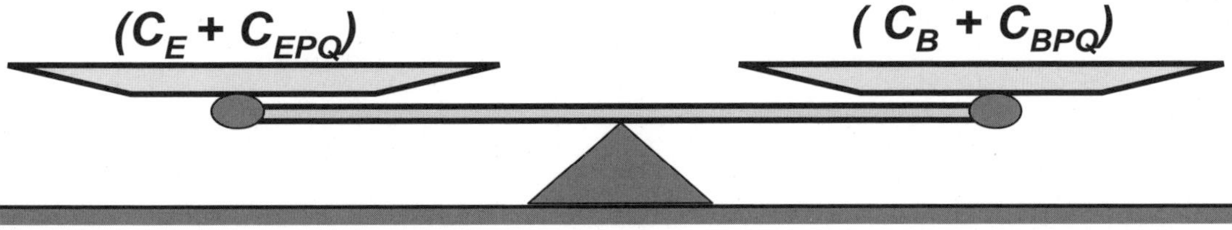

Figure 6.9 – The COPQ Calculator provides a rough estimate of the cost benefits of enhancing a process capability, based on the simplifying assumptions listed in the text. * Note that the cost of direct materials and labor included in these calculations are those embodied in the part being produced, not necessarily the direct costs for the entire product.

The trickiest terms in the C_Δ equation are the actual cost of poor quality for both the baseline and enhanced processes. Quantifying these values doesn't start off well; they depend, in part, on that blasted market forecast (wouldn't it be great if we could actually *believe* those sales estimates?). Assuming that we can get beyond our skepticism about V_T, we will need estimates of what the first-pass percent yield would be for both the baseline and enhanced process choices. It might be possible to get a good number for Y_B empirically; in fact, some valid data may already exist from products in your factory with similar tolerances. Getting a handle on the enhanced process yield, Y_E, is more of a challenge. You might try asking suppliers of enhanced process equipment for capability data, but these yield estimates might be even more "optimistic" than your market forecast. The best approach would be to perform a statistically significant pilot run on the actual equipment. The material in the next subsection will assist you in obtaining some decent values for Y_B and Y_E, although even under the best of circumstances, these numbers will be fuzzy.

Near the bottom of the COPQ Calculator is the calculation of C_{PQ} (note that the calculation for either the baseline or enhanced process looks the same). To keep it simple, I've included only the cost of wasted materials and labor due to variability-induced defects. Note that these costs should reflect just those embodied in the part or assembly that is being rejected, not the direct labor and materials for the entire product (unless, of course, the defect occurs at the final step in the manufacturing process). I've also included a rather insidious term that recognizes the potential *price impact* of poor quality. In some cases, the quality level of a product will be proportional to the price it will garner in the marketplace. Much like diamonds, a consistently flawless product can often command a much higher market price than those with a cloudy reputation. If this factor is not significant in your industry, you can neglect it, but don't move too quickly to scratch that term. First consider what opportunities might avail themselves if you *could* achieve near-perfect quality. Could your market be resegmented to target a higher-priced, higher-quality niche?

Finally, the pan-balance drawing at the bottom of the COPQ Calculator says it all. For any product type and economic situation, there is a "right" choice for process capability. It is not, I repeat *not*, necessary to pursue "six-sigma" quality for every product. Six-sigma variability is an ideal from a quality standpoint, but it is *not necessarily* an ideal from an economic standpoint. Your decision regarding investment in process capability enhancement must be driven by hard numbers, not hype. The exploration of Motorola's journey through this optimization process, provided in the next subsection, should arm you with a realistic and practical perspective.

Why "Six" Sigma?

In the early 1980's, engineers at the Motorola Company struggled with the very tradeoffs that were discussed above. In their case, however, traditional quality solutions seemed inadequate. This newfangled "pocket-pager" product had such huge profit potential that it justified taking a fresh look at traditional quality. Just how far could the quality envelope be extended? Could a $C_p = 1.0$ be achieved? Not a problem for a production line with almost 100% automation. As we've already seen, however, this supposedly "capable" production line would still have churned out defects at an unacceptable rate. Much higher capability would be needed if their goal of "no test or inspection" was to be realized.

After analyzing the variability distributions of their yield-limiting processes, the Motorola pioneers determined that the only way to truly eliminate the need for testing and inspection would be to approach an overall process capability of $C_p = 2.0$, as shown in Figure 6.10. Keep in mind that at the time, this was uncharted territory; traditionally, process capabilities had never been pushed to these extremes, particularly on a new and technology-intensive product.

As we learned earlier, at $C_p = 1$, defects occur at the three-sigma points in a variability distribution (assuming that the distribution is approximately normal, and that the mean of the distribution is at the nominal design value for the part in question). If we were to double C_p, what would that mean? Defects would now occur at the *six-sigma* points in the variability distribution. Sound familiar? Yes folks, an improvement buzzword was born and the rest is history...or is it? Actually, Motorola's initial attempts at achieving zero defects didn't work, *despite achieving $C_p = 2.0$ on all limiting processes.* Somehow, additional variability was creeping into their process and causing unexpected

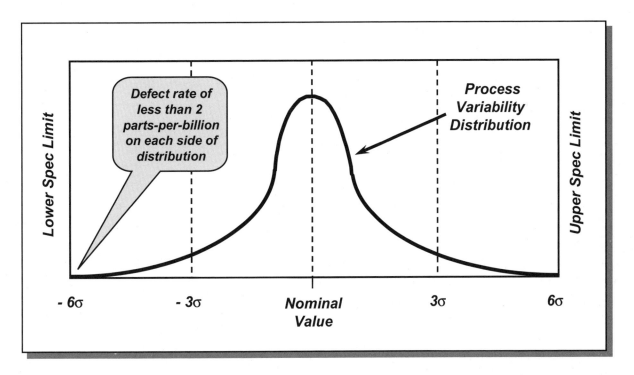

Figure 6.10 – Motorola coined the term "Six Sigma" in reference to the number of standard deviations (sigmas) between the nominal (desired) value for a process and the upper or lower specification limits, represented by a process capability of $C_p = 2.0$. Note that at this extreme, the number of projected defects from the process is only four parts-per-billion (ppb).

6.2

defects; not a lot of them, to be sure, but defects nonetheless. With their reputations on the line (not to mention their future chances of founding exorbitantly profitable consultancies), the Motorola team set to work troubleshooting their process.

To understand what was happening to these pioneers, you can perform a little experiment. Find a nice sharp wooden pencil. Now place a sheet of clean white paper on the floor directly below where you are standing. Hold the pencil by the eraser end so that the point is directly above the approximate center of the paper and roughly two feet off of the ground. Steady your hand and drop the pencil. It will make a small mark where it strikes. *Keeping your feet in exactly the same place*, pick up the pencil, hold it as closely as possible above your first dot, and drop it again. If you do this ten to twenty times, you will begin to see a distribution of dots forming about the center of the paper. This is representative of typical process variability – a cluster of data points with the highest density in the center and fewer events as you move outward from the "mean."

Now close your eyes and take two large steps backwards away from the paper, and then take two large steps forward again toward the paper. Plant your feet like they are in concrete, open your eyes, and start dropping your pencil again, being careful not to twist your body or move your arm from the position you were in during the previous exercise (*do not* try to line up with your previous set of dots). Almost certainly, your feet did not come back to exactly the same spot. Hence, although the new distribution of dots you create will show the same clustering as before, *the center of the distribution will not coincide with the center of the previous one*, as shown in Figure 6.11. What happened?

Obviously, since your feet are in a different location, the center of the dots for your new distribution will also be in a different location. Exactly the same thing happens when a machine is set up, changed over, and set up again. Or when a parts supplier sets up their line, changes it over, and sets it up again. Get the picture? Batch-to-batch variations can cause the mean of a process variability distribution to shift discontinuously over time, resulting in higher-than-expected defect rates. What we are dealing with here is the difference between *precision* and *accuracy* (if you thought these words were synonymous, move to the back of the class). *Precision* refers to the ability of a process to cluster tightly around a mean value (in your experiment, your ability to hold the pencil as close to the same spot as possible, drop after drop). *Accuracy* refers to how close the mean of a distribution is to the nominal (or desired) value for that process. It is therefore possible for a variability distribution to be highly accurate (the mean is dead-on the nominal value), but not precise (the individual dots are all over the paper). Likewise, it is possible for a distribution to be very precise (the dots are all clustered closely together), but way off on accuracy (the second cluster of dots is centered in a different spot than the first).

Hence, to ensure essentially zero defects, we must develop a process that has both excellent precision (which is, by the way, what C_p represents), and also excellent accuracy. Looks like we need a somewhat more sophisticated metric: the *Process Capability Index* (C_{pk}), as defined in Figure 6.12. C_{pk} takes into account both precision and accuracy, so that if a process is doing well in C_{pk}, it should meet our objectives for defect rates. In Motorola's case, although their precision was generally up to snuff ($C_p = 2.0$), the C_{pk} values they were

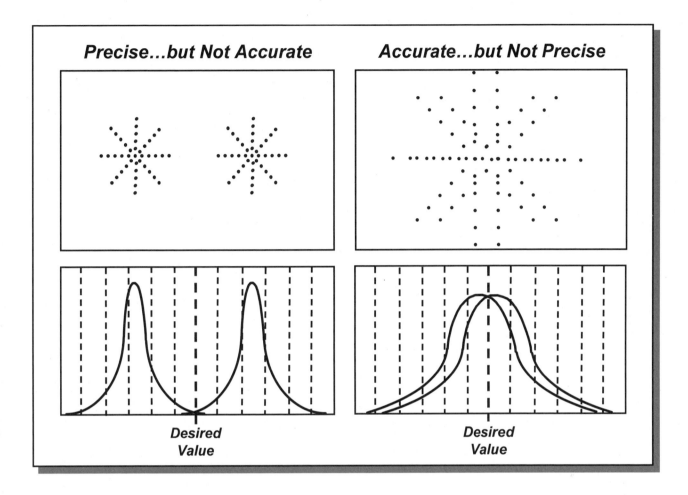

Figure 6.11 – A simple demonstration of the difference between *precision* and *accuracy*. Precision refers to the spread of a distribution about its center (i.e., its mean), whereas accuracy refers to how close the mean of a distribution is to a desired nominal value. It is possible to have an accurate distribution that is not precise, or a precise distribution that is not accurate. A balance of both is required to achieve exceptional quality.

able to achieve could not realistically be improved beyond $C_{pk} = 1.5$ (due primarily to supplier quality limitations). Although today we refer to the achievement of the Motorola team as a "six-sigma" breakthrough, they were actually able to achieve no better than +/- 4.5 sigma for their overall process. Somehow the name "Six Sigma" stuck, however. (I suppose that Jack Welch and other CEOs would have felt funny touting the benefits of "Four-Point-Five-Sigma" Design.) Despite falling short of their original goals, they still achieved a breakthrough success; at $C_{pk} = 1.5$, their average defect rate was roughly 3.4 parts-per-million (ppm). Good enough to allow Motorola to transfer all of those unneeded test engineers and quality inspectors over to their telecommunications equipment division, where they found much to keep them occupied.

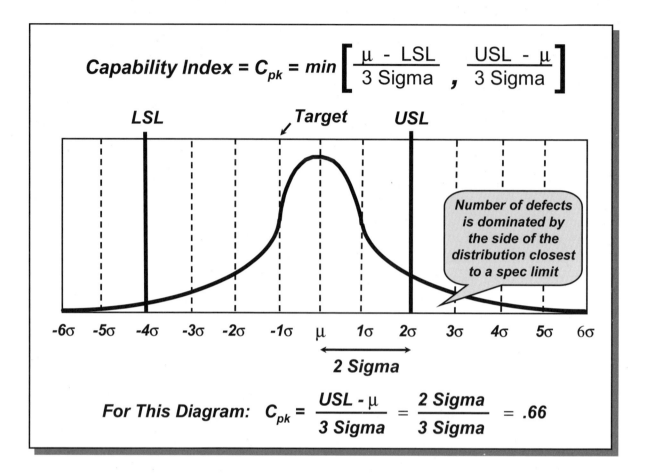

Figure 6.12 – The Process Capability Index (C_{pk}) is a realistic metric for process defect rates. Both the spread of a process distribution (its precision) and the variability of its mean about a desired nominal value (its accuracy) are represented.

We now have three ways that we can reduce process defects and improve first-pass yields. They are:

1) Improve the precision of a yield-limiting process (i.e., tighten the variability distribution, as measured by C_p).
2) Improve the accuracy of a yield-limiting process (i.e., move the mean of each distribution closer to the desired nominal value on a batch-to-batch basis, as measured by C_{pk}).
3) Loosen the product's design tolerances to become more "robust" to the variability of a yield-limiting process (best measured by C_{pk}).

Which of these opportunities to focus on depends upon your situation, but in general, I would always consider (and exhaust) any possibility of relaxing product design tolerances before I would spend time and money upgrading either precision or accuracy.

Before we leave this fascinating statistical stuff, there is one more critical topic to discuss. Recall that to utilize the Cost-of-Poor-Quality Calculator tool we must have an estimate of the first-pass yield for both the default process and for an enhanced version. How do we come up with these numbers? Suppose that you are able to take actual measurements on real equipment. You might set up an experiment in which a sampling of units is run through the default process, while a similar number of units are run through the enhanced approach. In principle, at least, some time spent with statistical tables should give you the percent-yield numbers you seek, *provided that your data is valid*. If the sample size of your experiment is too small, your results will be questionable. If you made several runs of the same experiment, on the same day, with the same people, and got different results, you should be skeptical of your data. Finally, if you came back the next day and ran the same experiment, but the results looked different, your confidence should be shaken.

The above concerns regarding the validity of statistical data are addressed in one of the fundamental tools of Six-Sigma Design, usually referred to as Gage Repeatability and Reproducibility or Gage R & R. *Repeatability* means that if the same person does an experiment over and over within a short period of time, they should get reasonably similar results. *Reproducibility* means that if a set of data is taken on one day, and then retaken on a different day, with a different person, and so on, it should again yield the same answer. To calculate COPQ (or any other statistical parameter, for that matter), we must have acceptable repeatability, reasonable reproducibility, and one more thing: *a large enough sample size to give us a high confidence level*.

You can determine your level of repeatability and reproducibility in a fairly simple way. Run a number of units through both your default and enhanced processes, and use a statistical-analysis software package to do the grunt work. How many samples should you take? In general, the statistical error in a measurement decreases in proportion to the square-root of the number of samples taken (this is what your local newscaster means when he points out that "this poll has a margin of error of four percent"). More samples always means higher confidence in the outcome, but a practical rule-of-thumb for determining process capabilities is to run ten samples at three different points in time. The data from these experiments can be entered into a simple statistical software tool such as Minitab, and out will pop your desired yield numbers, along with an estimate of "measurement variation." If this variation metric is less than 10%, your measurement system is acceptable. If the variation is between 10% and 30%, your confidence should be tempered, and if your experiment resulted in greater than 30% variation, you need to go to work on your empirical methods until this figure-of-merit improves.

Well, congratulations are due: You've survived a quick dip into statistical waters and have come away unscathed. Was it really as bad as you remembered from your summer-semester course in college? The remainder of this endlessly long section will focus on several of the important "hermit-crab" tools that have been appended to the Six-Sigma Design methodology over the past decade. Although these techniques deserve your attention, always keep in mind that Six-Sigma Design is really about *matching process capabili-*

ties to product tolerances on the factory floor. Don't get me wrong; it's great to extend powerful ideas into new and unrelated areas. But if your Six-Sigma consultants start talking about the number of defects (in parts-per-million, no less!) that occurred at your firm's most recent board-of-directors meeting, throw the rotters out.

A Toolbox for Reducing COPQ

One of the first tools to be added to the Six-Sigma toolbox was Quality Function Deployment (QFD). Fortunately for both the reader and the writer, we've already discussed this voice-of-the-customer tool in Section 2.1. Of course, most Six-Sigma mavens do not use the simplified Lean QFD approach that I recommend, but hopefully with the advent of Lean Six Sigma, the need to reduce wastefulness will drive practitioners toward this far more efficient tool.

The next enhancement to Six-Sigma Design worthy of mention is a systematic process for reducing variability and improving yield. This methodology is referred to as DMAIC (Define, Measure, Analyze, Improve, Control), and is shown graphically in Figure 6.13. They say that there is nothing new under the sun, and nowhere is this platitude more evident than in the world of improvement initiatives. If you have even a few grey hairs, you will likely remember the old "Plan-Do-Check-Act" cycle from the days when Continuous Measurable Improvement (CMI) was the new buzzword on the block. DMAIC is just a variant of the same cycle, but with more emphasis on realistic problem-solving steps; words like "measure" and "analyze" are far more specific than "do" and "act." Yet the general idea is the same; an iterative process for selecting improvement opportunities, attacking them systematically, and then ensuring that the gains you've achieved can be sustained.

The five key activities included in the DMAIC cycle can be described as follows:

Define – Precisely identify the process step(s) that contribute to a yield, defect, scrap, or other variability-related problem.

Measure – Use empirical methods (with validated Gage R & R) to determine the process capability for each contributing process step.

Analyze – What are the patterns in the data? Where are the weak links in the capability chain? Where is the highest leverage point for improvement?

Improve – Using one of several tools from the Six-Sigma Design toolbox, reduce the offending process variability (either by making the product design more robust, or by enhancing the capability of yield-limiting process steps).

Control – Once you've identified and verified a process improvement, how must the process parameters be controlled to assure that your gains won't degrade in the future?

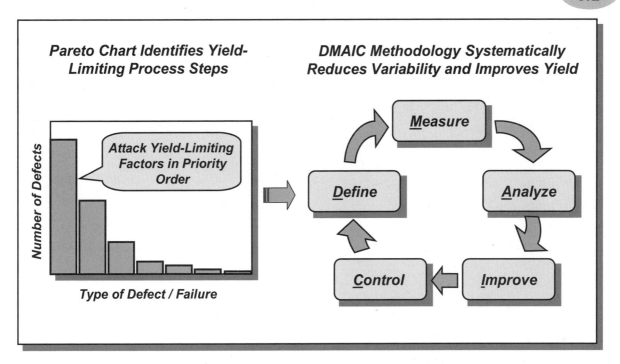

Figure 6.13 – The DMAIC cycle describes a systematic approach to process improvement. To make the best use of this methodology, opportunities for improvement should first be graphed Pareto-style, and the yield-limiting processes should then be attacked in priority order.

There is really not much more to be said about this fundamental problem-solving strategy, except that to be successful in process improvement, *you must use something similar*. A scattergun approach to problem-solving, in which your improvement teams behave more like volunteer firepersons than systematic problem-solvers, will probably create more damage than it will correct (we used to call this the "ready / fire / aim" mode). Good scientific method, careful measurements, and frequent sanity-checks are critical to improvement success. Before you start firing off silver bullets, be sure your team has the discipline to aim first.

Designed Experiments for the Fashionable Problem-Solver

Breaking news: *The whachamacallit team is in trouble!* Recall that we left our friends on the verge of a successful product launch, with full confidence that they had things under control. Unfortunately, while we've been off learning new tools, they've been floundering. Everything was going great until the pilot production run of the whachamacallit product. Having aggressively implemented product and process co-development, the "W-team" had every confidence that their first-pass yields through the factory would be 100%. When the quality data came back from the shop floor, however, they were shocked to find that something was terribly wrong. Variability was far higher than was predicted by process capability test data. In fact, the problem is so severe that if something can't be done, the entire product line will be in jeopardy.

6.2

Upon digging into the data, our apocryphal team discovers that the yield-limiting process for the whachamacallit production line is an adhesive-curing step that depends on two key parameters: temperature and time. Unfortunately, the behavior of the process is not well-understood, so guesswork is involved in tweaking these two parameters to achieve a high yield. Evidently there is some "hidden" interaction between temperature and time that is causing unexpected variability. How can the team sort out this mysterious behavior and fix their yield problem?

Fortunately for all concerned, the Six-Sigma Design toolbox includes a methodology so powerful that it deserves my providing a complete (albeit highly simplified) example. Most production processes depend on multiple process parameters. If the world was a sane and friendly place, these parameters would be *uncorrelated*, meaning that they can be changed independently of each other in a predictable way. For example, the controls on your television set allow you to change the channel independently of the volume, with each having no effect on the other. If this were the case for our W-team's process, they could perform some simple controlled experiments: hold one parameter fixed and vary the other to see which factor dominates variability and yield. But what if the two parameters affect each other in some subtle way; in other words, suppose they *interact*. The traditional approach to experimentation fails us under these conditions. We need a more sophisticated empirical methodology referred to as Design of Experiment (DOE).

The objective of DOE is to help process designers sort out highly complex interactions in a multivariable environment. Today, many production processes depend for their success on a pantheon of parameters. Semiconductor manufacturing, for example, is notoriously fickle. Achieving appropriate etch rates for a silicon wafer requires ultra-precise control of photoresist deposition, etchant chemistry, temperature / time profiles, rinse-fluid purity, and so on. To optimize such processes, it must be possible to deconvolve the interactions between parameters and identify the optimal settings that will result in the desired outcome. Fortunately, there is a rich variety of DOE types that can address even the most daunting multivariable situation. The complexity of the DOE, however, is proportional to the complexity of the process challenge being analyzed. The W-team's application of DOE is about as simple as this methodology gets, and is intended to illustrate the potential problem-solving power of this tool.

The first step that the W-team must take is to clearly define the experiment they wish to perform. To keep this simple, they decide to consider just the two key process parameters mentioned above (temperature and time), and to measure the process at only two different "levels." This type of experiment is referred to as a "two-factor, full-factorial DOE," as shown in Figure 6.14. Four "runs" will be performed, one for each possible combination of *factors* (i.e., one of the key process parameters) and *levels* (i.e., the setting of the parameters for each factor). The easiest way to establish two levels for each factor is to use extremes of reasonable process settings. For the whachamacallit example, the W-team's process engineer determines that the maximum temperature that the adhesive should experience during processing is 50 °C and the minimum reasonable temperature is 25 °C. These become the two temperature levels used for their DOE. Similarly, the two

Example of a Two-Factor, Full-Factorial DOE Matrix				
Run Number	Factor Settings		"Coded" Settings	
	A – Temp.	B – Time	A – Temp.	B – Time
1	25 °C	1 Hour	- 1	- 1
2	25 °C	4 Hours	- 1	+ 1
3	50 °C	1 Hour	+ 1	- 1
4	50 °C	4 Hours	+ 1	+ 1

Figure 6.14 – Experimental design matrix for a simple two-factor, full-factorial Design of Experiment (DOE). Note that all possible combinations of the two factors and two levels are represented in experimental "runs."

reasonable extremes of the time factor are a minimum of one hour of cure time and a maximum of four hours. The output (also referred to as the *response*) of the process that will be used as a gage of quality is adhesive bond strength, as measured in pounds-per-square-inch (psi).

You will notice in the figure that I've included both the actual factor settings to be used in the experiment, and an additional two columns, referred to as "coded" settings. By convention, the high setting for each factor is designated as "+1" and the low setting is indicated by "-1." This coding trick will allow the W-team to apply some simple matrix-multiplication rules to quickly generate usable results. Finally, to complete the design of the W-team's experiment, they must decide on the number of repetitions to be performed for each run number. Here is where statistical effects come into play; a greater number of repetitions means higher confidence in the conclusions of the experiment. This desire for confidence, however, must be weighed against available resources. Time, money, and equipment availability must all be considered when determining the scope of a DOE. A good rule-of-thumb is to perform between five and ten repetitions for each of the four runs, for a total of twenty discrete experiments.

The next step is to actually run the experiments. It is critical that the W-team maintain control of all process parameters other than the two key factors under test. The best way to do this is to create a "run sheet" with all possible variables explicitly identified and fixed. I have seen tremendously sophisticated and costly DOEs ruined by the lack of appropriate controls. Having different operators perform the runs, for example, can cause unexplained variations that will corrupt your data. Even running experiments at different times of the day can be a killer. In one case, the difference in electrical noise between day-shift (where all machines in a factory were operating) and nightshift (where only a few tools were in operation) caused a sensitive DOE on a satellite system to be rendered useless. It is also advisable to "randomize" the experimental runs, such that the first repetition of Run #1 would be followed by the first repetition of Run #2, and so on. Often this kind of cyclic randomization is not practical (the setup and changeover times might be prohibitive), but if this is not a problem, performing runs in random order is best from an error-reduction standpoint.

		Results of DOE Runs for the Whachamacallit Example		
Run Number	**Factor Settings**		**Adhesive Bond Strength Measurements (psi)**	**Run Average**
	A – Temp.	**B – Time**		
1	25 °C	1 Hour	110, 111, 113, 115, 117	113.2
2	25 °C	4 Hours	122, 121, 125, 120, 126	122.8
3	50 °C	1 Hour	113, 118, 122, 125, 114	118.4
4	50 °C	4 Hours	123, 122, 125, 128, 124	124.4

Figure 6.15 – The raw data generated by the W-team from their twenty experimental repetitions (four runs, with five repetitions each). Note that all other variables in the process must be carefully controlled to ensure that this data will yield meaningful results.

While we were chatting, the W-team has completed their twenty experimental runs, and they are quite satisfied with the results, as shown in Figure 6.15. After a quick look to verify that their outcomes are reasonable, they feel confident that their data is ready for analysis. At this juncture, there are a number of possible approaches they can employ. If there is a statistician among them (or at least someone who got an "A" in statistics), there are some sophisticated techniques that can be utilized to generate valuable results from their raw data. Both Analysis of Variance (ANOVA) and regression analysis can be employed for this purpose. Fortunately for the "C" students, there are some useful software packages available, including many spreadsheet applications, that can automate the number crunching. If your team is statistically challenged, you might want to start with a simple graphical technique such as the one described below, and move to more rigorous methods only if your results warrant additional attention.

From the data listed in Figure 6.15, the W-team can determine the *effect* (also known as "strength of effect" or "process sensitivity") of each of their two key process factors. They must first determine the average of all data points that were taken at the high temperature level (a total of ten points from Run #3 and Run #4), and then all data

	"Effects" of the Two Key Process Factors for the Whachamacallit Example			
Run Number	Factor Settings A – Temp.	B – Time	Adhesive Bond Strength Measurements (psi)	Run Average
1	25 °C	1 Hour	110, 111, 113, 115, 117	113.2
2	25 °C	4 Hours	122, 121, 125, 120, 126	122.8
3	50 °C	1 Hour	113, 118, 122, 125, 114	118.4
4	50 °C	4 Hours	123, 122, 125, 128, 124	124.4
	121.4	123.6	Average Bond Strength at High (+)	
	118.0	115.8	Average Bond Strength at Low (−)	
	3.4	7.8	Strength of Effect (Δ)	

Figure 6.16 – The W-team's experimental data has been used to calculate the "strength-of-effect" for their two key process factors: time and temperature. In this example, controlling time is more than twice as important as controlling temperature when attempting to reduce variability in the adhesive-bonding process.

points taken at the low temperature level (from Run #1 and Run #2). The averages are 121.4 psi for the high level and 118.0 psi for the low level, as shown in Figure 6.16. Similarly, they must average all data points from the high-time-level experiments and the low-time-level experiments, resulting in averages of 123.6 psi and 115.8 psi respectively. The individual effects of these two process factors can now be calculated by simply taking the difference between the appropriate averages, as shown in the figure. This strength-of-effect metric, usually symbolized by a delta (Δ), is an indication of how sensitive a process is to changes in a specific key factor. For the W-team's process, the strength-of-effect for time is over twice as strong as for temperature. Hence, controlling time will be significantly more important than controlling temperature in reducing process variability. A useful conclusion to be sure.

We can take this example one step further, however. Can the W-team determine whether there is any *interaction* between the two key process factors? A simple graphical approach can provide some preliminary insights, as shown in Figure 6.17. The adhesive bond strength (i.e., the process response) is plotted along the y-axis, while either one of the process factors (it doesn't matter which one you choose) is displayed along the x-axis. Once the four run-averages are plotted, two lines will result, representing the high and low

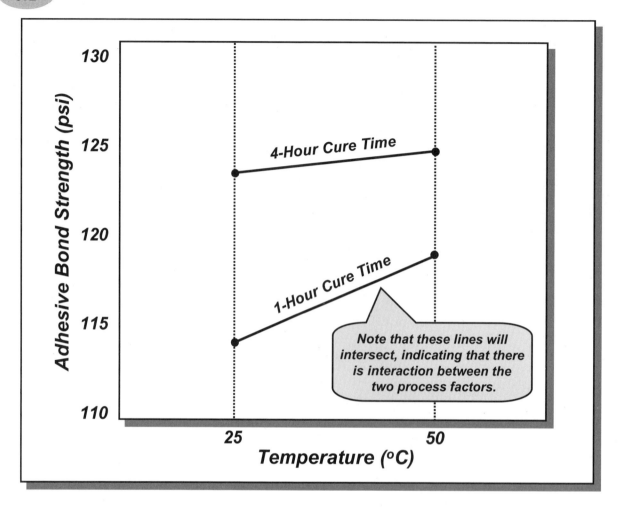

Figure 6.17 – A simple graphical technique allows the W-team to determine whether the two key process factors that they have selected are independent of each other, or if they interact in some way. Parallel lines indicate no correlation between the two factors, while lines that will intersect (such as those shown) imply that there is at least some interaction between the process factors.

levels for the other process factor. If these lines are perfectly parallel, the W-team can conclude that the two process factors are completely independent of each other (like the volume and channel controls on your TV). After examining their graph, however, they discover that the two lines will eventually intersect, meaning that there is some interaction between time and temperature for their process. Is this a strong effect, or can it be ignored?

Here is where those "+1" and "-1" codes that I defined in Figure 6.14 come into play. Even though the whachamacallit example is a simple one, it can still be treated as a *two-by-two matrix*. Hence, we can use matrix algebra to determine the "cross terms," usually designated as the "AB interaction," as shown in Figure 6.18. We "multiply" the coded designations for the runs where both the A and B factors are high (i.e., multiply +1 times

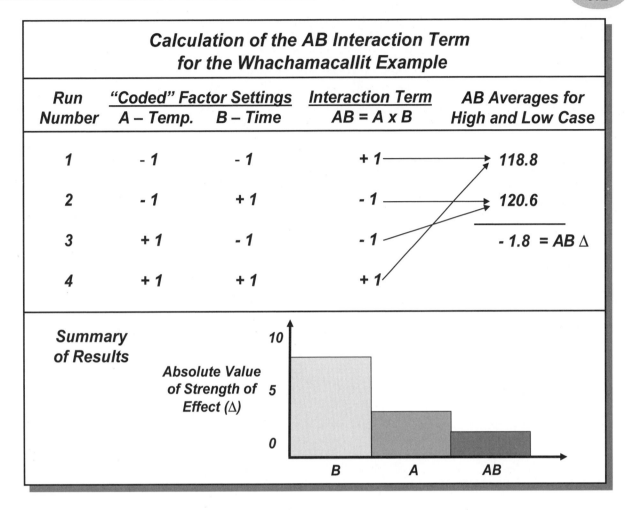

Figure 6.18 – The final step in the W-team's DOE process improvement effort; the calculation of the strength of interaction between the A and B process factors, designated as AB. In this case, the interaction term is small relative to the effects of either the A or B factor, as shown in the summary histogram at the bottom of the figure.

+1 to get a +1), and enter the result under the AB column. When the A and B factors are of a different sign (e.g., A is -1 and B is +1), the AB value will be -1. We then take the average of those data for which AB = +1 and the average of those data for which AB = -1. The difference between these two averages represents the strength of the interaction between A and B.

For our intrepid W-team, the results are now fairly clear. The B factor (time) has a significantly stronger effect on bond strength than either the A factor (temperature), or the interaction between the two factors, AB. This might be sufficient analysis to allow them to get started on process improvement, beginning with establishing tighter controls on the curing time of the adhesive. If the simple graphical approach used above proves to be too coarse for effective action, they can take their analysis further. A "prediction equation" can be derived, for example, that would allow the team to define a specific bond strength and determine the optimal factor levels necessary to achieve the desired response. They could also utilize regression analysis or Analysis of Variance (ANOVA) to gain additional insights and determine confidence levels for their results. In any case, I think we can finally wave goodbye to our W-team with the assurance that they will solve their problem. Time to place your advance orders for whachamacallits.

Failure Modes and Effects Analysis

The final Six-Sigma add-on tool that is worthy of specific mention is in such common use that I would be surprised if you haven't heard of it. Failure Modes and Effects Analysis (FMEA) is not only a mainstay of Six Sigma, it is also firmly embedded in the very popular Advanced Product Quality Planning (APQP) process that has become the standard in many industries. Nonetheless, it is important enough that a brief overview is warranted, for those readers who may still be uninitiated.

FMEA is essentially a design-review process that focuses on proactive identification and mitigation of product risks. Its most frequent application is as a method for ensuring product safety – in our litigious society, the cost of liability can be a major factor in some products (such as stepladders). As I've roamed the industrial landscape, I've come across lots of almost-funny-but-really-tragic stories about the misuse of products. Like the guy who decided that it was a waste of money to buy a power hedge trimmer; instead he used his rotary power mower for that purpose. Unfortunately, he managed to trim more fingers than branches.

It would be a mistake, however, to relegate FMEA to serving as a stopgap tool for protecting your firm against liability claims. FMEA reviews should be performed iteratively, in much the same way as Target Costing, Value Engineering, and other lean design tools. A complete deployment of FMEA could involve at least four levels of application, as shown in Figure 6.19. At the early concept-design stage of product development, a system-level (also referred to as "concept-level") FMEA might be held to shine a timely spotlight on overall product failure risks. Once a design concept has been selected, important subassemblies and components could receive similar treatment, through the completion of one or more design-level FMEAs. In parallel, a process-level FMEA can be held to identify weaknesses in the production plan, potential safety or defect risks, and so on. Finally, a service-level FMEA might be scheduled to address the supportability of the product in the field, along with consideration of human factors, maintenance and repair, etc.

There is a fair amount of overlap between the benefits of holding an FMEA review and those derived from some of the other lean design tools within this guidebook. A process-level FMEA, for example, is really not much different than a "How's it Built?" Review. That being said, FMEA is entirely focused on future-risk mitigation, and that is such a critical consideration during product development that some "belt and suspenders" behavior can be forgiven.

Here's how a typical FMEA review is executed. The usual suspects are gathered in a room for a half-day affair (you know...core design team, other smart people, a minimum

FMEA Level	Objectives / Benefits
System	• *Uncover safety issues* • *Identify reliability limiters* • *Verify all configurations / versions* • *Verify HW / SW compatibility*
Design (Component)	• *Detect weaknesses in design* • *Highlight tolerance / interface issues* • *Identify potential point failures* • *Verify operation under use environment*
Process	• *Match process and design tolerances* • *Verify design for manufacture / test* • *Rank-order process defect issues* • *Make design "error proof"*
Service	• *Ensure that product is supportable* • *Consider human factors and reliability* • *Verify installation and maintenance processes*

Figure 6.19 – Failure Modes and Effects Analysis (FMEA) reviews should be held at several key points within the product development process. Typically, the system-level FMEA is conducted at the very beginning of the project, with the design- and process-level reviews occurring at about the midpoint. The service-level FMEA can bring up the rear, provided that the design is still fluid enough to benefit from its recommendations.

of managers, and no elephants). The product is reviewed in some logical and systematic way (such as by system hierarchy, by bill-of-materials structure, etc.), with each design element being the subject of a brief discussion. The goal of these brainstorming sessions is to list as many potential *failure modes* as possible for each element. A failure mode is simply a way in which the product (or process, as the case may be) could fail to perform its function properly, reliably, and safely. For example, a possible failure mode for an electric table fan would be "wires short." Not all failure modes need be the fault of the product; incorrect use of the product can also result in a failure, and may jeopardize customer satisfaction and safety if no corrective action is taken. (Incidentally, the findings of FMEA meetings often cause manufacturers to put lots of seemingly ridiculous warnings on their products, such as, "Do not use your new lawnmower as a hedge trimmer.")

Once failure modes have been identified for all major design elements, the team returns to the first failure mode listed and identifies any possible effects which might result from that mode of failure. If, for example, our table fan's "wires short," we might expect that: a) the circuit breaker will blow, making the customer unhappy, b) the wires will melt, making the customer *very* unhappy, or c) the wires will burn, putting the customer at risk. All of these effects are possible, but clearly they don't have the same importance to customers. If a circuit breaker blows, your customer may be a bit peeved, but it's a minor inconvenience. A burning fan is more than an inconvenience, and could easily become a tragedy. For this reason, a ranking system is used to prioritize the negative effects of a given failure mode, as shown in Figure 6.20. The *severity* of the effect is ranked on a 1-10 scale, with "10" implying risk to human life, and "1" reflecting an insignificant risk.

FMEA Rates on a Scale from 1 (Low) to 10 (High):

   Severity(S) - The seriousness (effects) of the failure
   Occurrence (O) - The frequency of the failure
   Detection (D) - The probability of a defect NOT being detected prior to shipment

Risk Priority Number = RPN = S x O x D

Some Extreme Examples:

| Numerical Rating | | | Nature of Failure | Action Needed |
S	O	D		
1	1	1	Ideal situation (goal)	None
10	1	1	Failure does not reach user	None
10	1	10	Failure may reach user	Yes
1	10	1	Frequent failures - detectable / costly	Yes
1	10	10	Frequent failures that reach the user	Yes
10	10	1	Frequent failures with major impact	Yes
10	10	10	TROUBLE!	YES!!!

Figure 6.20 – Three rankings are used in an FMEA review to determine the priority of a failure mode. The severity, occurrence, and detectability of a failure are all quantified using a 1-10 scoring system. Some examples of how the extremes of these scores might be interpreted are provided.

After identifying the possible effects for a specific failure mode, the potential *causes* of that failure are listed. The cause of our doomed table fan's burning wires could be: i) no strain relief on the wires, ii) poor soldering of the contacts, or iii) poor insulation. Again, these possible failures are not equal; each has a different likelihood of *occurrence*. This calls for another 1-10 ranking, with a "10" score implying a very high probability of occurrence, and a "1" score indicating no chance whatsoever. As if we aren't already overdosed on rankings, FMEA provides for one final variable: *detectability*. How can each of the proposed causes of the failure mode be eliminated or guarded against? If we can't elimi-

A Template for Failure Modes and Effects Analysis (FMEA)

Failure Mode / Condition	Potential Effect(s)	Severity (S)	Potential Cause(s)	Occurrence (O)	Detection Method	Detection (D)	RPN	Action Assigned
Wires Short	Circuit Breaker Blows	3	No strain relief on wires	8	Design issue	10	800	Add strain relief to design
	Wires Melt	7	Poor soldering	5	Inspection	3	150	Define inspect. criterion
	Wires Burn	10	Poor insulation	3	Inspection	1	30	None required

Figure 6.21 – A template for the execution of an FMEA review. The example of a table fan with a failure mode of "wires short" is provided for illustration.

nate it, can we detect it before it gets into our customers' hands? For the table-fan example, the lack of strain relief on the wires is actually a design weakness, and can therefore be solved prior to product launch. Hence, "lack of strain relief" would receive a "10" score for detectability. For the cause identified as "poor soldering," some inspection would be required in the factory to detect potential problems prior to shipment. Since this inspection will be only partially effective at detecting bad solder joints, the detectability score for this cause might be a marginal "3."

Once severity, occurrence, and detectability scores have been selected for each potential cause of a failure mode, they are multiplied together to arrive at a "risk priority number (RPN)." The highest possible RPN is 10 x 10 x 10 = 1000 and the lowest score would be one 1 x 1 x 1 = 1. The RPN is used to determine which failure modes should be addressed first, and which can be considered less significant to customer satisfaction and safety. A template for executing an FMEA review is provided in Figure 6.21, with the above table-fan example used for illustration. As can be seen, the failure mode "wires short" is most likely to be caused by no strain relief on the wires. This is a design issue, and is therefore completely preventable. Since the severity of the failure mode is high (S = 10), the probability of occurrence is significant (O = 8), and the risk can be mitigated easily (D = 10), the priority to make this design change (RPN = 800) is extremely high.

As with many of the Six-Sigma tools, FMEA is often made to be far more complicated and time-consuming than it needs to be. I've personally found this to be an exceptionally valuable tool, particularly when a product is new to the market, or is being targeted for a new application. If you happen to be the manufacturer of products that have high liability potential, your future could depend on the use of this technique. How do you think that stepladder in your garage got all of those red stickers on it that read, "This is Not a Step," "This is REALLY Not a Step," and so on?

The Six-Sigma Cost-Reduction Guide

You might have noticed that we have traversed a number of pages without one of my "At-a-glance" tool summaries popping up. To some extent, this is a reflection of the relative maturity of Six-Sigma Design. I am loath to modify tools that are already successfully deployed in firms around the world. Instead, I will offer a lean design tool that can help the reader select which Six-Sigma method is most applicable to their cost-reduction challenge. All quality-improvement tools impact product cost in one way or another. However many do not attack costs *directly*, or may only be suitable for a specific subset of cost problems. If your challenge is a lack of synergy across your product lines, for example, Six-Sigma tools will be of little help to you. If, on the other hand, your problem is an unstable manufacturing process and a mountain of customer returns, you're smack in the middle of Six-Sigma territory.

The Six-Sigma Cost-Reduction Guide, shown in Figure 6.22, allows the reader to select which of the major Six-Sigma tools fits their specific situation. Since this tool is essentially an "At-a-glance" overview of the Six-Sigma Design toolset, you'll have to wait

Six-Sigma Cost-Reduction Guide

Twenty Cost Levers \ Six-Sigma Tools	Quality Function Deployment	Gage R & R	Process Capability Analysis	Design-of-Experiment (DOE)	ANOVA / Regression Analysis	Design / Process FMEA	Statistical Process Control
I. Direct Labor							
A. Simplify Processes				■		■	■
B. Reduce Skill Level	■	■	■	■	■	■	■
C. Automate Processes			■	■	■	■	■
D. Reduce Test Costs	■	■	■	■	■		■
II. Direct Material							
A. Reduce Scrap			■	■		■	
B. Eliminate Parts	■					■	
C. Low-Cost Materials	■					■	
D. High-Volume Parts							
III. Assignable Capital							
A. Eliminate Batches			■	■	■		■
B. Outsource Processes			■			■	■
C. Optimize Tooling	■			■	■	■	
D. No Dedicated Equip.							
IV. Design Costs							
A. Design Reuse			■		■	■	■
B. Eliminate Complexity	■			■		■	■
C. Avoid Gold Plating	■		■			■	
D. Optimize Make vs. Buy						■	■
V. Factory Overhead							
A. No Factory Changes				■	■	■	■
B. Reduce WIP							
C. Reduce Handling							
D. Reduce Consumables							

Figure 6.22 – The Six-Sigma Cost-Reduction Guide provides an "at-a-glance" overview of the major Six-Sigma tools, as they directly relate to the Twenty Cost Levers. At the juncture between a tool and a cost lever is an indication of how applicable that tool would typically be to that cost factor. The darkness of the square indicates the level of applicability.

6.2

until Section 6.3 for one of my pithy tool description boxes. Instead, we will quickly survey the Six-Sigma Cost-Reduction Guide on our way across the border into Design-for-Manufacture-and-Assembly land.

I've attempted to organize the Six-Sigma toolset shown in the figure in chronological order of application, running from left to right. Most of these tools can (and should) be used at multiple points in the development process, but there is a "sweet spot" where their use is most effective. Quality Function Deployment (QFD), for example, is at its best as a front-end pathfinder. Rather than dwell on this now-familiar tool, however, I will refer the reader back to Section 2.1 for more detail. Note, however, that QFD primarily impacts design-related costs, while the other cost levers are more weakly affected. Reducing design complexity, avoiding overshoot of customer needs, and paring of mis-targeted features are its strong suits (along with having a significant impact on the price side of the profit equation). Its ability to solve factory overhead problems, on the other hand, is negligible.

Gage R & R is equally skewed in its applicability. This is fundamentally a measurement validation discipline, designed to assure that empirical data can be used with confidence. Hence, it must be paired with another tool to be of any value in the cost arena. Where Gage R & R hits home runs is as a partner with Process Capability Analysis, Design of Experiment (DOE), Analysis of Variance (ANOVA), and even Statistical Process Control (SPC). It's like the auto-focus on your camera; no matter what's in the picture, the value of a photo will be greatly enhanced if the details are sharp.

The next three Six-Sigma tools listed in the Six-Sigma Cost-Reduction Guide can be thought of as an escalating continuum. If process variability is your challenge (as indicated by an unacceptable scrap rate or other quality issues), your first weapon of choice should be Process Capability Analysis. Which steps in your manufacturing flow are the yield-limiters? Where are product tolerances putting a strain on equipment and labor? What is the optimal tradeoff between the cost of poor quality and the cost of process upgrades? If the answers to these questions are straightforward, there is no need to use more advanced tools. If, on the other hand, your answers are masked by a complex maze of process variables (and believe me, even *two* process variables can be a miasma if their behavior is psychotic enough), then you'll need a bigger gun: Design of Experiment. Set up some matrices, perform a statistically valid set of experiments under carefully controlled conditions, and take a look at the data. Are the process factors under consideration independent of each other, or is there a strong interaction? Which factor has the strongest effect on the process response (i.e., the quality metric you've chosen to represent your yield-limiting process step)? If simple graphical analysis is adequate to provide you with actionable insights, there's no need to escalate your attack. If, on the other hand, the data is muddy, inconsistent, or otherwise contrary, it's time to drop a nuke. Statistical data-reduction techniques such as ANOVA and regression analysis are powerful, but can be time-consuming and confusing to the novice. If it has been necessary to escalate your problem to this level, some formal training is highly recommended. Alternatively, you could consider hiring a...I just can't say that C-word, but you know what I mean.

The next-to-last Six-Sigma tool listed in Figure 6.22 has the broadest applicability of the bunch. Failure Modes and Effects Analysis (FMEA) can be applied during concept development, detailed design, process definition, service and maintenance planning, and at just about any other point in development that would benefit from risk mitigation. It is like a set of headlights for your project, helping your team avoid the potholes on your way to success.

Finally, once the product is in the factory, Statistical Process Control (SPC) can enable quality levels to be maintained effectively and economically. In a sense, SPC is the "go-do" output of Process Capability Analysis, DOE, etc. Once you understand which factors impact process capability and yield, how can they be controlled? Can inspection or testing be eliminated by establishing appropriate control limits on the process itself?

Well, it's time to take out your government-issued ID for one last border-crossing. Before we leave Six-Sigma territory, however, I must pause for a moment to editorialize. Improvement programs, in general, remind me of the old adage, "The operation was a success...but the patient died." I've seen major corporations, for example, that have set up separate internal organizations to deploy Six-Sigma and Lean, and *then encouraged them to compete with each other for turf*. Other firms have invested so heavily in Six-Sigma training that they now have gangs of underutilized blackbelts hanging around the office cooler, waiting to pounce on the first sign of variability. Some extremely costly Six-Sigma projects have been justified by such fanciful and optimistic numbers that a corporate investment in the Brooklyn Bridge would seem savvy by comparison.

My point is this: Make sure that Six-Sigma Design, or any other improvement initiative, doesn't get away from you. More than any of the other tools discussed in this book, Six Sigma can grow to be costly and time-consuming. Don't let it become a religion, or at least give all improvement religions equal stature. A secular organization can achieve great things, so keep an eye out for the extremists. Your aim should be a balanced application of all lean design tools.

Notes

Section 6.3 — Design for Manufacture and Assembly (DFMA)

The last stop on our journey to product cost excellence is, in a sense, also where we began (see, you just *knew* I was guiding you in circles!). Design for Manufacture and Assembly (DFMA) is the closest thing out there to a true cost-reduction methodology. Moreover, it spans much of the same broad scope adopted for this guidebook. Beginning with fundamental cost drivers and ending with checklists of cost-reduction recommendations, DFMA provides a practical and almost universally accepted toolset. So why wait until the very end of this guidebook to discuss it? Actually, *it has already been discussed*; Parts I, III, IV, and V span the same space and incorporate many of the key techniques of DFMA. All that's left to do is clean up a few loose ends.

The "Design for ..." terminology has been around the manufacturing world for decades, but the real fathers of DFMA are Geoffrey Boothroyd, Peter Dewhurst, and Winston Knight, the authors of a landmark book, suggestively titled *Product Design for Manufacture and Assembly*. Oh, one might quibble that the Boothroyd Dewhurst, Inc. approach (what a surprise, these former University of Rhode Island professors started their own consultancy) is too auto-industry focused. It might even be said that they are somewhat obsessed with touch (i.e., direct) labor, and therefore miss many of the strategic, cross-product-line opportunities. These are minor eccentricities of an otherwise overwhelmingly useful and practical methodology.

My personal "first time" with DFMA was cathartic. Back in the "good old days" of aerospace (when our enemies really *did* have weapons of mass-destruction), my design team was chosen as a guinea pig for this relatively new idea of Design for Manufacturability. Some (very good) consultants came to our facility for a few days of training, and we were then unleashed to attack costs on an important new weapon system. In retrospect, the two-day event we conducted was remarkably similar to the Quick-Look Value Engineering (QLVE) event described in Section 4.2. Originally, our charter was to slash costs throughout the entire product; *all 2500 parts of it*. Fortunately for my team, more realistic heads prevailed, and we were allowed to focus our first DFMA review on just a single, relatively simple design element. The results were (for me at least) astonishing, as can be seen in Figure 6.23. Less than a fifth as many drawings, a third the number of parts, and a 74% direct-material cost savings. Most of us arrogant engineers couldn't believe our eyes.

6.3

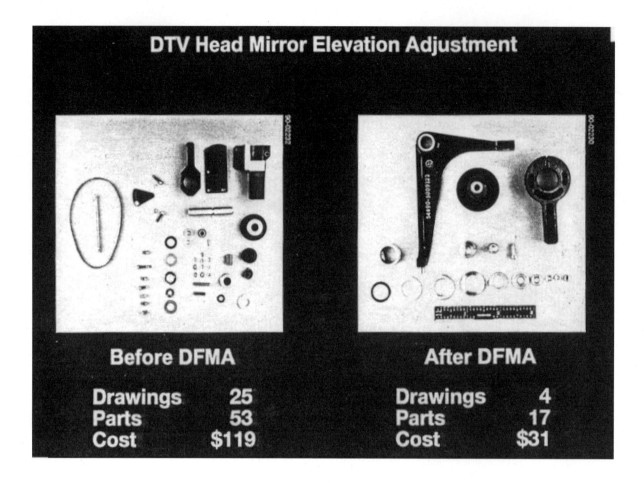

Figure 6.23 – An illustration of how DFMA techniques can dramatically reduce the complexity and cost of a product design. The subassembly shown is a mirror-tilting mechanism for an optical system.

Perhaps this first exposure to cost reduction was the genesis for my writing this guidebook, but in truth, I hadn't thought about that ancient experience until just now. What can be said for certain is that DFMA is the foundation upon which this guidebook's cost-reduction philosophy is based. Today, there are tons of DFMA resources available to support virtually any industry and product type. A "short" list of my personal favorites is provided in Figure 6.24. Since so much has been written about the basics of this methodology, I'll avoid redundancy. Instead, I'll discuss two aspects of DFMA that are less well-trodden; the last two pieces in the puzzle, so to speak. First, we'll consider a broadening of the "Design for..." perspective, followed by the introduction of a lean design tool that will help you institutionalize DFMA in your design organization. Incidentally, I wonder why no one has coined the term "Design for Profitability"?

Selected DFMA Resources

***** **Product Design for Manufacture and Assembly, 2nd Edition**
G. Boothroyd, P. Dewhurst, and W. Knight
2002, Marcel Dekker, Inc., ISBN 0-8247-0584-X

***** **Design for Manufacturabililty Handbook, 2nd Edition**
J. Bralla
1999, McGraw-Hill, ISBN 0-07-007139-X

***** **Engineering Design and Design for Manufacturing**
J. Dixon and C. Poli
1995, Field Stone Publishers, ISBN 0-9645272-0-0

***** **Tool and Manufacturing Engineers Handbook
(Vol. 6: Design for Manufacturability)**
R. Bakerjian, C. Wick, J. Benedict, et al. (Editors)
1992, Society of Manufacturing Engineers (SME), ISBN 0-87263402-7

***** **Tool and Manufacturing Engineers Handbook (All Volumes)**
Society of Manufacturing Engineers (SME), www.sme.org

**** **Design for Excellence**
J. Bralla
1996, McGraw-Hill, ISBN 0-07-007138-1

**** **Concurrent Engineering and Design for Manufacture of Electronics Products**
S. Shina
1991, Van Nostrand Reinhold, ISBN 0-442-00616-0

*** **Design for Manufacturability & Concurrent Engineering**
D. Anderson
2003, CIM Press, ISBN 1-878072-23-4

*** **Design for Manufacture**
J. Corbett, M. Dooner, J. Meleka, and C. Pym
1991, Addison-Wesley, ISBN 0-201-41694-8

Figure 6.24 – Several recommended resources for obtaining additional information on DFMA. These references contain a wealth of ideas, tricks, guidelines, checklists, and other practical enablers of manufacturing cost reduction.

6.3

Design for…Just About Everything

It wasn't long after Design for Manufacturability came on the scene that it became apparent designers required a broader perspective to ensure that all stakeholders in a product were considered. Sure, the voices of machine operators and assemblers on the factory floor were now being heard (at least in theory – unfortunately, being *heard* is not the same thing as being *listened to*), but what about all those others who have an impact on the cost and quality of a product? Don't the test and inspection folks deserve a "Design for" of their own? How about the service and maintenance people? And while we're on the subject, shouldn't designers be tasked with optimizing a product's reliability and cost of ownership *over its entire lifecycle*, from its cradle in the factory to its grave in a landfill?

One of the first organizations to recognize that DFMA didn't go quite far enough was AT&T's Bell Telephone Laboratories. In the late 1980's, several workers at Bell Labs coined the term "Design for X" (or DfX for short), implying that there were multiple attributes of a product that must be addressed to maximize value over the full product lifecycle, as shown in Figure 6.25. Since the DfX abbreviation always begged the question, "What's the 'X' stand for?" some clever individual at AT&T finally responded, "The 'X' stands for 'Excellence'." Hence, the name Design for Excellence has come to represent a methodology that addresses all aspects of design optimization, spanning the entire lifecycle of a product.

Design for Testability, for example, can be a major factor in reducing both the non-recurring and recurring cost of complex system products. Despite the idealism of Six-Sigma Design, virtually all products require some level of testing and inspection, and for multi-tiered systems, this can represent the largest single contributor to direct labor. Moreover, test equipment is expensive, test fixturing can be both expensive and product-specific (a cost no-no, as you might recall), and the cost per labor hour for test engineers may be well above the factory average. So what can be done?

First and foremost, a product must be designed to be fully testable, meaning that physical access should be provided for testing and inspection, and any "hidden functions" (e.g., seals for pressure vessels, electromechanical controls, software, embedded firmware, integrated circuits) must have 100% coverage for possible faults or failures. If the economics of the product warrant an even more aggressive stance, it might be designed to include built-in test (often referred to as BIT) and / or built-in diagnostics. As with all design considerations, there is a tradeoff that must be made between the cost of such sophisticated solutions and the cost of poor quality for the type of product involved. Keep in mind, however, that Design for Testability can return dividends to your firm even before the product hits the factory, by enabling rapid and effective prototype validation and qualification. More cost-saving benefits may be accrued after the product is in the field, particularly if your firm is responsible for service and repair.

Another heavy-hitter in the DfX constellation is Design for Reliability. Initial product quality is no longer sufficient to ensure long-term customer satisfaction, and more important, customer retention. Your product must continue to perform to high standards

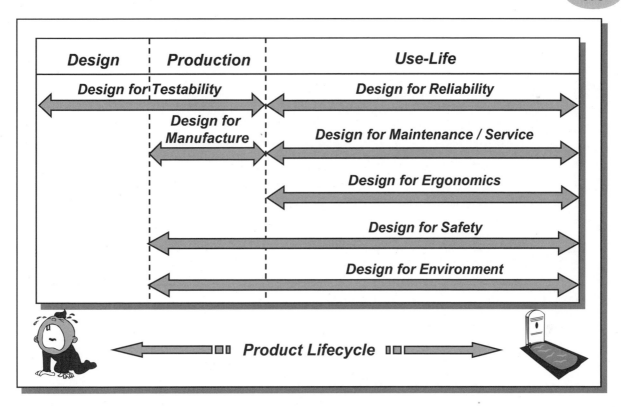

Figure 6.25 – The "Design-for-Excellence" perspective on product design acknowledges the entire lifecycle of a product from cradle to grave. This balanced approach ensures that all stakeholders in the product, from designers and factory workers to end users, will have their needs addressed.

throughout its expected life...whatever that is. Every market segment has different expectations regarding product reliability. It is critical that your designers know their targets for reliability, including infant mortality (out-of-box failures, which should be targeted at *zero*), use-life failures, and end-of-life wear-out and replacement. Fortunately, many of the cost-reduction recommendations included in this guidebook will also tend to support Design for Reliability. Complexity is the enemy of long product life, so parts-count reduction and simplification efforts performed ostensibly to reduce cost will likely also bear fruit in improved reliability.

There are endless other "Design for X" attributes that can (and should) be considered by designers: Design for Maintenance and Service, Design for Ergonomics, Design for Safety, Design for Environment (also known as Green Design), and so forth. How on earth can a design team keep all of these considerations in mind, while racing to the product-launch finish line? The most common solution is to create lots of checklists. DFMA and DfX are characterized by checklist after checklist, such as the samples provided in Figure 6.26. You should know by now that I am a major cheerleader for checklists, but the broad and general ones that are offered in most DFMA references leave me a bit cold. The

6.3

A Sampling of Design-for-Excellence Checklist Items (Page 1 of 4)

Design for Testability –

- ☐ Minimize or eliminate manual adjustments.
- ☐ Employ a single test connection wherever possible.
- ☐ Provide self-adjusting or self-optimizing design elements.
- ☐ Allow sufficient space around critical nodes for probe access.
- ☐ Provide for design-element isolation and partitioning.
- ☐ Use standardized interfaces and circuit board dimensions (e.g., compatible with standard test equipment).
- ☐ Standardize power and ground connections (pin locations) across product lines.
- ☐ Provide sufficient controllability of separate design elements.
- ☐ Provide high-frequency test points as close to the signal source as possible.
- ☐ Provide 100% access and coverage of board features through edge connectors wherever possible.
- ☐ Provide automated alarms or signals to communicate failures.
- ☐ Provide quick-disconnect fittings for pressure testing.

Design for Reliability –

- ☐ "Always look for the weakest link"
- ☐ "Keep it simple"
- ☐ Reduce parts count (e.g., fewer fasteners)
- ☐ Reduce or eliminate interconnections (e.g., bends vs. welds)
- ☐ Avoid wear-out mechanisms:
    - ☐ Corrosion
    - ☐ Mechanical wear
    - ☐ Electromigration
    - ☐ Abrasion
- ☐ Reduce stress wherever possible:
    - ☐ Balance mechanical and electrical loads
    - ☐ Avoid "hot spots"
    - ☐ Reduce thermal loads everywhere
    - ☐ Avoid high-pressure nodes

Figure 6.26 – "Design-rule" checklists are critical to successfully incorporating DFMA / DfX into your product development process. The generic examples provided are by no means complete, but should serve as a good starting point for your own, more product-specific checklists.

A Sampling of Design-for-Excellence Checklist Items (cont.) (Page 2 of 4)

Design for Safety –

- ☐ Design products to include fail-safe features.
- ☐ Avoid sharp corners, edges, points, etc.
- ☐ Provide guards or covers to avoid contact between persons and any moving parts.
- ☐ Guards should be permanently mounted to product to prevent insertion of foreign objects, and should not interfere with use.
- ☐ Avoid shearing or crushing points that could trap body parts.
- ☐ Anticipate the environment in which the product will be used.
- ☐ Utilize proper grounding and electrical interlocks.
- ☐ Incorporate warning devices that detect hazards when present.
- ☐ Avoid awkward positioning of the user's hand, wrist, arm, etc.
- ☐ All safety markings must be clear, concise, and long-lasting.

Design for Service and Maintenance –

- ☐ Ensure that components that will require replacement / service are easily accessible and clearly visible.
- ☐ Design short-lived parts to have easy removal and replacement.
- ☐ Allow for both preventative and breakdown maintenance.
- ☐ Design with field service conditions in mind (e.g., minimize tool requirements, avoid small fasteners, etc.).
- ☐ Consider designing the product with easily replaceable modules, often called "field-replaceable units."
- ☐ High-maintenance parts should either be commercially available or meet all common industry standards.
- ☐ Failure annunciation / alarms should be included to warn users of failures and provide diagnostic assistance.
- ☐ Design for rapid diagnostics and fault isolation.
- ☐ Provide spares of high-wear parts with new-product shipments.
- ☐ Access covers should be self-supporting when open.
- ☐ Verify that service / maintenance procedures are free of hazards!

Figure 6.26 – (Continued)

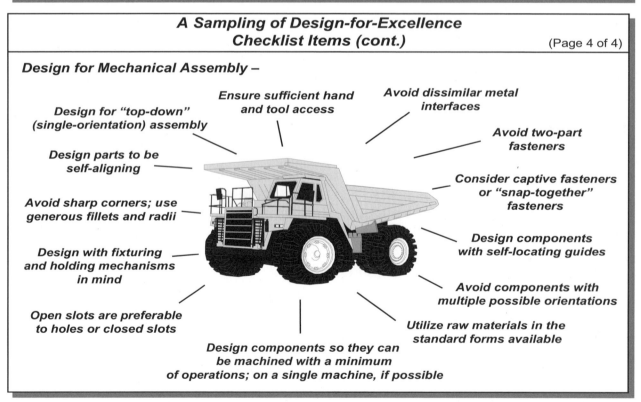

Figure 6.26 – (Continued)

examples that appear in the figure *are barely starting points* for what your design team *really* needs to successfully implement DFMA / DfX. The time invested by your engineering organization in developing *product-specific, firm-specific, market-specific* checklists will pay for itself a hundredfold.

When should these checklists be employed? The best time to trot out your DfX laundry list is during the early stages of concept design, when product functions are being defined and prioritized (see Part II). It is entirely reasonable for your product's function list to include: "last ten years," "be fully testable," "avoid injury," etc. As the development process progresses, the checklists can be influential at design reviews and other gate-type events. Naturally, as with all knowledge-management tools of this type, a process should be defined for updating (and also scrubbing) your DFMA / DfX checklists to ensure that they steadily improve over time.

Although checklists are like candy to me, I must admit that there is actually a *better way* to institutionalize DFMA / DfX in your product development organization. The problem with checklists is *context*, or perhaps I should say, the *lack of context*. Typically one set of lists is applied to every type of part in every type of product. If a firm is somewhat more sophisticated, it might develop process-specific lists: one for electronic assemblies, one for mechanical parts, and so on. Why not take this to its logical conclusion? What designers really need are part- or product-specific *design guidelines*. An integrated set of recommendations and design "best practices," spanning all applicable DFMA / DfX attributes, that focuses on what designers actually design. The lean design tool presented in the next subsection will help you develop your own library of Design "Best-Practice" Guidelines.

Defining a "Region of Goodness" for Product Design

A few years ago, I worked with an aerospace firm on the West Coast that specialized in airframe components, including engine nacelles and other big pieces of things that fly. These guys were intensely committed to achieving a lean enterprise, and had considered a number of approaches to lean design, some more effective than others. The one success story that impressed me most was their library of "design guidelines." They had created a standard template for capturing design best practices, and after each development project was completed, they assigned key individuals to fill out one or more of these templates. At the time of my visit, they had over 250 guidelines in a searchable database. The unspoken rule for their designers was that unless they had a compelling justification, the guidelines must be honored for any new design.

The beauty of these guidelines is that they pulled together design rules for manufacturability, performance, reliability, safety, testability, and more, all in one place, and specific to one design element at a time. In other words, both DFMA and DfX recommendations were presented in the context of individual product types and market segments. A new engineer could join this firm and within weeks be spooled up on the "right way" to do airframe design. This is not to say that these guys just turned the crank during new product development. They simply focused their clever minds on problems that could not be solved using their existing best practices. How better to maximize their design-teams' productivity? (Recall that I've already given you my dire warning about "best practices," so I won't belabor the point here. Just remember that the word "best" is just a figure of speech, not a license to stop thinking.)

The Design "Best-Practice" Guideline template tool summarized in Figure 6.27 and presented in Figure 6.28 can enable your firm to build its own repository for design excellence. These resources need be no more than a few pages in length, and should take only a few hours to complete. At the end of each development project, select one or more of the involved team members to fill out a template. Focus on aspects of the product design that were particularly successful (e.g., low production cost, higher-than-expected performance, improved synergy with other products, etc.). Establish a location on your intranet (or in your file-server directory if you are still living in caves) to store these gems, ideally with a search-engine interface to allow rapid access to needed information. True, it will take a couple of years to build a comprehensive library. Some strategic, visionary, progressive

---

"At a Glance" – Design "Best-Practice" Guideline

Overview –
The mandates of DFMA and DfX are often implemented in the form of endless checklists that provide no context for designers. As a result, important considerations are often ignored or neglected until late in the development process. The Design "Best-Practice" Template allows a host of design rules and cost-reduction considerations to be incorporated into a simple, designer-friendly format.

Primary Benefits –
Provides a practical way to deploy DFMA and DfX mandates, while defining a "region of goodness" for product designers. Can also serve as a powerful resource for knowledge capture and management, allowing new employees to rapidly come up to speed.

Best Suited Products –
Works for any product or service that requires non-recurring design.

Advantages –
Quick and easy to implement, and relatively non-threatening to designers. Allows an "exception management" approach for the incorporation of cost-reduction measures into new product designs.

Disadvantages –
Requires a small time investment to complete a template, so this method is best implemented over an extended period of time. As always, teams must have discipline to use this tool.

Impact on the Twenty Cost Levers –

I. Direct Labor				II. Direct Materials				III. Capital				IV. Design Cost				V. Overhead			
1a	1b	1c	1d	2a	2b	2c	2d	3a	3b	3c	3d	4a	4b	4c	4d	5a	5b	5c	5d
◉	○	○	●	●	◉	◉	◉	○	○	◉	○	●	●	●	○	○	○	○	○

Figure 6.27 – "At-a-glance" overview of the Design "Best-Practice" Guideline template lean design tool.

thinking is required here. Actually, I'm just trying to butter you up. It's really not that big of an investment, and the payback begins the first time you hire a new designer, or when one of your "irreplaceable" gurus walks out the door with everything they know.

The Design "Best-Practice" Guideline template shown in the figure provides space at the top for title and authorship. If you plan to create a comprehensive set of these templates, it might make sense to use a numbering convention similar to that of a drawing tree for one of your typical products. If not, a set of searchable keywords should suffice to allow rapid access to desired topics. It is also important to indicate the context in which the guideline must be considered: a specific "exhibit" should be identified for each guideline (i.e., an actual component or assembly upon which the best practice is based), and the model number of the product in which the "exhibit" is incorporated. All technical documentation should be identified under the "Reference Documents" heading, and if any other good examples of the best practice exist, they should be indicated as well.

The "Overview" should be a single terse paragraph. Just enough information for the user to understand what is being designed. Save the detail for the specific recommendations that will follow. At the bottom of the first page, I like to provide space for a digital photo or simple drawing. The annotations that I've shown in the figure are optional, but they can be quite useful if the part is not visually familiar to other designers.

Beyond this introductory information, the remainder of the guideline should consist of rules-of-thumb, recommendations, suggestions, even specific mandates if necessary. It is not essential that a Design "Best-Practice" Guideline be only two pages long, but I recommend putting an upper limit on page count. The longer the document, the less likely it will be that designers will use it. Focus on only the high-value stuff and everyone will be better off. The categories of recommendation that you include are entirely up to you: any DFMA or DfX attribute is fair game. Certainly performance suggestions are a must, along with manufacturability design rules. Anything that makes your product challenging to design, difficult to produce, or potentially dissatisfying to customers is grist for the mill.

A good way to obtain willing participation from your designers is to offer a symbolic reward for completing a Design "Best-Practice" template. Perhaps a little recognition at a company function, or an "I submitted a Design 'Best Practice,' and all I got is this stupid tee-shirt" gift. Inject a little fun into the process, and you'll have no trouble persuading designers to contribute to your firm's strategic future.

6.3

Design "Best-Practice" Guideline (Page 1 of 2)

Title: Printed Circuit Board for DC Motor Control
Author: Ron Mascitelli   **Date Created:** 4/24/2010
Guideline No.: RM101-2010
Key Words: Circuit, Board, Electronic, Motor, Control, Wave, Solder
Applications: All products with DC motors less than one horsepower, and 115 VAC input power.
Exhibit Part Number: XYZ23456-3
Incorporated into Model Number: Megamotor A-123
Reference Documents:
   Drawing No. ABC123
   Specification XYZ456
   Test Procedure 22222.44
   Industry Standard AB-CD

Overview:

This guideline describes a successful, low-cost design approach for printed circuit boards (PCB) whose function is to control DC motors of less than 1 hp. The XYZ23456-3 PCB is an excellent exhibit for this guideline, having displayed production yields of > 99.9% at volumes of > 10,000 units per month. The manufacturing process is assumed to be through-hole / wave-solder, with automatic parts insertion and no secondary (hand) assembly. A four-layer polyamide board is used, as a balance between cost and quality. Automated "in-circuit" testing is provided for in the design.

Simplified Drawing:

- All through-holes are the same diameter
- Edge connector with 100% test coverage
- Large test pads are provided for in-circuit testing
- Four layers maximum
- Ground layer doubles as noise shielding
- IC xxx-4 is standard for all Megamotor controllers

Figure 6.28 – The Design "Best-Practice" Guideline template provides a simple and highly effective way to capture DFMA / DfX-type recommendations in a user-friendly format.

Design "Best-Practice" Guideline (Page 2 of 2)

Recommended Process Equipment and Suppliers:
1) Boards-R-Us standard four-layer polyamide circuit board
2) X-2000 component auto-insertion machine
3) QRB-23 wave-solder machine
4) Organic chemical wash and deionized water rinse
5) F-467 in-circuit tester with standard configuration test rack

Material Selection Guideline:
1) Avoid tantalum capacitors for this application
2) Note maximum temperature for all components must be > 50 °C
3) Carbon resistors in standard values are preferred
4) All components must be available on tape-and-reel for auto-insertion

Critical-to-Quality Factors:
1) Ground noise must be handled by a continuous ground layer connected at multiple points to the master ground
2) Avoid placing ICs next to tall vertical components (to reduce possibility of damage during auto-insertion)

Recommendations for Yield Optimization:
1) Spacing of through-holes must be > 0.3 inch on center
2) All ICs should be positioned near center of board
3) Axial components should be positioned in parallel
4) Polarized components should be aligned in parallel, with poles oriented in the same direction

Recommendations for Cost Reduction:
1) Never use jumper wires or other manual operations
2) Eliminate chip carriers – solder ICs directly to board
3) All through-holes should be the same diameter
4) Use lower-tolerance passive components when possible
5) Gold-plated edge connectors are not required for this application

Recommendations for Test / Inspection:
1) Pads for in-circuit testing must be > 0.05 inch square
2) Logic should be provided on board to allow 100% fault testing of control commands through the edge connector
3) Functional nodes should be separable from each other to allow independent testing and diagnosis

Figure 6.28 – (Continued)

Notes

Section 6.4 — Achieving Continuous Cost Improvement

Well, folks, your guided tour of the lean design landscape is complete. It's time to head for baggage claim...except for one final unanswered question. We have journeyed through virtually every aspect of product cost reduction, gathering along the way eighteen lean design tools that can be applied immediately to maximize your profits. What should your next step be? How can these ideas be converted into action by yourself, your team, and if you're a corner-office type, your entire organization?

This is not a trivial challenge (those of you who have held the thankless job of "change agent" at some point in your career are no doubt shouting "amen"). I certainly have no fairy dust to offer you here, but I can share my experience in implementing these and other lean methods in firms spanning several industry sectors. Two scenarios will be considered: 1) you are a team member or leader who is interested in reducing cost on a specific new product, and 2) you are an organizational leader with a desire to implement lean design across your entire group or business unit. Before addressing these situations, however, I'll offer a few platitudes about change that might help bolster your resolve:

1) True organizational change happens gradually and inconsistently, despite the banners, tee shirts, and endless pep talks. This can be immensely frustrating to those who are championing the change. Keep this in mind: if you're pushing a giant boulder up a mountain, you can't see the progress you've made until you look behind you. Take every opportunity to celebrate the (albeit disappointing and woefully inadequate) successes you've achieved, rather than dwelling on how "our culture just won't accept new ideas." Sometimes it takes a little success to breed more success.

2) Be *persistent*, not *insistent*. A good analogy for organizational change is to compare it to braces on your teeth. Slow, steady pressure will eventually yield substantial improvement. A quick, hard hit to the jaw, on the other hand, rarely results in an improved smile.

3) Finally, recognize that change is scary to just about everybody. So why not implement new ideas below people's radar screens? If your designers don't know they're changing, their guard will be down. Try slipping new ideas into your development process "on the spur of the moment." Don't imply that the idea is a permanent change; just a neat tool

that's worth a test drive. Ask people's opinion afterward, and if the response is positive, let it appear as though it was their idea to use the tool. You can accomplish almost anything in an organization if you don't take personal credit for it.

Ok, enough of the banal generalities. We will first consider how you might implement lean design if you're the leader of a single development team, or just the master of your own daily work.

A Kaizen Approach to Lean Design Deployment

Let's assume for the moment that you are a product development team member or team leader. You are likely immersed in specific design issues, cost tradeoffs, and process challenges; the last thing on your mind is trying to change the world (or even your business unit). You want to be successful at your assignment, and that means you need a quick and easy way to gain major cost savings. Fortunately, the toolbox format presented in this guidebook is ideally suited to your situation. All that's required is a method for selecting the best tool(s) for the job.

Rather than inventing something new, let's steal a page from the lean folks on the shop floor and use a *kaizen* approach. The word *kaizen* literally means "continuous improvement," but there is a strong connotation to this word that I find irresistible: *don't talk about it, do it*. *Kaizen* events are typified by intensive, hands-on activity that yields immediate results. To achieve this high benefit-to-time ratio, opportunities to improve a specific process are gathered, and a simple priority-ranking approach is used to guide the *kaizen* team down the most lucrative path. Since we already have a nice list of lean design tools (see the Lean Design Tool Quick-Reference Guide at the beginning of this guidebook), all we need is a way to sort them out. The *kaizen* priority-ranking approach is a perfect fit.

Gather your core design team together for a one-hour meeting. Begin by informally discussing the major cost challenges that you will face during development of your specific product. Now create a template such as the one shown in Figure 6.29 on a flipchart or whiteboard. Since there are only eighteen lean design tools, you could easily consider all of them in a one-hour meeting. You might, however, decide to trim the obvious non-starters from the list and perhaps add a few of your own improvement ideas. Once you have selected an appropriate list of candidate tools, spend a minute or two discussing how each tool might apply to the cost issues you've identified. After this brief dialog, have the group rank the tools using two subjective criteria. The first is its potential *impact* on product cost. A 1-5 scale works quite well, with a "1" implying little or no impact and a "5" being a direct hit. Use a similar scale to evaluate the tool's *ease of implementation*. Some of the best ideas in the world are just too darned hard to make happen. This second score helps ensure that your team's lean design efforts won't stumble at the starting gate. Note that a "5" score in this category means that the tool under consideration is *easy* to implement, whereas a "1" score indicates a very difficult road ahead.

Promising Lean Design Tools	Ratings (1-5)		Priority
	Impact (I)	Ease (E)	(I x E)

Figure 6.29 – A simple *kaizen* template that can help your team select the lean design tools that will provide the greatest immediate benefit. Two subjective 1-5 scores are used to prioritize the most promising cost-reduction techniques. The product of the *impact* and *ease of implementation* scores serves as a useful priority ranking.

Once all of the lean tools on your list have been given scores for both impact and ease of implementation, multiply the two scores together (by now you know the drill); the result will be a useful priority ranking. Assign individuals to be responsible for implementing the top one-to-three tools on your list, and you're on the way to cost-saving nirvana. This approach can be used repeatedly throughout a given project, or can be used organization-wide as a surgical tool to solve intractable cost problems. Either way the value added will far outweigh the time spent. You won't achieve much organizational change, however, other than an increase in tribal knowledge. To aggressively move your firm toward lean design (and therefore cost-reduction) excellence, you'll need a systematic deployment plan, such as the one described in the next subsection.

6.4

Lean Design as a Corporate Improvement Initiative

One of the greatest advantages of lean design is that deployment doesn't require major organizational disruption. Improvements to the *process* of product development can impact virtually every function within a firm, and can be a major pain to sell, train, document, measure, and enforce. On the other hand, getting designers to use lean design tools requires nothing more than education, discipline, and a positive attitude toward cost improvement (I make it sound so easy). Sure there will be resistance, but most lean design tools are fun, quick, and show such dramatic and immediate results that even the biggest concrete-heads in your firm should eventually be swayed.

How might a corporate-wide lean design initiative be executed? The first step is to identify the order in which the tools should be deployed. Please don't try to deploy all of the tools at once. I've found that a typical organization can only absorb three-to-five tools at a time, with perhaps a year or more between "waves" of deployment. Hence, the strategy that I recommend involves three "phases," with each phase consisting of a select group of tools. The order of rollout is entirely up to you, and should be driven by your firm's most pressing cost challenges. Everything else being equal, however, there is a logical order that you might consider, as shown in Figure 6.30. Think of the pyramid depicted in the figure as a lean design "maturity model" for your organization (not unlike Maslow's "Hierarchy of Needs").

At the base of the hierarchy, listed under Phase I, are individual- and team-level tools that are fundamental to successful cost control. A lean design effort *must* begin with a target cost and a practical cost model. Otherwise, how would your team know if they've gained or lost ground? The Twenty-Cost-Lever tool is also a basic building-block, since it can be used in almost any tradeoff situation to validate cost-saving opportunities. Finally, I've included two high-leverage tools in Phase I that address basic cost issues: the Quick-Look Value Engineering event focuses on optimization of conceptual design, while the "How's it Built?" Review ensures that at least some basic product and process co-development occurs.

As your firm matures in lean design, more aggressive tools can be rolled out, based on the needs of the time. I've recommended eight possibilities, but I would only include about half that number in your Phase II program. The remainder can be held back for Phase III, or set aside indefinitely if they seem to be of low applicability. My personal choices, if I had to select only four tools for Phase II, would be the "Seven-Alternatives" Process, the Lean QFD, Must / Should / Could, and the Design "Best-Practice" Guideline.

Finally, once you've raised your firm's level of cost consciousness well above the water line, you can begin considering strategic cost-saving opportunities. In Phase III, you would establish a Product-Line Optimization Team and get them started building a Platform Plan and Product-Line Roadmap. You might also consider a serious program to train and implement Six-Sigma Design methods. It is important to note that the deployment of Six Sigma could easily be the *first* thing that you do after a foundation of Phase I tools is in place. You will have to assess the opportunities yourself, but keep in mind that

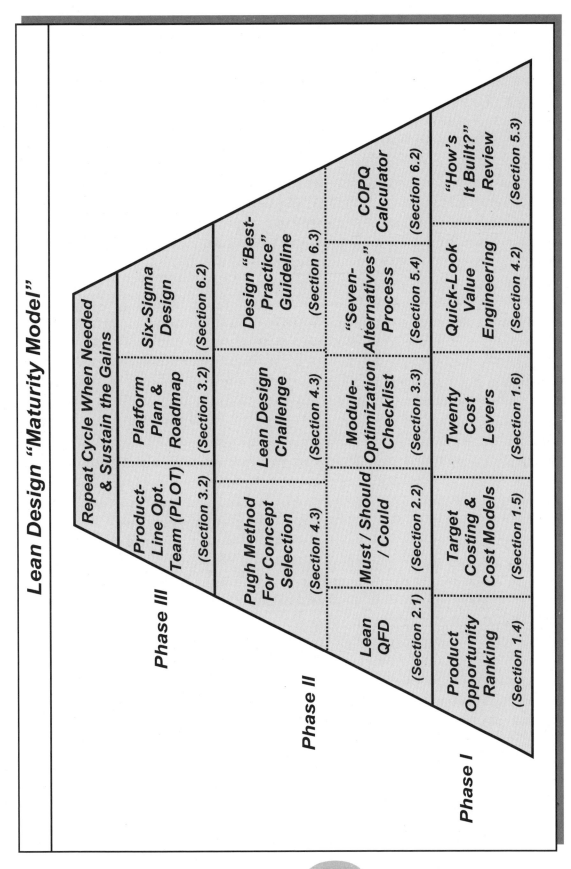

Figure 6.30 – The tools of lean design can be deployed in any order, but there is a logical hierarchy that should be followed if you are "starting from scratch" in the area of product cost reduction. Phase I builds a strong foundation of team-level cost-management tools, Phase II adds in some powerful tactical methods, while Phase III completes the picture with strategic, cross-product-line initiatives.

6.4

Six-Sigma Design requires major organizational commitment, so if you follow this path, it is likely that deployment of all other lean design tools will be delayed for at least a year or two.

Now that we have an idea of the order in which the tools should be deployed, all we need is a viable plan that can make it happen. One of the best techniques that I've observed involves selecting a *showcase project* for initial validation of each wave of tools. A showcase project can be any new product development activity, provided that the project team is open to new ideas, the team leader is relatively strong and effective, and the project has enough visibility and credibility to serve as a useful showcase. Your goal is to work the bugs out of the tools within each phase, and demonstrate to the rest of the organization that lean design can work in *your* culture, and on *your* products. A schedule for a three-phase deployment of lean design that incorporates this showcase-project approach is shown in Figure 6.31.

The first steps indicated in the schedule are the establishment of a deployment plan and the selection of a showcase project, as discussed above. Once these preliminaries are complete, the showcase team should receive training in the lean design tools selected for Phase I. As the project progresses, a series of interim debriefings is advisable so that functional and executive management can keep a pulse on the team's progress with the tools. It is critical that the showcase team be allowed to adapt and modify the tools as needed to ensure a positive outcome. A success here will open the door to broader acceptance and adoption, but word of a failure will spread like wildfire throughout your organization, poisoning the waters for further deployment.

After the showcase project is complete (or at least far enough along to feel confident with the tools), a "lessons-learned" meeting should be held to document any modifications to the tools that seem warranted. Training materials should then be updated accordingly and used to train the entire design staff. Now *all* projects should begin using Phase I tools, and it is time to kick off Phase II. Another showcase project is selected (or perhaps the same project might be used a second time, if it's of long duration), and the team is trained in the Phase II toolset. It is a good idea to select a Phase II showcase team that includes at least a few members from the first showcase project, to serve as lean-design advocates within the group. After Phase II is complete, the same process can be repeated for Phase III, until all tools have been trained and all project teams are using them appropriately.

Keep in mind that a deployment of this magnitude takes time, so be patient. You should begin to see improvement almost immediately, and that success will tend to accelerate the acceptance of additional tools. Be sure to assign an individual to be the champion for the entire deployment initiative (don't ask for volunteers, just pick the best person for the job). You cannot expect anything to happen if it is the responsibility of "the team." If you want results, make it somebody's job-one. Finally, don't be afraid to add your own twists to this process. If you have an alternative approach to deployment that has been successful, use it. If you know of in-house tools that should be added to the lean design toolbox, include them. If you discover the secret to successful organizational change, *tell me!*

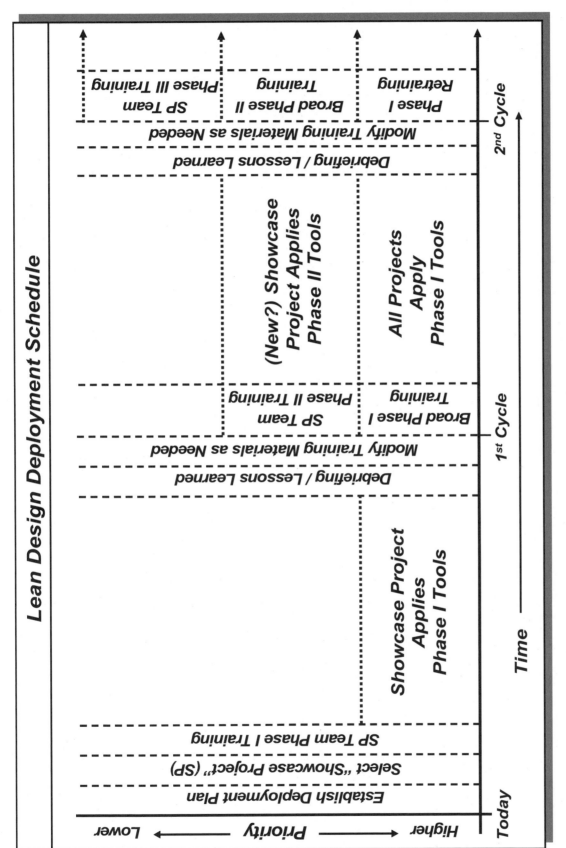

Figure 6.31 – A reasonable approach to the rollout of lean design tools throughout an organization. A "showcase project" is selected at the beginning of each "phase" to serve as a pathfinder. Once the tools have been validated by the showcase team, they are deployed more broadly throughout the organization. Note that the tools selected for each phase are entirely up to you, but consider the recommendations shown in Figure 6.30.

Notes

Recommendations for Further Learning

Here is my last set of recommendations. Please note that references for Design for Manufacture and Assembly (DFMA) and Design for Excellence (DfX) are listed separately in Section 6.3, Figure 6.24. Good luck in your studies!

Six-Sigma Design

***** *Design for Six Sigma: A Roadmap for Product Development*, Yang, K., and B. El-Haik, 2003

If you can get beyond the steep price tag, this is a truly great guide to Six-Sigma Design. It gets rather deep in spots (which is not necessarily a bad thing if you desire such detail), but is understandable through and through.

**** *Design for Six Sigma*, Chowdhury, S., 2002

Don't get this book confused with the one mentioned above (with almost the same title). The presentation is not as effective, and the scope is a bit narrower, but it is otherwise a good resource. Unless you are counting pennies, however, I'd fork over the dough for Yang, et al.

**** *The Vision of Six Sigma: Tools and Methods for Breakthrough*, Harry, M. J., 1994

Mikel Harry was one of the founding fathers of Motorola's original Six-Sigma methodology. Since that time, he has built a major consultancy that is a world leader in Six-Sigma training. Therefore, it is not surprising that this book is essentially a training manual, filled with "viewgraph-style" figures and virtually no text. I like the graphics (except for Harry's penchant for cluttering up figures with meaningless clipart), and some of the examples are excellent. You definitely need a second, more explicit resource to pair with this one, however.

*** *Six Sigma*, Harry, M. J., and R. Schroeder, 2000

I wish that this was the book to pair with the other by Mikel Harry mentioned above, but it just isn't. A broad-brush look at corporate deployment of Six Sigma, and definitely *not* applicable to product designers. I included it on my list because some of you might be at a level in your firm where corporate-wide initiatives are the topic of discussion around the cappuccino machine.

**   *Lean Six Sigma*, George, M. L., 2002

This is the only two-star reference in this guidebook, and its inclusion is more of a warning than a recommendation. You would be far better off reading a good book on Lean Thinking and a good book on Six Sigma, and figuring out how to combine these two philosophies yourself. There is certainly merit to a merger of these highly synergistic and effective programs, but most of the books on this topic are such superficial rehashes that they may give Lean Six Sigma a bad name. I don't mean to single out Michael George's book; my opinion is applicable to the entire genre (as of this writing).

Taguchi Methods / Robust Design

*****   *Engineering Methods for Robust Product Design*, Fowlkes, W. Y., and C. M. Creveling, 1995

There are lots of good books on Taguchi Methods (some of which are actually *by* Taguchi), but this one stood out to me as the most comprehensive and pragmatic. If you are interested in gaining a practical understanding of the subject, you won't be disappointed. Just remember that Taguchi Methods are relatively complex, so don't start whining when you see integrals and differential equations.

Design of Experiment (DOE)

*****   *Understanding Industrial Designed Experiments - 3rd Edition*, Schmidt, S. R., and R. G. Launsby, 1992

As you might have guessed, I'm only recommending one book on each of the single-tool topics. Why? Because there is only so much you can say about DOE (or Robust Design, or FMEA), and a *great* reference is far better than three or four mediocre ones. This book is fairly sophisticated in its treatment; any more depth and you would need to breathe a helium-oxygen mixture to avoid the bends. Yet it is a very comprehensive and understandable book. If you are frightened by matrices (and the manipulation thereof), you will be horrified by the topic of DOE in general, so be forewarned.

Failure Modes and Effects Analysis (FMEA)

*****   *Failure Mode and Effect Analysis*, Stamatis, D. H., 1995

If there were no other books on the subject of FMEA, the world would be none the worse off. Another excellent resource, and there's some good news…*no heavy math*. My only question for the author would be, "Why does your book's title use singular rather than plural forms for 'mode' and 'effect'?" You know, it's one of those "writer things."

Conclusion

A Word About Lean and Green

Now that you have completed your intellectual journey, I hope you are convinced that there is a wealth of opportunity to reduce costs through the methods of lean design. For the pragmatists among you, this should be sufficient for you to feel excited and empowered. I join you in that excitement, as I'm all in favor of making money as well. On the other hand, as my own journey through life has progressed, I've discovered that not all profits are created equal. Simply making money is relatively easy, particularly if you have little concern for the impact of your enterprise on the "greater good." Yet those of us who design products for a living have an immense impact on the world as a whole, beyond the narrow perspectives of paying customers. Hence, if your mercenary tendencies are tempered by a social conscience, I have very good news. In almost every sense, *lean design is really green design*. By eliminating the waste from new product designs, we are very likely reducing the negative impact of those products on the natural world. As Phil Crosby used to say, "Quality is free." If industry truly embraces lean design, it may turn out that saving our planet can be "free" as well.

A little history lesson is in order. The first and second industrial revolutions (the introductions of steam power and electricity respectively) were characterized by breakthroughs in production efficiency. The factors of production (i.e., the raw materials, energy, and labor) that enabled industrialization in the nineteenth and twentieth centuries, however, were generally extracted from our poor unsuspecting planet. The energy and materials needed to propagate and automate manufacturing came with an abysmal environmental price tag. Fouled air and water, strip mines, clear-cut forests, destroyed habitats, and global warming are the sad but familiar legacy of our early days of industrialization. Indeed, even today developing countries are going through the same destructive cycle (albeit at an accelerated rate). Witness the irreversible and breathtakingly rapid annihilation of rain forests in Indonesia and Brazil, the incalculable impact of China's Three Gorges Dam project, and so on. Is this simply the price of modern society; an acceptable penalty for an increased standard of living? Perhaps we should ask a different question: Is it standard of living that is important, or is it really *quality of life*? We have certainly made notable progress on the former, but in my opinion, we have failed miserably in guaranteeing the latter.

Conclusion

Now for the good news. As the industrial marketplace has become more sophisticated, competition has driven firms to look for new and deeper efficiencies. Mass production is no longer enough. Quality is no longer enough. Firms must now provide *true value*; performance and quality delivered at the lowest possible price. As a result of this mandate, the profit-driven goals of business are finally beginning to merge with the altruistic demands of environmental protection. We no longer need to justify green (i.e., environmentally friendly) design, *because the cost savings justify themselves*. If your firm standardizes parts to reduce production cost, it also reduces the energy and materials that would have been wasted in producing a variety of different parts. If your designs enable your factory to make better use of its capital equipment, the Earth need not be robbed of the materials and energy required to build more machines. If your operations team is able to streamline their manufacturing processes, they will consume less space, energy, and materials. Further lean design improvements can reduce scrap, consumables, and other forms of industrial waste that the planet must ultimately deal with. The bottom line is that wasteful designs are costly to both the Earth *and* the balance sheet.

The optimists among us might say that we have arrived at the beginnings of a virtuous cycle; lean designs yield cost savings that drive competition toward even leaner designs, with each cycle resulting in reduced environmental impact. Perhaps we product designers can soon hold our heads high in our pursuit of profits. Through lean design, we may finally have found a way to increase wealth without destroying the beautiful planet that has, for so long, abided our self-serving neglect.

Respectfully,

Ron Mascitelli
April 10, 2004

Glossary

Accuracy – The ability of a process to achieve a mean value that is close to the nominal (target) value. If you were a perfect marksperson who owned a perfect rifle (one that had ideal precision), your target-shooting accuracy would be determined by how well the gun sight was aligned with the aim-point of the gun. Move the gun sight and the "perfect" cluster of holes in the target would move to a new central value. To take this example into the non-perfect world, see the entry in this glossary under "precision."

Activity-Based Costing (ABC) – An informal enhancement to standard accounting methods that provides insight into the *actual* consumption of indirect overhead costs by individual products. It can significantly improve a firm's decision-making ability with respect to new product opportunities.

Assignable Costs – Costs that can be allocated to a specific product, rather than lumped into operational overhead.

Balanced Scorecard – An approach to performance measurement that recommends combining several distinct metrics when evaluating a situation. This technique avoids the potential skewing of results due to unrealistic emphasis on only a single metric.

Batch Process – A manufacturing process that acts on a relatively large number of parts at a single time, or with a single setup. Batch processes are a no-no in lean manufacturing; one-piece flow is considered the ideal.

Benefits – What customers actually pay for. Benefits are not requirements; they are high-level concepts (worded in the customer's own language) that usually involve saving time, saving money, improving quality of use, or delivering entertainment, prestige, or esteem.

Breakeven Number – The number of units of a new product that must be sold before a firm's non-recurring investment can be considered to be "paid back."

Consumables – Stuff that gets used up as part of the manufacturing process. Examples include paints, adhesives, abrasives, cutting tools, etc. The cost of consumables is usually lumped into operational overhead, making it invisible to everyone but the shareholders.

Glossary

Cost Buildup – The accumulated costs of a product, including all direct, indirect, and assignable non-recurring cost items.

Cost Knobs – Five high-level factors that can (and must) be optimized to gain maximum profits from a new product.

Cost Levers – Specific factors that can impact overall product cost. In this guidebook, I have suggested "twenty cost levers" but there could easily be alternatives that should be considered for a given product situation.

Cost Model – A simple calculating tool (often just a spreadsheet) that allows product designers to iteratively compare their current knowledge of product costs to the target cost for that product.

Cost of Poor Quality (COPQ) – A metric of product cost that focuses on lost profits due to poor manufacturing quality. Contributors to COPQ can include the costs of scrap, rework, delays, warrantee charges, service and repair, etc.

Dedicated Equipment – Capital equipment that will be used for the manufacture of only a single product (or set of related products). The cost of dedicated equipment must be "paid back" from the profits of the specific products that utilize it.

Design for Excellence (DfX) – A broader perspective on product design than Design for Manufacture and Assembly (DFMA). This concept was first proposed by AT&T Bell Telephone Laboratory as a way to consolidate a number of "Design for…" mandates, including DFMA, Design for Testability, Design for Environment, etc.

Design for Manufacture and Assembly (DFMA) – An improvement methodology that focuses on reduction of manufacturing cost through decreasing touch labor and material waste. Tends to have an auto-industry flavor, since the originators used this sector for their initial focus.

Design of Experiment (DOE) – An experimental methodology usually associated with the Six-Sigma Design suite of tools and techniques. DOE allows an experimenter to analyze the behavior of multivariable systems in which there may be dependency among the variables (such as in complex chemical processes, semiconductor manufacturing, pharmaceuticals, etc.).

Design Overshoot – A "gold-plated" design that provides more performance or features than a given market segment would be willing to pay for.

Design Undershoot – A substandard design that fails to completely solve the "customer problem" for a specific market segment.

Direct Labor – Labor hours that are required to produce a single unit of a product, counting only those activities that directly "touch" the product during manufacturing. (The remaining factory labor costs are generally included in operational overhead.)

Direct Materials – All materials that are directly incorporated into a single unit of a product during manufacture.

Discount Rate – A term used in the calculation of net present value that takes into account the future value of money (i.e., it reflects the financial risk of an investment in a new product by comparing it to what could have been earned if the same money had been earning interest).

Economic Risk – A risk associated with new product development that is related to economic factors such as inflation, economic growth (or the lack thereof), changes in interest rates, etc.

Economies of Scope – A beneficial situation in which multiple (and potentially very different) products within a product line share common parts, processes, capital equipment, and so on. Often referred to in the text as "cross-product-line synergy."

Failure Modes and Effects Analysis – A design review methodology that focuses on identifying the potential failure modes of a product, and subsequently determining ways to mitigate each risk of failure.

Finite Capacity – An occurrence characterized by a firm having more money-making opportunities than they have resources to pursue them. A factory is said to have finite capacity if demand for its products exceed its maximum output per period. A design organization has finite capacity if there are more profitable projects for designers than they can realistically handle.

First-Pass Yield – The percentage of products that pass through the manufacturing process with zero defects on the first try (no rework, in other words).

Five Principles of Lean Thinking – From the book, *Lean Thinking*, by Womack, et al. (see Bibliography). These are the guiding principles of the Lean Thinking improvement philosophy, with a focus on value, value stream, flow, pull, and perfection.

Glossary

Fixed Costs – Product-related costs that are independent of the volume of products that are produced. Capital equipment is a typical example of a fixed cost.

Flow-Line – A lean manufacturing mandate that involves elimination of wasted material and worker movement, along with any other interruptions to the "flow of value." Often a "one-piece-flow" strategy is employed in conjunction with flow-lines.

Function – Something that a product must deliver or perform to provide benefits to a customer.

Functional Silos – The tendency of organizations to form high-walled functional departments that can be obstacles to communication and can inhibit the ability of design teams to perform true cross-functional development.

Generally Accepted Accounting Principles (GAAP) – Accounting guidelines that are used as a foundation for validating a business' financial practices. One might argue that some aspects of GAAP are out-of-date when it comes to handling high-mix, high-customization manufacturing firms (see Activity-Based Costing).

Gold Plating – The act of overshooting customer requirements in a way that will not generate additional price or market share, either by incorporating excessive performance or undesirable features. That little paperclip animation that constantly pops up in MS Word to interrupt your work is a particularly annoying example of gold plating.

Innovation – The ability to think independently and creatively. From the market's perspective, a thimble-full of innovation is worth a railcar-load of turn-the-crank designs.

Interface – The point at which two or more "modules" of a product connect together. Typically, a standardized interface is an enabling factor in modular product design. Simple interfaces are always preferred.

Just-in-Time (JIT) – An improvement philosophy developed by Toyota Motor Company and other Japanese manufacturers during the 1980's. Involves minimizing inventory carrying costs by having materials delivered to a factory "just-in-time" to be consumed by the production process.

Kaizen – The Japanese word for "continuous improvement." Has a connotative meaning of "take immediate action." Is often used in the context of "*kaizen* events" that can result in dramatic reduction in non-value-added waste.

Lean Enterprise – An extension of the Lean Thinking improvement philosophy to an entire business enterprise.

Lean Manufacturing – A highly efficient approach to manufacturing, based on the methods developed by the Toyota Motor Company. Characterized by elimination of waste in all aspects of production, from inventory levels to movement of materials.

Lean Six-Sigma – A "Frankenstein" improvement philosophy that attempts to merge the "best of Lean" with the "best of Six Sigma." The result is (as of this writing) not much more than a convergence of buzzwords.

Learning Curve – A characteristic of direct (touch) labor that reflects the improved efficiency of workers as they become more experienced in manufacturing a product. It is typically represented by an exponential function, wherein each doubling of the total number of products produced results in a fixed percentage decrease in the direct labor required.

Market Forecast – A piece of fiction upon which most firms bet their futures. A projection of how many units of a product will be sold in which markets at what price over how long a period.

Market Risk – A risk to the success of a new product development project that reflects the uncertainties associated with market acceptance, price, competition, etc.

Mass Customization – A manufacturing strategy that attempts to capture both the cost advantages of mass production and the price benefits of customization. The operative word here is postponement – the customization of a product should be postponed as long as possible in the manufacturing process. In special cases, the customization might be performed by the customers themselves after purchase.

Mean – The weighted average of all points within a distribution. For a standard normal distribution, the mean value is at the center of the distribution.

Modular Design – A platform-based strategy in which the functionality of a product can be easily changed through the selection of appropriate modules. Modular product architecture requires standardized interfaces to enable maximum flexibility in the resulting product family.

Muda – The Japanese word for waste.

Glossary

Net Present Value (NPV) – A financial metric that represents the "total discounted future cash flows of a proposed product, minus the initial investment required." A positive NPV means that investment in a new product opportunity will be profitable to the firm. A negative NPV means the product opportunity should not be pursued.

Non-recurring Design Costs – The cost of design labor and materials consumed during the development of a new product. This is a fixed cost, and is therefore independent of the volume of the product that will ultimately be produced.

One-Piece Flow – An ideal of the lean manufacturing philosophy, one-piece flow avoids batch processes to enable improved production cycle-times and reduced work-in-process inventory.

Outsourcing – Delegating the production of some element of a product to an outside supplier. This strategy can range from the manufacture of minor components to the fabrication of an entire product (also known as "contract manufacturing").

Overhead – Also referred to as "operational overhead." All operating costs that cannot be directly assigned to specific products are lumped into an overhead "burden rate." This burden rate represents a "tax" on the profits of every product produced in a factory.

Pareto Principle – The famous "80 / 20" rule, which states that the vast majority of benefit from an activity (80%) can be achieved in the first 20% of the time invested. This "rule" applies to many aspects of business, including time invested in problem-solving, information-gathering, and so on.

Partitioning – The act of dividing a system into logical subsets or subsystems. A complex product might be "partitioned" into major subassemblies, minor subassemblies, components, etc. Typically a partitioning activity is needed when some "common" element of a system must be allocated among several design elements.

Platform – Any subset of a product (from the entire product to a single component) that can be shared across multiple models within a product line.

Positioning – A marketing technique that involves establishing a clear differentiation between a firm's products and their competitors' offerings.

Precision – The ability of a process to achieve minimal variability about a mean (or central) value. If you clamp a rifle into a vise and fire off a number of rounds at a target, the diameter of the cluster of holes that results would reflect the precision of the rifle. See "accuracy" for the other half of the story.

Production Process Preparation (3P) – An integrated and highly detailed approach to product and process co-development. This strategy is a mainstay of Toyota Motor Company's product development process.

Productivity – The profit (or revenue) output of an employee per period worked (often referred to as "output per labor hour").

Process Capability – The ability of a manufacturing process to hold tolerances when producing a specific product. Process capability is usually reported in terms of either the Process Capability Ratio (C_p) or the Process Capability Index (C_{pk}).

Process Capability Index – A measure of both the precision and accuracy of a production process, usually denoted by C_{pk}.

Process Capability Ratio – A measure of the precision of a production process, usually denoted by C_p.

Profit Margin – The difference between the total cost buildup of a product and the price received by the firm that produces it (note that this definition refers to "pre-tax profits").

Pull System – An approach to manufacturing that was pioneered by Japanese automobile manufacturers such as Toyota. Simple *kanban* (signal) cards are used to communicate what is needed (and *only* what is needed) by downstream processes. In a sense, a pull system starts at the shipping dock and works its way backwards through the factory, ultimately to raw materials inventory. A Just-in-Time (JIT) production system uses pull for both internal and supplier workflow management.

Quality Function Deployment (QFD) – Also known as the "House of Quality." A methodology for capturing the "voice of the customer," developed in the 1980's as part of the Total Quality Management movement. Allows customer-driven prioritization and tradeoffs to be performed on product functions and requirements.

Risk – The uncertainties that keep you from profits. Risk can be related to technical challenges, resource limitations, market uncertainty, economic turmoil, or any other unpredictable factors that can ruin your day.

Risk-Corrected Net Present Value – A modification of the traditional net present value calculation that incorporates "discount percentages" to account for market and technical risks.

Glossary

Robust Design – A design that is tolerant of the inherent variations in the manufacturing process. Taguchi Methods focus on achieving robust product design.

Scalability – A platform-based design strategy in which one or more design parameters of a product can be scaled through a range of possible values without an increase in the cost of each customized version.

Scenarios – Alternatives that provide insight into the range of possibilities for a given situation. In the context of product design, one might consider a "performance-maximized" scenario, a "cost-minimized" scenario, and so on.

Six-Sigma Design – A powerful and well-developed improvement methodology based on the breakthrough work performed by designers at Motorola Company in the late 1980's. The primary focus is on reduction of process variability to improve yield, reduce waste, and accelerate time-to-market.

Statistical Process Control (SPC) – A quality-assurance methodology that establishes control limits on process equipment and workers to ensure a high yield of quality parts. The goal of SPC is to reduce or eliminate in-line testing and inspection.

Strategic Product - Either: a) a product that is not likely to be profitable, but could have a significant positive effect on the future of a firm, or b) a money-loser that your boss just won't admit was a terrible idea.

System – A set of components or design elements that work together toward a common purpose, with some form of feedback. A "system product" usually connotes a fairly complex and multifunctional product.

Systems Thinking – A philosophy proposed by Peter Senge in his book, *The Fifth Discipline*, that applies fundamental systems-analysis concepts to the broader topics of business, leadership, management, and even personal productivity.

Taguchi Loss Function – One of the so-called "Taguchi Methods" for product quality improvement. Taguchi observed that the cost of poor quality does not behave like a step-function (i.e., either a part is "in tolerance" or "out of tolerance"). Instead, he suggested that *any* deviation from the nominal (target) value for a part will have a negative impact on overall product quality and customer satisfaction.

Takt Time – "*Takt*" is the German word for musical meter. The *takt* time of a product is related to how fast each unit must be produced to meet production quotas. For example, if a firm has orders for 1000 units per month of a specific product, the *takt* time would be: 160 hours per month / 1000 units = 9.6 minutes per unit (assuming a twenty-day month and a single, eight-hour shift).

Target Cost – The (realistic) market price projection for a product, minus the desired profit (or target) margin. The target cost should be calculated at the very beginning of a new product development project, and then compared to actual cost estimates throughout development to ensure that the desired margin can be achieved once the product is in production.

Target Margin – The minimum profit margin that is desired for a new product. This should be at least equal to the average gross margin for all products within a business unit.

Technical Risk – A risk to the success of a new product development project that results from the application of new or challenging technologies.

Thingamajigs – A relative of the widget that replaced the thingamabob in most geographic locations.

Tooling – A category of capital investment that is almost always product-specific (i.e., assignable capital). Tooling can include fixtures, molds, jigs, dies, test racks, holders, plates, and so on.

Total Quality Management – One of the first truly global improvement initiatives. Its source was the statistical quality methods first proposed by Deming and Juran, and successfully deployed by Japanese firms in the 1970's and 1980's.

Touch Labor – (see Direct Labor)

Toyota Motor Company – The fountain of all wisdom and enlightenment (or so one might believe, based on the rhetoric of lean consultants).

Value – Something that a customer would willingly pay for. In other words, value is performance (a solution to the customer's problem) delivered at a specified price. The value of a product is related to both the importance of the problem that is being addressed (from the customer's perspective) and the effectiveness of the product at solving that problem.

Glossary

Value Analysis – (see Value Engineering)

Value Engineering – One of the most effective methods for reducing the cost of a product, typically applied during initial conceptual design. Utilizes structured brainstorming on possible design alternatives to allow delivery of customer-mandated performance at the lowest possible cost.

Value Stream – A theoretical ideal for how value can be created most efficiently. The value stream is the flow of events necessary to accomplish a value-creating activity. For the case of products, there are two primary value streams involved: the non-recurring design value stream and the manufacturing value stream.

Variability – The enemy of all that is good and just. Variability exists in every manufacturing process, and is the predominant cause of quality defects in products. A "robust" product design is highly tolerant of manufacturing process variability, thereby assuring acceptable quality even when process precision and accuracy are marginal.

Variable Costs – Costs which increase as the production volume of a product increases.

Whachamacallits – A relative of thingamajigs, but with far greater therapeutic value.

Widgets – An obsolete product that was all the rage among authors of business and technical books. Once a high-price, high-profit product, now you can get a top-of-the-line widget for a just a few bucks on eBay.

Wonderjig – A highly successful variation of the basic thingamajig.

Workcell – An area of the factory that is set up to perform a series of process steps. Workcells can be organized around specific products or subassemblies, or can perform a common activity for multiple products (e.g., a painting workcell). Often, workcells are organized in a "U" shape to reduce material and worker movement, and to optimize factory workflow.

Work-in-Process (WIP) Inventory – All the stuff laying around the factory that should have been processed and shipped long ago. Excessive WIP costs a firm money, takes up space, gets in the way of flow, and generally turns your "pipeline factory" into a cluttered and costly warehouse.

Anderson, D. M., 1997, *Agile Product Development for Mass Customization*, Irwin Professional Publishing.

Anderson, D. M., 2003, *Design for Manufacturability & Concurrent Engineering*, CIM Press.

Baldwin, C. Y. and K. B. Clark, 2000, *Design Rules: The Power of Modularity*, The MIT Press.

Ballis, J., 2001, *Managing Flow: Achieving Lean in the New Millennium to Win the Gold*, Brown Books.

Barnes, T., 1996, *Kaizen Strategies for Successful Leadership*, Financial Times Pitman Publishing.

Belliveau, P., Griffen, A., and S. Somermeyer, 2002, *The PDMA Toolbox for New Product Development*, John Wiley & Sons.

Bicheno, J., 2000, *The Lean Toolbox – 2nd Edition*, PICSIE Books.

Bicheno, J., 2001, *The Quality 75*, PICSIE Books.

Boothroyd, G., Dewhurst, P., and W. Knight, 2002, *Product Design for Manufacture and Assembly – 2nd Edition*, Marcel Dekker.

Bossidy, L., and R. Charan, 2002, *Execution: The Discipline of Getting Things Done*, Crown Business Press.

Bralla, J. G., 1996, *Design for Excellence*, McGraw-Hill.

Bralla, J. G., 1999, *Design for Manufacturability Handbook – 2nd Edition*, McGraw-Hill.

Brown, J., 1992, *Value Engineering: A Blueprint*, Industrial Press.

Chow, W., 1998, *Cost Reduction in Product Design*, Van Nostrand Reinhold.

Chowdhury, S., 2001, *Design for Six Sigma*, Dearborn Trade Publishing.

Clark, K. B., and S. C. Wheelwright, 1993, *Managing New Product and Process Development: Text and Cases*, Harvard Business School Press.

Cohen, L., 1995, *Quality Function Deployment: How to Make QFD Work for You*, Addison Wesley.

Cokins, G., 1996, *Activity-Based Cost Management: Making it Work*, Irwin Professional Publishing.

Cooper, R. G., 1993, *Winning at New Products*, Addison Wesley.

Cooper, R. G., 1995, *When Lean Enterprises Collide*, Harvard Business School Press.

Cooper, R. G., and R. Slagmulder, 1997, *Target Costing and Value Engineering*, Productivity Press.

Cooper, R. G., Edgett, S. J., and E. J. Kleinschmidt, 1998, *Portfolio Management for New Products*, Perseus Books.

Corbett, J., et al., 1991, *Design for Manufacturing: Strategies, Principles and Techniques*, Addison Wesley.

Cowley, M., and E. Domb, 1997, *Beyond Strategic Vision: Effective Corporate Action with Hoshin Planning*, Butterworth Heinemann.

Bibliography

Criner, E. A., 1984, *Successful Cost Reduction Programs for Engineers and Managers*, Van Nostrand Reinhold.

Dimancescu, D., and K. Dwenger, 1996, *World-Class New Product Development*, AMACOM.

Dimancescu, D., Hines, P., and N. Rich, 1997, *The Lean Enterprise*, AMACOM.

Dixon, J. R., and C. Poli, 1995, *Engineering Design and Design for Manufacturing: A Structured Approach*, Field Stone Publishing.

Erhorn, C., and J. Stark, 1994, *Competing by Design*, Oliver Wright Publications.

Fallon, C., 1971, *Value Analysis to Improve Productivity*, John Wiley & Sons.

Forrester, J. W., 1971, *Principles of Systems*, Productivity Press.

Fowlkes, W. Y., and C. M. Creveling, 1995, *Engineering Methods for Robust Product Design*, Addison Wesley.

Gawer, A., and M. A. Cusumano, 2002, *Platform Leadership*, Harvard Business School Press.

George, M. L., 2002, *Lean Six Sigma*, McGraw Hill.

Goodpasture, J. C., 2001, "Make Kano analysis part of your new product requirements," *PM Network*, May Issue, pgs. 42-45.

Gorchels, L., 2000, *The Product Manager's Handbook*, NTC Business Press.

Groppelli, A. A., and E. Nikbakht, 1995, *Finance – 3rd Edition*, Barron's Educational Series.

Harry, M. J., 1994, *The Vision of Six Sigma: Tools and Methods for Breakthrough – 4th Edition*, Sigma Publishing Company.

Harry, M., and R. Schroeder, 2000, *Six Sigma*, Currency Doubleday.

Heineke, J. N., and L. C. Meile, 1995, *Games and Exercises for Operations Management*, Prentice Hall.

Hooks, I. F., and K. A. Farry, 2001, *Customer-Centered Products*, AMACOM.

Horngren, C. T., Foster, G., and S. M. Datar, 1994, *Cost Accounting: A Managerial Approach*, Prentice Hall.

Hyman, B., 1998, *Fundamentals of Engineering Design*, Prentice Hall.

Ichida, T., 1996, *Product Design Review*, Productivity Press.

Imai, M., 1997, *Gemba Kaizen*, McGraw-Hill.

Jackson, T. L., 1996, *Implementing a Lean Management System*, Productivity Press.

Kaplan, R. S., and D. P. Norton, 1996, *The Balanced Scorecard*, Harvard Business School Press.

Kaplan, R. S., and R. Cooper, 1998, *Cost & Effect: Using Integrated Cost Systems to Drive Profitability and Performance*, Harvard Business School Press.

Koenig, D. T., 1994, *Manufacturing Engineering – 2nd Edition*, Taylor & Francis.

Laraia, A. C., Moody, P. E., and R. W. Hall, 1999, *The Kaizen Blitz*, John Wiley & Sons.

Lareau, W., 2000, *Lean Leadership*, Tower II Press.

Lareau, W., 2003, *Office Kaizen*, ASQC Quality Press.

Leach, L. P., 2000, *Critical Chain Project Management*, Artech House.

Lee, H. I., et al., 1997, "Getting ahead of your competition through design for mass customization," *Target Magazine*, Vol. 13, No. 2.

Lencioni, P., 2002, *The Five Dysfunctions of a Team*, Jossey Bass.

Liker, J. K., 2003, *The Toyota Way: 14 Management Principles from the World's Greatest Manufacturer*, McGraw-Hill.

Lipnack, J., and J. Stamps, 1997, *Virtual Teams*, John Wiley & Sons.

Mascitelli, R., 1999, *The Growth Warriors: Creating Sustainable Global Advantage for America's Technology Industries*, Technology Perspectives.

Mascitelli, R., 2000, "From experience: Harnessing tacit knowledge to achieve breakthrough innovation," *J. Prod. Innov. Manag.*, Vol. 17, 179-193.

Mascitelli, R., 2002, *Building a Project Driven Enterprise: How to Slash Waste and Boost Profits Through Lean Project Management*, Technology Perspectives.

McConnell, S., 1996, *Rapid Development*, Microsoft Press.

McConnell, S., 1998, *Software Project Survival Guide*, Microsoft Press.

McGrath, M. E., 1995, *Product Strategy for High-Technology Companies*, Irwin Professional Publishing.

Meyer, M. H., and A. P. Lehnerd, 1997, *The Power of Product Platforms*, The Free Press.

Michaels, J. V., and W. P. Wood, 1989, *Design to Cost*, John Wiley & Sons.

Mikkola, J. H., 2003, "Managing modularity of product architecture: Toward an integrated theory," *IEEE Transactions on Engineering Management*, Vol. 50, No. 2.

Miles, L. D., 1972, *Techniques of Value Analysis and Engineering – 2nd Edition*, McGraw-Hill.

Monden, Y., 1992, *Cost Management in the New Manufacturing Age*, Productivity Press.

Monden, Y., 1995, *Target Costing and Kaizen Costing*, Productivity Press.

Mudge, A. E., 1989, *Value Engineering: A Systematic Approach*, J. Pohl Associates.

O'Guin, M. C., 1991, *The Complete Guide to Activity Based Costing*, Prentice Hall.

Park, R., 1999, *Value Engineering: A Plan for Invention*, St. Lucie Press.

Pine, B. J. II, 1993, *Mass Customization*, Harvard Business School Press.

Pugh, S., 1991, *Total Design: Integrated Methods for Successful Product Engineering*, Addison Wesley.

Reinertsen, D. G., 1997, *Managing the Design Factory*, The Free Press.

Rother, M., and J. Shook, 1999, *Learning to See*, Lean Enterprise Institute.

Sakurai, M., 1996, *Integrated Cost Management*, Productivity Press.

Schmidt, S. R., and R. G. Launsby, 1992, *Understanding Industrial Designed Experiments – 3rd Edition*, Air Academy Press.

Sekine, K., and K. Arai, 1994, *Design Team Revolution*, Productivity Press.

Senge, P. M., 1990, *The Fifth Discipline*, Currency Doubleday.

Bibliography

Shina, S., Graham, A., and D. Walden, 1993, *A New American TQM: Four Practical Revolutions in Management,* Productivity Press.

Shina, S. G., 1991, *Concurrent Engineering and Design for Manufacture of Electronics Products*, Van Nostrand Reinhold.

Smith, P. G., and D. G. Reinertsen, 1998, *Developing Products in Half the Time – 2nd Edition*, John Wiley & Sons.

Sobek, D. K. II, et al., 1998, "Another look at how Toyota integrates product development," *Harvard Business Review*, July-August Issue.

Sobek, D. K. II, et al, 1999, "Toyota's principles of set-based concurrent engineering," *Sloan Management Review*, Vol. 40, No. 2.

Stamatis, D. H., 1995, *Failure Mode and Effect Analysis*, ASQC Quality Press.

Stamatis, D. H., 1998, *Advanced Quality Planning: A Commonsense Guide to AQP and APQP*, Productivity, Inc.

Suri, R., 1998, *Quick Response Manufacturing*, Productivity Press.

Suzaki, K., 1987, *The New Manufacturing Challenge: Techniques for Continuous Improvement*, The Free Press.

Suzue, T., 2002, *Cost Half: The Method for Radical Cost Reduction*, Productivity Press.

Terninko, J., 1997, *Step-by-Step QFD – 2nd Edition*, St. Lucie Press.

Thomas, R. J., 1993, *New Product Development: Managing and Forecasting for Strategic Success*, John Wiley & Sons.

Thrun, W., 2003, *Maximizing Profit*, Productivity Press.

Ulrich, K., 1995, "The role of product architecture in the manufacturing firm," *Research Policy*, Vol. 24, pgs. 419-440.

Ward, A., et al., 1995, "The second Toyota paradox: How delaying decisions can make better cars faster," *Sloan Management Review*, Vol. 36, No. 3.

Womack, J. P., Jones, D. T., and D. Roos, 1990, *The Machine That Changed The World*, Harper Perennial.

Womack, J. P., and D. T. Jones, 2003, *Lean Thinking: Revised and Updated*, The Free Press.

Yang, K., and E. El-Haik, 2003, *Design for Six Sigma: A Roadmap for Product Development*, McGraw-Hill Professional.

Index

A –

accuracy, 247-256
action lists, 172-174
Activity-Based Costing, 28, 29
activity centers, 28
Advanced Product Quality
 Planning (APQP), 195, 260
alpha customers, 70
Amazon.com, 21
Analysis of Variance (ANOVA),
 256-260
analysis paralysis, 147
andon lights, 193
architecture, of product, 108
Argus Charts, 143, 144
assignable capital, 61, 172-174
assignable costs, 22, 23, 36
assumptions, 9, 11, 150-171
AT&T Bell Telephone
 Laboratories, 270-275
automation, 26, 46, 52, 58, 60, 61,
 124, 211

B –

balanced scorecard, 75, 114, 115
baseline design, 151-171
batch processes, 53, 191-193
benchmarking, 80
benefits, 67-69, 73-75, 148-151
beta customers, 70
bill-of-materials, 49
blackbelt, Six-Sigma, 237-266
boundary-spanning object, 70
brainstorming, 164-174, 210,
 213-218
breakeven number, 25
built-in test (BIT), 270-275
bus modularity, 121-124

C –

CAD / CAM, 46, 127, 198
cancellation of projects, 43
capability, of process, 52
capacity, of factory, 198-200
capital depreciation, 23, 25, 52
capital equipment, 23, 26, 33, 53, 55, 61, 97,
 129-131, 203-206, 211-221
capital investment, 31, 46, 54, 243-251
catch phrases, 199
change, organizational, 8, 281-287
checklists, 100, 101, 120, 121, 124-126,
 164-171, 199, 206-210, 267-279
commodity, 139
commonality, 212, 108, 109, 117, 122
competition, 80
complexity, of design, 54
component-sharing modularity, 121-124
component-swapping modularity, 121-124
concept selection, 175-185
conceptual design, 175-185
concurrent engineering, 9
consumables, 56
continuous cost improvement, 86-88,
 281-287
Continuous Measurable Improvement
 (CMI), 252
contract manufacturing, 58, 61
cooperation, among products, 95, 96
corporate improvement initiative, 284-287
cost accounting, 21, 28, 45
cost buildup, 21, 22, 48
cost drivers, 28
Cost Improvement Recommendation
 template, 172-174
cost knobs, (see "five cost knobs")
cost levers, (see "twenty cost levers")
cost model, 45, 47, 88, 89
cost of poor quality (COPQ), 237-266
Cost-of-Poor-Quality Calculator, 237-245
cost-reduction loop, 88, 89, 145, 146
could-haves, 81, 82
cross-functional teams, 9
customer feedback, 67, 70-72
customer intimacy, 68, 71, 73
customer problem, 67, 69-73, 148-151
customer satisfaction, 83
customer-sensitivity map, 81
customer surrogates, 75
customization, 104, 107, 118, 124, 127-132
cut-to-fit modularity, 121-124

Index

D –

Daimler Benz, 107
dedicated equipment, 54
default design, 151-171
defects, 227-233, 237-266
defect rates, 243-256
delaying decisions, 178-181
deployment, of lean design, 281-287
deployment plan and schedule, 284-287
design alternatives, 58, 175-185
Design "Best-Practice" Guideline, 275-279
Design Challenge Announcement, 182-185
Design Challenge Response template, 182-185
design for electronic assembly, 274
design for environment, 270-275, 291
Design for Excellence (DfX), 270-275
Design for Manufacture and Assembly (DFMA), 52, 53, 267-279
design for mechanical assembly, 274
design for reliability, 270-275
design for safety, 270-275
design for service and maintenance, 270-275
design for testability, 52, 270-275
design guidelines, 275-279
design loop, 88
Design of Experiment (DOE), 203, 237, 253-260
design reuse, 32, 54
design rules, 131
design team, 45, 69, 101, 150-174, 181-185
design tolerances, 191
detectability, of failure modes, 262-264
differentiation, 81, 85
direct costs, 22, 267-279
direct labor, 18, 24, 30, 31, 46, 52, 61, 170-174, 267-279
direct materials, 22, 24, 46, 170-174, 267-279
discount rate, 38
DMAIC process, 252-253

E –

economies of scope, 123
esteem value, 138, 139, 159
exchange value, 138, 139, 159
expected commercial value (ECV), 35

F –

factory layout, 55
factory model, 198, 204-207
factory walk-through, 203-210
failure modes, 261-264
Failure Modes and Effects Analysis (FMEA), 237, 260-264
fasteners, 52, 97
feedback, of a system, 96, 97
finite capacity, 9, 40
first-pass yield, 52, 243-251
five cost knobs, 25, 26, 29, 51, 56, 57, 59, 60
fixed costs, 21, 23, 31
flexibility, of design, 118-123, 144
floor space, factory, 31
flow-lines, 191-193, 195-200
Ford Motor Company, 180-182
fully-burdened costs, 24
Function Analysis System Technique (FAST), 143, 144
functions, naming, 150-171
functions, product, 18, 45, 49, 68, 69, 73-76, 97, 117, 119, 120, 140, 150-171

G –

Gage Repeatability and Reproducability (Gage R&R), 251-256
General Motors, 109
Generally Accepted Accounting Principles (GAAP), 27
gold-plating, of design, 55, 82
"good-enough" strategy, 85
graphical user interface, 70
Green Design, 271, 272, 291
gross profit, 24, 25
Grumman Corporation, 152-154

H –

hazardous materials, 56
hierarchy of complexity, 108
high-volume parts, 53
Home Shopping Network, 34, 38, 58
House of Quality, 72
"How's it Built?" Review, 201-210, 260

I –

implementation, of lean design, 267-273
improvement champion, 281-287
incentives, 101, 182-185
indirect costs, 22

Index

information gathering, 147-151
innovation, 7, 9, 19, 54, 70, 178-185
integral design, 119
integration, 48
interaction effects, 253-260
interfaces, 48, 118, 123, 124
internal rate of return, 35
inventory turns, 191
iterative prototyping, 70, 72

J –

job plan, for Value Engineering, 137-144
Just-in-Time (JIT), 9, 15, 55, 191-193

K –

kaizen, 15
kaizen event, 200, 204, 282-283
kanban cards, 191-193
Kano, Noriaki, 81
Kano Model, 81-83
Kennedy Challenge, 152

L –

Lean Design Challenge, 175-185
Lean Design Deployment Schedule, 284-287
Lean Design Maturity Model, 284-287
lean enterprise, 15, 97, 140
lean factory, (see "lean manufacturing")
lean manufacturing, 56, 191-193, 195-200
Lean QFD, 70, 73-77, 83, 140, 147, 160
Lean Six Sigma, 13, 252
Lean Thinking, 12, 15-17, 142, 237
Lean Thinking, Five Principles of, 17
learning curve, 30, 31
line extensions, 98, 99, 103
Lunar Excursion Module (LEM), 152-154
lunar landing system, 152-154

M –

make vs. buy, 55, 220-221
manufacturability, 201-210, 227-233
manufacturing engineering, 201-210, 227-233
manufacturing process, 52
market forecast, 33, 34
market price, 43-45
market risk, 85

market segmentation, 102, 104, 149
market share, 41, 42
Maslow, Abraham, 12
mass customization, 117, 128-132
material handling and movement, 55, 198
Method of Five Whys, 11
microplatforms, 109, 110
Miles, Lawrence, 140
Mister Potato Head, 107, 123
modular design, 53, 117-126, 132
Module-Optimization Checklist, 120, 121, 124-126
Motorola Company, 237-251
muda, 15
Mudge, Arthur, 140
multifunctional products, 48
multivariable analysis, 253-260
Mustang automobile, 180-182
must-haves, 81, 82
Must / Should / Could, 82-88, 140, 147, 160

N –

narrowing funnel, 195-200
net present value (NPV), 34-36
network effects, 80, 118
network externalities, 118
new products, prioritization, 33
non-recurring design, 23-26, 30-33, 36, 54, 55, 114, 172-174
non-value-added, 15, 52
nth-look stages, of Value Engineering, 142-144

O –

occurrence, of failure modes, 262-264
one-piece flow, 45, 191-193
opportunity costs, 45, 127
outsourcing, 54, 60, 61, 86, 220-221
overhead, factory, 22, 24, 27, 53, 55, 61, 172-174
overshoot, of design, 11, 44, 53, 55, 137, 139

P –

parametric design, 127, 128
Pareto, 77
Pareto Principle, 148
partitioning, 46-50, 119, 120
parts count, reduction of, 53, 97
Pathfinder, 152-155
phases and gates, 44
platform design, 53, 98, 103, 104, 107-120, 127-132

Index

platform effectiveness, 114, 115
platform efficiency, 114, 115
Platform Integration Schedule, 111-113
Platform Matrix, 111-113
platform metrics, 114, 115
Platform Plan, 110-113
point-of-use customization, 130
positioning, 80, 81
postponement, 128-132
precision, 247-256
preconceptions, 150-171
price, maximizing, 7
primary functions, 154-164
prioritization, of products, 9, 33-38, 40, 112
prioritization, of requirements, 70, 73, 74, 76, 79-89, 104, 140, 150-164
problem-solving system, 48
process alternatives, 200, 203-221
process capability, 191, 227-233, 237-251
Process Capability Index (C_{pk}), 248-250
Process Capability Ratio (C_p), 229-233, 246-251
process response, 253-260
process variability, 227-233, 237-251
producibility, (see "manufacturability")
product, (see "new product")
product and process co-development, 191-193, 195-221, 239-251, 267-279
product architecture, 104
product description, 68
product development process, 7, 36, 44, 88, 142, 193, 195-200
product family, 98
Product-Line Optimization Team (PLOT), 99-102, 110, 111, 120
Product-Line Roadmap, 99, 102-105, 110
product solution, 67
product tolerances, 229-233, 241-251
product value, 70
Production Preparation Process (3P), 54, 142, 191, 195-221
productivity, 40
profit-maximizing system, 95, 96, 98, 117
profitability, 54, 89, 97, 100
profitability index, 35
profits, maximizing, 25, 36, 41, 43, 44, 46, 88, 89
prototyping, 70, 203
Pugh, Stuart, 175-179
Pugh Method for Concept Selection, 175-179, 215-217
pull system, 129, 191-193

Q –

quality assurance, 227-233, 237-266
Quality Function Deployment (QFD), 72, 266-266
quantity discounts, 30
Quick-Look Value Engineering (QLVE) event, 140-178, 267

R –

ranking, of opportunities, 34-40
raw materials, 53, 55, 97
regression analysis, 256-260
reliability, of product, 238, 270-275
requirements, design, 67, 69, 73, 76-85, 151-164
risk, discounting, 36
risk, economic, 36, 38
risk, market, 36, 38, 85
risk, technical, 36, 38, 85
risk-corrected NPV, 40-42
risk priority number (RPN), 264
robust design, 52, 237-251

S –

scalable design, 53, 117, 127-129, 132
scaling, of lean design tools, 142-144
scarcity value, 138, 139, 159
scenarios, 46, 58
scrap, 24, 52, 227-233, 237-250
secondary functions, 154-164
sectional modularity, 121-123
Set-Based Concurrent Engineering, 175, 179-181, 196-198
setup and changeover, 52
"Seven-Alternatives" Process, 54, 200, 211-221
severity of effect, 262-264
should-haves, 81-82
showcase project, 284-287
Six-Sigma Cost Reduction Guide, 237, 264-266
Six-Sigma Design, 13, 52, 142, 231-233, 237-266
six-sigma variability, 243-250
skill level, 52
slot modularity, 120-122
Smith, Adam, 137, 138
Sobek, Durward, 178-181
software, 48, 107, 108, 118, 129, 156, 227
specifications, (see "requirements")
Spirit / Rover Mars lander, 152-155, 183-185

standard cost, 45
standardization, 32, 45, 53, 83, 97, 100, 108-111, 122
standardized interfaces, 118-126
Statistical Process Control (SPC), 237, 239
strategic products, 41, 42, 45, 220-221
strength of effect, 256-260
subjective scoring, 215-217
sunk costs, 45
suppliers, 55
SWOT analysis, 80
synergy, among products, 95-97, 102, 109, 117
system, 48, 95-97, 108
system hierarchy, 110, 155
system products, 46-49
systems thinking, 46, 49, 95, 108, 109

T –

Taguchi, Genichi, 240
Taguchi Loss Function, 241-243
Taguchi Methods, 237, 240-242
takt time, 191-193, 198
target cost, 43-51, 70, 79, 80, 88, 89, 145, 181
target margin, 43
teamwork, 95
testing and inspection, 48, 52, 97, 239-251
thingamajigs, 24, 34, 58
third-party manufacturers, 118
time, minimizing, 7
time base, 102
time-to-market, 7, 75, 114
tolerance stackup, 241-243
tolerances, (see "product tolerances")
tooling, 46, 54, 129, 213-221
tooling optimization, 213-221
top-down assembly, 52
Total Quality Management (TQM), 13, 72, 81, 178
touch labor, (see "direct labor")
Toyota Motor Company, 54, 140, 175-181, 191, 195-200, 211
tradeoffs, design, 56, 59-61, 76, 79, 80, 151-171, 201-210, 211-221
translation, of requirements, 68, 73, 141
Twenty-Cost-Lever tradeoff tool, 56-61, 88, 151-171
twenty cost levers, 51, 56-61, 72

U –

undershoot, of design, 11, 139
use value, 137, 138, 159

V –

value, defining, 16, 137-139, 150-171
value, product, 16, 150-171
value-added distributor, 55
Value Analysis, (see Value Engineering)
Value Engineering, 9, 18, 137-174
Value Paradox, 137, 138
value stream, 97, 98
variability, (see "process variability")
variable costs, 21, 31
verb / noun function description, 68, 144, 150-171
Viking Mars lander, 152
voice of the customer, 67
volume, production, 29, 31
volume discounts, 53

W –

waste, reduction of, 16, 17
Wealth of Nations, The, 137
weighting factors, 56, 58, 75
whachamacallits, 146-174, 253-260
widgets, 24
Wonderjig, 34, 38, 39
work-in-process (WIP) inventory, 55, 61, 129, 172-174, 191, 198
workcells, 97, 191-193, 195-200

Y –

yield-limiting process, 243-256
yield loss, 229-233, 243-256

About the Author

Ron Mascitelli, PMP (Project Management Professional, Masters Degree Solid State Physics, University of California, Los Angeles) is the Founder and President of Technology Perspectives. Ron is a recognized leader in the development of advanced product design and development methods. He presents his workshops and seminars internationally, and has created company-specific lean product development training for a number of leading firms, including Lockheed-Martin, Boeing, Parker-Hannifin, Harris Corporation, Goodrich Aerospace, Hughes Electronics, Rockwell Automation / Allen-Bradley, and Applied Materials.

Ron served as both Senior Scientist and Director of Research and Development for Hughes Electronics and the Santa Barbara Research Center. His industry experience includes management of advanced product development projects for the Department of Defense, the Defense Advanced Research Projects Agency, Lawrence Livermore Laboratory, NASA, and the Department of Energy.

Since founding Technology Perspectives in 1994, Ron Mascitelli has published over twenty papers and technical articles in major journals, including the *International Journal of Technology Management* and *The Journal of Product Innovation Management*, and is a contributing author for IEEE's *Technology Management Handbook*. He has written two previous books, including the critically acclaimed, *Building a Project-Driven Enterprise: How to Slash Waste and Boost Profits Through Lean Project Management*, and is the author of *The Lean Guidebook Series*, of which this book is the first installment. Ron currently lives with his wife, Renee, and their many pets in Northridge, CA.

For *Everything* Your Firm Needs to Implement *Lean Design*, Visit Our Website:

www.Design-for-Lean.com